THE DIGITAL FRONTIER

FRAMING THE GLOBAL

Hilary Kahn and Deborah Piston-Hatlen, *editors*

THE DIGITAL FRONTIER

Infrastructures of Control on the Global Web

Sangeet Kumar

INDIANA UNIVERSITY PRESS

This book is a publication of

Indiana University Press
Office of Scholarly Publishing
Herman B Wells Library 350
1320 East 10th Street
Bloomington, Indiana 47405 USA

iupress.org

Manufactured in the United States of America

First printing 2021

Cataloging information is available from the Library of Congress.

ISBN 978-0-253-05647-4 (hardback)
ISBN 978-0-253-05649-8 (paperback)
ISBN 978-0-253-05648-1 (web PDF)

For my parents, Pramod Dev and Suman Devi,
whose lives of simplicity and idealism
have been my most enduring education.

CONTENTS

PREFACE

THIS BOOK IS AN ATTEMPT TO RESUSCITATE AND centralize the global within the thriving scholarship on digital media and culture. Once a prominent field of interdisciplinary investigation and a legitimate vantage point from which to understand and critique the global dynamics of production, circulation, and consumption of media and cultural texts, theories of global cultural power—even in their subsequent nuanced and complex versions—have largely ceded space to locally situated and deeply contextualized narratives of creativity, power, and resistance focused on subjects' relationships with media technologies and texts. These narratives have added complexity to our understanding of how we engage with media, but they have often done so at the expense of the global scale of analyses about how media, power, and culture are enmeshed within axes of geopolitics, postcoloniality, history, and the North/South divide. The recession of questions about the global dynamics of media and cultural power, even as we witness the rise of arguably the most global media technology ever, is paradoxical but precisely so a phenomenon worthy of interrogation.

There are many reasons for this changing dynamic within media studies, including the networked and locally situated nature of digital media technologies that makes their global dimension a seemingly less determining factor in subjects' usage and interactions with the medium. This book is intended to show that, far from disappearing, that global dimension is key to shaping and structuring the role of digital media technologies in our lives. It does not give to the global the primacy that erstwhile theories of cultural dominance did (and were justifiably critiqued for); instead, it shows the global to be in a continuous negotiation with the local to determine the meaning, usage, and role of the digital ecosystem that increasingly envelops us. The global's seeming invisibility in an immersive and immanent medium makes it a more elusive object of analysis, but that should not lull us into diminishing its role in the assertion of cultural power in the digital realm. The global approach continues to grow but is still a narrower stream in comparison to the gushing tides of other approaches to the study of digital media technologies. In situating this book as a part of that relatively narrower stream, my attempt here is to strengthen its flow and help expand its reach and scope.

Sidestepping the global vantage point functions to gloss over questions of scale and structure, geopolitics and sovereignty, and power and history as they play out in the digital domain. Most importantly, it allows us to remain blind to the raging controversies and events unfolding in the contemporary world that situate the digital realm centrally within clashes over international political supremacy and global dominance. The deployment of seemingly neutral platforms, sites, and digital media corporations in the ongoing battles to shape the global order provides grist to the idea that those entities are firmly entrenched within international geopolitics in ways that current scholarship on the subject is yet to fully address. We would be remiss to ignore digital media entities' central role in the ongoing global power games as well as how they emerge as sites where ongoing battles for dominance—such as in the realm of ideologies, culture, subjectivity, epistemology, and sovereignty—are played out.

In centralizing the global perspective within scholarship on digital media technologies, this book hopes to address this seeming imbalance and serve as a reminder that even though we experience the web locally, it has a global arc. A media technology that is global by default must be analyzed at that scale in order to fully capture its role in our world. While prior media technologies were made global through deliberately planned expansion, digital media's setting is global by default, meaning that efforts must be made not to globalize it but to contain its global sway by keeping it out of national borders. If left untampered with, its manifestation (e.g., websites, platforms, applications, and other digital services) can transgress boundaries far more effortlessly than any media technology of the past. Starting with that global premise, this book's argument seeks its place alongside other equally valuable and locally situated studies of digital media technologies that have enriched our interdisciplinary field of media and communication studies. In rejuvenating the narrower rivulet, its goal is to enrich and strengthen the flow of the river itself.

ACKNOWLEDGMENTS

A BOOK OF THIS SCOPE IS THE CULMINATION of a long trajectory com-prising innumerable moments of learning, both formal and informal. In acknowledging those pivotal moments as well as the people who shaped them, I pay homage to the many scholars, mentors, friends, and collaborators who played formative roles in the evolution of the ideas explored within these pages. I would like to begin by thanking my coadvisors in graduate school at the University of Iowa. I extend my thanks to Timothy Havens, whose reminders about the importance of structures and the subjects that shape them has remained a continuing thread in my work. To Mark Andrejevic, whose unapologetic critical perspective has been a source of inspiration, especially as that position is increasingly called out to justify itself. To John Durham Peters, whose towering and kind presence at Iowa and beyond has touched many students' lives—including mine—in enduring ways. To the late Bruce Gronbeck, who left an indelible print on a generation of students at Iowa and on its historical rhetoric program. To Priya Kumar, who helped historicize and deepen my early interest in the field of postcolonial studies and was a go-to resource for all research related to South Asia. And to Meenakshi Gigi Durham, whose pivotal presence at the School of Journalism and Mass Communication at Iowa (across the bridge from the Becker building that housed the communication department) helped sharpen the critical edges of my scholarship and thinking.

Beyond my committee, faculty members in the department of Communication Studies and beyond played nurturing roles for me and other graduate students. I would like to especially thank David Depew and his classes on the intersections of rhetoric and philosophy that enabled and facilitated my (and countless others') entry into key philosophical texts and debates. My gratitude also to Kembrew McLeod, whose innovative scholarship, unconventional ways of thinking, and activist engagements and critiques have fostered in many students a culture of activism about key issues. Thanks to Steve Duck, whose guidance in the rigors of teaching and evaluation during my first semester as his teaching assistant helped shape an important dimension of my experiences during graduate school. David Hingtsman has been a kind and enduring presence in the Department of Communication Studies, and his openness for conversations with graduate students on a range of interests is much appreciated. Thanks to Ece Algan for her seminar on global media where some of these ideas germinated. Additionally, immense gratitude to Rita Zajacz, Joy Hayes, Kristine Munoz, Leslie Baxter, Virginia Dominguez, Balmurli Natarajan, Sujatha Sosale, Russell Valentino, and David Wittenberg, who at different moments each touched and enriched my presence at the University of Iowa with support and guidance. Beyond the department, I would like to especially thank Philip Lutgendorf for his support and mentorship over the years (both during and after graduate school). My gratitude also to the South Asian Studies Program, which provided an enduring intellectual fraternity and created grounds for conversations (over chai and samosas) on key theoretical and real-life issues specific to South Asia. Frederick Smith, Meena Khandelwal, and Paul Greenough were all instrumental in building and nurturing that community over the years.

My time at Iowa, while rewarding beyond measure, would not have been so without the training and preparation received during my MA at the University of New Mexico (UNM). I was lucky to have been taken under the tutelage of the late Everett Rogers and to have been his last research assistant. No words can capture my gratitude toward Ev for his early mentoring of me in the discipline. I would like to offer my gratitude to my MA thesis advisor, Krishna Kandath, and committee members Glenda Balas and Mark Peceny, who were instrumental in shaping my time at UNM. Additionally, faculty members including Kenneth Frandsen, Karen Foss, John Oetzel, Brad Hall, John Condon, Judith Hendry, and Janet Cramer all played important roles at the institution for me.

Perhaps the most invaluable social reward of graduate school is the friendships forged there, and the interdisciplinary nature of the humanities and social sciences at the University of Iowa ensured that those friendships cut across disciplinary boundaries: Amit Baishya, Peter Schaefer, Margaret Schwarz, Katherine Bishop, Michael Albrecht, Alina Haliliuc, Xinghua Li, Jesse Schlotterbeck, Young Cheon Cho, Kristina Gordon, David Morris, Minkyu Sung, Meryl Irwin, Sydney Yueh, Gerald Voorhes, Zachary Stiegler, Evelyn Bottando, Chitra Akkoor, Joseph Steinitz, Hsin-Yen Yang, Renu Pariyadath, Jong-in Chang, Sam McCormick, Kim Nguyen, Arpita Kumar, Samantha Joyce, Michael Lawrence, Aaron Sachs, Adam Roth, Ania Spyra,

Steve Schubert, Anup Kumar, Ben Basan, Sarah Goffstein, Brooke Budy, and Vinu Warrier were all close friends who made the travails of graduate school far more tolerable and even memorable. Friends at the University of New Mexico including Avinash Thombre, Ruben Ramirez, Ignacio Gallegos, Susan Podshadley, Monica Yancey, Adolfo Garcia, Radi Simeonova, Divya Srinivas, and Bhavna Upadhyay, among many others.

Life beyond graduate school requires rebuilding afresh local systems of support and networks of friendship. My colleagues at Denison University have gradually taken on the role of that community both at the social as well as at the intellectual level. In particular, my colleagues in the Department of Communication, such as Suzanne Condray, Jeff Kurtz, Lisbeth Lipari, John Arthos, Amanda Gunn, Bill Kirkpatrick, Laura Russell, Alina Haliliuc, Hollis Griffin, Omedi Ochieng, Sharon Chuang, Kristen Cole, Alan Miller, and Sally Scheiderer, have played key roles in their own ways by inspiring me and lending their shoulders or ears as needed. Their kind and supportive presence has ensured my smooth transition between the corridors of Becker and Higley by providing a continuity between them. Beyond the Department of Communication, colleagues (current and former) in other departments at Denison, including John Cort, Kirk Combe, Steve Vogel, Anna Nekola, Tony King, Nestor Matthews, Francesco Lopez, Isabelle Choquet, Andy McCall, Clare Jen, Gary Baker, Raj Bellani, Fadhel Kaboub, Taku Suzuki, Megan Threlkeld, Isis Nusair, Quentin Duroy, Jack Shuler, and many others, have provided a social and intellectual community for debate and exchange of ideas, many of which found their way into the book.

Just as important are the friends, collaborators, and mentors within the broader academia who have provided me with a community of scholars and researchers that is annually reaffirmed through meetings at conferences, symposia, workshops, and other events. Radhika Parameswaran, Aswin Punathambekar, Shanti Kumar, Arvind Singhal, Stuart Cunningham, Devika Chawla, David Craig, Limor Shifman, Aasim Khan, Sahana Udupa, Daya Kishan Thussu, Dilip Gaonkar, Vibodh Parthasarthi, Sumandro Chattopadhyay, Kiran Jonalagadda, Kalyani Chadha, Radhika Gajjala, Debashis Aikat, Joyojeet Pal, Payal Arora, Amit Prasad, Shefali Jha, and Rakesh Batabyal are just a few names from a large group of like-minded scholars who are pursuing similar questions in the region of South Asia and beyond. I feel lucky to have their critical and intellectual input on my work, shared over the years in conversations, conference panels, and many

笑"""

""""""

ongoing and completed collaborative projects. This continuously growing list of friends and interlocutors continues to energize and expand my scholarship through a cross-fertilization of ideas, theories, and methods.

The world of academia, by providing a welcoming and supporting community, has been a second home for me. My first home in the professional world will always be the journalistic and media world of Delhi, where I started my working career and spent a few rigorous years gaining experiences that continue to percolate into my academic life. It is only natural that my first community of friends and mentors should belong to the media world in Delhi. I do not have enough words to thank each of them for continuing to accept me as a part of their world through the travails of graduate school and academic life. I would like to especially thank Ajit Kumar Jha for being a mentor who started me on this journey and facilitated my entrance into graduate school in the early days of my journalistic career. The late Diptosh Majumdar touched more lives in deeper ways than he ever knew, and I consider myself fortunate to have come under his tutelage during my early days at the *Indian Express*. Sonu Jain, my first boss and mentor at the newspaper, took a chance on me first with a job and then with trusting me with the prized beats (environment and infrastructure) that had become synonymous with her name. Indrajit Hazra, Bobby Mathur, Sunil Menon, Raj Kamal Jha, Unni Rajan Shanker, Rupa Sarkar, and Ranjit Bhushan all played formative roles when I was starting out, and I owe much of my journalistic career to them. In addition to these mentors, enduring and invaluable friendships with Shubhajit Roy, Himanshi Dhawan, Shobita Dhar, Sandeep Phukan, Esha Roy, Toufiq Rashid, Megha Bahree, Ajay Panicker, Anant Baveja, Tina Baruah, Divya Vashisht-Kumar, Dalip Singh, Prarthna Gahilote, Kavita Chaudhary, Manish Kumar, Aastha Sahdev, Sukriti Chaudhari, Merlin Francis, and countless others (whom I am sure I have missed) have made my network of friends in India a continuing, rewarding presence in my life.

The process of preparing a book from its initial idea to its final form is impossible without professional help from experts who know the minutiae of the process. Editors at Indiana University Press have played that role for me, and I would like to express my deep gratitude to them for the time, perseverance, and patience with which they have helped in the evolution of this project. The late Rebecca Tolen was an early supporter of the idea; driving this project and its final shape would not have been possible without her early endorsement. Stephanie Smith, Jennika Baines, Allison Chaplin, Nancy Lightfoot, and Sophia Hebert all played vital roles during important moments in the transition of this project from idea to its published form, and I am immensely grateful for their advice and patience. Leigh McLennon's fine eye and diligent editing has made this a much better manuscript. Additionally, there are two short revised extracts from prior published work included in the book, and I would like to thank the publishers Taylor and Francis and Sage Publications for allowing their inclusion in chapters 3 and 5. And while the mentors, teachers, and collaborators get all the credit for the ideas in the following pages, any inadvertent errors that may have slipped in are entirely mine.

Lastly, the support of my close and extended family members (uncles, aunts, siblings, and cousins) scattered around the world has been invaluable in completing this project. They are far too many to name them all, but they know who they are, and I express gratitude to them for patiently understanding my seemingly unconventional career choices. Two of them whom I have affectionately called Vinod Bhaijee and Photo Baba deserve special mention for being continuous sources of inspiration. Lastly, completing this long project would have been much tougher without the affection of my nephew Soham and niece Ira. Transmitted in person and across various digital platforms, their voices have been a part of my life all these years, and I thank both of them for their unconditional love and support.

THE DIGITAL FRONTIER

1

INFRASTRUCTURES OF CONTROL

Introduction

Justifiably presented as a transformative media technology, the web and its global emergence have arguably been the defining phenomena of the past two decades. The changes wrought by this global media technology are yet to be fully understood, and recent studies have emphasized both its emancipatory potential and its disciplinary dimensions. Key bodies of recent scholarship account for the seepage of the web and its digitized culture into all aspects of life globally. Emerging critical studies have analyzed the web's unalterable effects on our quotidian lives including the transformation of politics, business, cultural production, human relationships, and knowledge as well as the enhanced modalities of surveillance and the power it embodies. While deepening our understanding, these studies have also opened avenues for public deliberation and policy discussions that have pushed against attempts to compromise the egalitarian ideals and promises that the internet started out with. Invoking those early promises, scholars have posed questions about power and inequity, cautioning us that the digital ecosystem could be reinforcing the very preexisting hierarchies that the web was intended to challenge. This book adds to those existing meta-critiques of the World Wide Web to conceptualize the inevitable ways in which it is reconfiguring key dimensions of global culture. It extends the critical questions posed about the social effects of digital culture to a global scale to understand the transnational consequences of the web's gradual global adoption.

Inspired by critiques that have emphasized dimensions of discipline, control, and power on the web, my attempt here is to capture a fuller account of how significant aspects of global culture are being transformed inexorably by the speed and scale of digital culture and the related rise of networked norms of sociality. I ascribe these transformations to a gradually expanding form of networked cultural power instantiated on the web. This modality of power functions akin to Deleuzian control that inheres within and *modulates* through the conventions, protocols, default settings, and algorithmic regulation that, by forming key components of the digital infrastructure that regulate online sociality, determine the essential preconditions for accessing and participating in global digital culture. This book seeks to present the operation of such a networked form of control, delineated in the ensuing pages, as the successor to earlier forms of global cultural hegemony that were previously acknowledged as key determinants of global inequities and asymmetries. As the web expands globally, the frictions created between its universalizing codes and conventions and the local cultural milieus irreducible to it open up sites of contestation that reveal the operation of this power. These sites instantiate a familiar and historical dynamic between the center and the periphery, the developed and the developing, and the erstwhile colonies and metropoles. This reenactment of a familiar historical trope wherein an overriding system claiming universal values can act in the name of the larger common good (Hardt and Negri 2000) by masking its contingent origins and parochial interests is given an entirely new valence by a networked modality of power that the web heralds and concretizes. Hence, despite the similarity between historical forms of cultural dominance and their contemporary digital iteration, especially in their claims of embodying universal values and ideals, this recent operation of power is also different from its historical avatars. That difference can be ascribed, among other reasons, to the self-presentation of digital networks as a centerless and neutral overarching entity whose diffused and horizontal architecture allows it to conceal its cultural, political, and ideological core and present itself as a potentially egalitarian network.

Expectedly, the proliferation of this emerging form of power through the web's expanding sinews is continuously contested and negotiated by competing worldviews, values, and visions that collide with the dominant cultural and political ideals embedded within the web's cultural architecture. While these contestations have a longer history in the Euro-American West (given the web's longer presence there), they are visibly pronounced today in large parts of the non-Western world and the Global South as they gradually come on board the digital network. This book's analysis proceeds by interrogating four such sites (described below) where the cultural power of the overarching digital ecosystem engenders confrontations between the universalizing codes of the global network and the irreducible local particularities that resist them. The goal is to show how these sites reveal moments of tug of war between the resilient preexisting cultural milieus located at differing stages of networked digitization and the newly assertive modality of networked cultural power. Undoubtedly, the heterogeneous nature of these conflicts at each site also reveals how local cultures and histories intertwine with global affordances of the networked technology in radically different ways to create distinct digital worlds (e.g., "national webs" [Rogers 2013]).

To be sure, the web's architecture inscribes a dialectical logic on this form of power wherein its ability to regulate, shape, and constrain rides on the ruse of emancipatory promises of expression, association, and subversion. Hence, pointing to its assertive force is not to deny the obvious advantages of connectivity, access, and collaboration but to show that those rewards are parts of a package that come along with the constraining impositions of conventions, protocols, algorithmic regulation, and behavior design that inherently privilege particular social, cultural, and political values over others. Embedded within the design, conventions, and modulating algorithms that function akin to soft infrastructures (Peters 2015) shaping digital culture, these ideological values reveal that, far from being some neutral enablers of human interaction, the web's affordances structurally incentivize particular norms, epistemologies, and cultures while disincentivizing others. By privileging particular ways of being, knowing, and belonging, these systems of rewards and penalty, sanctions and seductions, concretized by the web's architecture, share their modalities with prior regimes of power (Rose 1990, 1998) that sought to bring about social modulation through a similar system of incentives and penalties. The web's novelty lies in its ability to mask its directionality as well as its cultural and political core by rendering them invisible behind a horizontal, centerless, and diffused modality that helps support perceptions about its flexibility, emptiness, and apolitical nature.

It is this very center—and the cultural, political, and social directionality embedded within its incentive structures—that repeatedly collides with the preexisting norms and values at each of the four sites and instances of global contestations analyzed here. The book locates the first instance of this imposition within the expanding private enclosures of the global digital oligopolies that, in replicating a discourse similar to the colonial one of spreading progress and civilization beyond the frontier, instantiate how the logic of the global common good is being deployed as a ruse to expand private corporate interests. Next the analysis focuses on how the rules, protocols, and conventions that regulate knowledge production on collaborative online knowledge sites (such as Wikipedia), far from enabling diverse epistemologies and ways of knowing, have an exclusionary effect by strictly policing what counts as legitimate knowledge. In the same vein, the book's next site of interrogation underscores the ways in which the affordances, design, and algorithmic regulation on social media platforms help enable and foster emerging norms of global selfhood whose irrefutable origins can be located within Euro-American modernity, where these aspirational ideals of subjectivity were institutionalized. Lastly, the book focuses on a series of recent conflicts between the global web and nation-states to show how the former's cultural and political power poses unprecedented challenges to national sovereignty. This challenge is experienced disproportionately by countries depending on their differential power in the off-line world and due to preexisting asymmetries aligned along the North/South, the colonial/metropole, and the developed/developing world axes. These phenomena, with a chapter devoted to each, represent a common logic wherein the seemingly decentralized, horizontal, and diffused network reveals the cultural, political, and ideological valences embedded within the conventions and protocols that form the digital ecosystem's architecture.

This exploration of the global consequences of the web learns from extant critiques of power inequities within the globalization of culture that have occupied scholars making a case for difference, plurality, and heterogeneity (Jameson 1998) in the global cultural order. The book's core is animated by critical perspectives, such as postcolonial theory (Spivak 1999; Bhabha 1997; Said 1979; Fanon 2008; Parameswaran 2008), that have sought to subvert the universalizing narratives of post-Enlightenment Europe (Chakrabarty 2007) in the realm of knowledge and culture. This argument also extends critical scholarship about the process of cultural globalization (Kraidy 2007) that has theorized inequities within global cultural transfers, first through a lens of cultural imperialism (Schiller 1992; T. Miller 2005) and then through corrections to that lens that deployed more complex analyses of power (such as hybridity). Critiques of hegemonic moments within the global cultural order form key precursors to this project, which interrogates the iteration of those same asymmetries within the digital domain today. This book's contention that the globalizing cultural architecture of the web should nudge us to reconsider the relevance of those prior critiques of cultural dominance, long advanced by critical scholars of globalization, challenges the myth that globally expanding digital networks represent a globally representative summative mean and hence are without a particular center of their own.

Global Power in the Era of the Digital

Situating itself within a lineage of scholarship that has analyzed inequities within the global cultural ecosystem, this book seeks to extend to the digital domain critical insights about how processes of cultural production and consumption can function as sites of global contestations between ideologies, values, and norms. Prior attempts to theorize global dimensions of cultural power have shown how the dominance of particular cultural industries, institutions, and texts shape the symbolic, discursive, cultural, and ideological ecosystems at distant sites by overriding local values and norms and molding the trajectories of desire in recipient societies. Such interrogations of globalization through the lens of culture have complemented other related perspectives—such as the economic, political, historical, or technological—through which the structures of global hegemony have also been studied. Analyses of global economic disparities, for instance, have brought together Marxist critiques of the exploitative nature of capitalism with the historical fact of colonialism to argue that the modern economic system created distinctions between the higher and lower value modes of production to create a "core-periphery" (Wallerstein 2004, 17) relationship within the world economy. As seen by the world systems theory, colonialism was a logical consequence of the exploitative impulse within capitalism (Wallerstein 2004) since it realized the inherent instinct within capital to expand outward in pursuit of markets and raw materials.

This project deepens and broadens that critical cultural lens on globalization by pivoting its focus onto the digital domain to better interrogate the cultural consequences of what is arguably the most transformative media technology of our age. Such an examination, through questions about cultural power, must learn from prior understandings of the material, political, and economic consequences of cultural dominance while also remaining attentive to the unique ways in which the networked digital domain allows for a diffused, immanent, and hence invisible operation of power. The web's radical modality and architecture necessitate that we go beyond previous understandings of cultural dominance that have focused on political economy (T. Miller 2005; Schiller 1992), technological dominance (Adas 2009; Balwin 2016), or the ideological values inhering within the text itself (Liebes and Katz 1994). One of the most trenchant and powerful critiques of such dominance comes from the field of postcolonial studies (Said 1979; Spivak 1999; Kumar and Parameswaran 2018), which has sought to unravel how the cultural, symbolic, and discursive realm created the mandate for the physical and material subjugation of large parts of the world. Focusing on areas as distinct as identity (Bhabha 1997; Fanon 2008), knowledge (Connell 2014; Spivak 1999), language (Fanon 2008; Viswanathan 1997), media (Shome and Hegde 2002; Shome 2019; Gajjala 2013), and culture (Said 1994; Parameswaran 2002), threads within postcolonial theory have sought to understand the powerful effects of the symbolic and discursive structures in legitimizing cultural and political domination and control. The continuing ways in which those vestigial structures shape cultural, political, and ideological choices in the postcolonial era (Harindranath 2003; Kumar 2016) underscore the abiding contribution of this body of work in understanding global power relations today.

In addition to the historical analysis of postcolonial studies, the field of cultural globalization has similarly pointed to the continued influence of former imperial powers in the world through a manifest and measurable dominance in the production and distribution of culture (Schiller 1992; Dorfman and Mattelart 1975). Critical inquiry along these lines has asserted that the economic and technological advantages of former imperial powers allowed them to continue their cultural and ideological hegemony over still-developing nations, in an argument categorized as the "cultural imperialism" thesis (Dorfman and Mattelart 1975; T. Miller 2005; Schiller 1992; Tomlinson 1995). Here, global cultural flows were shown to represent a new imperialism of ideas, reinscribing the worn paths of military imperialism. The cultural imperialism thesis was obviously a product of its time, since a polemical attack on Western cultural domination of the world and an unmasking of its collusion with capitalism was much needed during the gradual process of decolonization in the twentieth century. In so doing, the thesis reminded observers that the end of de jure colonialism did not necessarily end the dynamics of global domination. Even though its theorizations have proven largely correct, it is worth underscoring that cultural imperialism was a phenomenon that, in a convoluted, perhaps ironic way, contained the roots of its own transcendence. Cultural reprogramming has been spectacularly successful driven by various causes but also by people's (often educated) desire to embrace a certain idea of modernity (Appadurai 1996). In this new context, scholars posing a correction to the cultural imperialism thesis made a case for theories of hybridity, arguing that cultural export, even in conditions of less than total equality, did not result in homogenized, look-alike cultures but rather a productive and empowering fusion referred to as "hybridity" (Bhabha 1984; Appiah 2006; Canclini 2006; Pieterse 2006). In consonance with active-audience theorists such as John Fiske and Elihu Katz (Fiske 2010; Liebes and Katz 1994; Appadurai 1990), those making a case for hybridity argue that global audiences remake the culture they consume, in a process of adaptation by which, it is suggested, they can assert collective power great enough to mitigate the potential homogenizing power of the dominant culture industries.

Locating Cultural Power in Digital Conventions

The rise of the digital domain and the consequent transformation in the economic, cultural, and media ecosystems it has engendered necessitates extending and going beyond these prior paradigms of global power in order to understand how the older power dynamics morph within the digital ecosystem today. The global span of networked digital media creates the conditions for an altered modality of cultural hegemony that is irreducible to singular causes such as political economy, technological prowess, distribution networks, or cultural texts. In responding to the exigencies of the digital era, this book goes beyond those extant factors to locate cultural power within the conventions, protocols, and algorithmic regulation that form the infrastructural backbone of digital culture globally. It advances the contention that the constraints on social interactions in the digital ecosystem that manifest themselves through a system of rules and affordances, which distribute rewards and penalties, have powers to shape norms, ideological values, and social behavior similar to the dominant cultural industries of yore, thus forging a new vantage point for understanding the nature of global power today.

In emphasizing the ways in which standards, conventions, and algorithmic modulation (elements defined as *infrastructures of control* below) regulate human behavior on the web, this book seeks to move the dominant paradigm through which to analyze global cultural power from an ideological and disciplinarian modality to that of control (Deleuze 1992), which also helps us reconcile the power-centric narratives of the web with its democratizing and enabling dimensions. In merging the critical threads of cultural dominance and postcolonial theory with the Deleuzian notion of control, this book continues similar engagements with Deleuze (Bignall and Patton 2010; Bensmaïa 2017) that allow it to underscore the dialectic of global connectivity heralded by digital and new media technologies by simultaneously pointing to its cultural and ideological costs. The emerging picture of a networked form of power that advances through seemingly necessary and invisible conventions holds true within a schema that places freedom and control in an eternal seesaw wherein the latter's promise of the former makes it seductively effective and deceptively invisible. The tantalizing narrative of enabling expression, democratizing production, and facilitating solidarities over time and space often renders invisible the structured sinews and pathways through which digital culture channels online human behavior. We see this duality of freedom and restraint play out in specific case studies such as the deployment of emancipatory discourses to usurp the digital commons, legitimizing certain epistemologies as truer than others, elevating particular notions of selfhood as aspirational, and presenting a variable challenge to national sovereignty—ideas that the subsequent chapters of this book are respectively devoted to.

An analysis that focuses on the ideological and cultural effects of seemingly neutral conventions, designs, and algorithmic modulation must carefully refute claims that present those elements as acultural, unbiased, and hence unable to assert any cultural, political, and ideological influence of their own. In presenting these protocols as a necessary and uncoercive background that merely facilitate communication instead of shaping it, the web is often presented as an aggregation of the global zeitgeist rather than an assertive force whose interactive promise is expediently premised on accepting innumerable conditions that privilege particular cultural and ideological values, nudging users toward behavior change. Even as studies have rightly emphasized phenomena such as the democratization of cultural production through digital platforms, political empowerment through social-media-enabled uprisings, and a growing global digital ecosystem of expression and collaboration, there are also conspicuous omissions such as the "deafening silence when it comes to the legacy of US Empire" within scholarship about global digital media and culture (Aouragh and Chakravartty 2016, 560). In addressing those gaps within studies of the global dimensions of the web, this book pays homage to and extends the work of prior scholars who have centralized asymmetries and inequities within the production, consumption, and circulation within global culture.

In countering unidimensional and celebratory visions of the web, this analysis maneuvers through critical theories of technologies (Heidegger 1977; Feenberg 1991; Ellul 2014; Ihde 1979; Marcuse 2014) that underscore the cultural and political orientations of technological infrastructures thus making a strong case for their deep imbrication within relations of power. Their insights on the irrefutably normative dimensions of technologies anchors this book's excavation of the cultural architecture of the World Wide Web, allowing it to pose corrections to claims about the value-neutral and apolitical nature of the web's architecture, often imagined as representing some ground-up organic global desire. The book's argument takes into account the rich history of media scholarship (McLuhan 2003, 2011; Innis 2008; Carey 1992; Kittler 1999; Peters 2015) that has conducted close analyses of the nature of the medium, including its affordances, technological features, and design, in order to challenge the primacy of content. Situating my analysis in that lineage, this study interrogates the cultural values and ethos embedded within the web's architecture—a point underscored by key recent scholars of the internet (van Dijck, Poell, and de Waal 2018; Hillis, Petit, and Jarrett 2013; Turner 2010) who reveal how the contingencies surrounding the web's origin shaped the dominant values of the medium. When transposed onto the global context, these codes and conventions have cultural and political ramifications far beyond their sites of origin.

Philosophy of Technology

An exploration into the ways in which the seemingly neutral and acultural medium of the web conceals a cultural and political core can be significantly enriched by a philosophical understanding of the relationship between technology and the social world. Debates about the philosophy of technology have explored the cultural, political, and social orientations of technological structures and interrogated their relationships to social life. If we concede that technologies are cultures (Mumford 1934), what, then, are the cultural values embedded within the architectures and affordances of the web? If, like all technologies (Kittler 1999; McLuhan 2011; Innis 2008), digital media alter and influence key aspects of social life within which they operate, then what are those cultural changes arriving on the coattails of networked digital media? This question has been posed and responded to by several recent scholars who have analyzed the societal changes arriving with the adoption of and immersion within digital culture (Carr 2011; Boyd 2014; Turkle 2017). By extending their insights to the global level, this project goes beyond the local, regional, or national effects of cultural change to get at processes and phenomena that are most starkly illuminated at sites where the web's global spread encounters difference, resistance, and backlash.

It is pertinent to ask that if technology were an empty medium, as the instrumental view would argue, would its "rational" character and the "universality of the truth it embodies" (Feenberg 1991, 6) ensure that it can easily be transferred from one social context to another seamlessly while performing its assigned role and being entirely subservient to human agency? This view, often echoed in threads of scholarship about the web and digital platforms, faces a strident challenge from the substantive view of technology that, taking inspiration from Martin Heidegger's explorations of the essence of technology (or *techne*), emphasizes its content and culture. Heidegger's critique of the neutrality of technology (conceding it to be seemingly correct but not true—the ontic but not the ontological) is premised on the argument that technology is in fact "a mode of revealing" (Heidegger 1977, 13) that brings forth something that has hitherto remained concealed. Heidegger positions technology as a means to a particular end but with a directionality of its own that frames or structures what is brought forth. He illustrates this through his now famous example of how a hydroelectric plant on the Rhine reveals a hitherto concealed aspect of the river as a standing reserve of energy, "as something at our command" (16), thus transforming the way we look at it. Given technology's agentic directionality, assertions about its neutrality, adaptability, or plasticity are seemingly correct but not true (Ihde 1979) since these arguments mask the ideologies and values that operate under the garb of that very neutrality. Claims to neutrality therefore conflate the ontic, which is only the "partial truth" (105), with the ontological, which is the "the field of the conditions of possibility" (106). The telos of technology, according to Heidegger, is to "relentlessly" (Feenberg 1991, 7) overtake us, driven by a "nihilistic will to power, a degradation of man and Being to the level of mere objects" (7). Heidegger's critique of technology as a "*mode of truth*" (Ihde 1979, 106; italics in original) whose eventual triumph leads to a regime of instrumental rationality foregrounds its agency and forms the starting point of key debates within the philosophy of technology.

This notion of technology emphasizes it as an active force in shaping social interests and culture rather than being subservient to human control and thus forms the driving core of this project, which interrogates the global effects of the technological agency of the web. In doing so the project thinks with scholars (Ellul 2014; Feenberg 1991; Ihde 1979; Dusek 2006; Mumford 1934; Winner 1980) who have elaborated on the specific ways in which technology intervenes within social and cultural milieus in order to shape them. This exploration is driven by posing similar Heideggerian questions to the techne of the global digital network: What is the nature of the global order that the techne of the Internet is bringing forth? What is the cultural architecture that the global digital network is revealing for us? The social and cultural effects of technology are best understood by locating it in an interactional position between the deterministic view taken by Jacques Ellul (2014), who ascribes an unyielding and autonomous character to technology that "maps its own route" (Ellul 2014, 430), and the instrumental view that makes it totally subservient to human control. Ellul's emphasis on technology's self-sufficiency does not discount the effect of economic, political, and cultural factors on its progress but argues that in the conflicts frequently played out between technology and the forces that seek to shape it, the latter eventually lose out. He concedes that the technological imperative evolves dialectically but asserts that the counter forces in society eventually align with technology's goals. Others such as Winner (1980) take a less deterministic position to distinguish between technologies that can be arranged or used for political purposes and those that are inherently political. The latter, according to Winner (1980), necessitate particular arrangements of power that then percolate beyond the specific institution to the broader social life with enduring effects. Hence, while it would seem wrong and counterintuitive "to discover either virtues or evils in aggregates of steel, plastic, transistors, integrated circuits, and chemicals," (122), the invariable social, cultural, and political effects of technological systems not only are far reaching but endure through time.

This project embraces the interactional path to emphasize the cultural agency of technologies while also allowing for their social modulation (Peters 2017; Feenberg 1991), thus keeping the insights of substantive theories without their pessimistic determinism. It aligns with scholars such as Feenberg (1991), whose critical theory of technology concedes that technologies restructure our world while not entirely giving up on human agency in shaping that process of restructuring. Valid critiques of determinism that call out tendencies to ascribe overarching and absolute causality to media technologies must not deter us from conceding that "form, delivery, and control, as well as storage, transmission, and processing, all matter profoundly" (Peters

2017, 13). This interactive middle ground is visible at sites of conflict, tugs-of-war, and tussles that form the case studies investigated in the chapters of this book, which allow us to acknowledge both the normative dimensions of the web and resistances to them. These sites of contestation represent "accidents and breakdowns" where the underlying infrastructure "comes out of the woodwork" (Peters 2015, 52) and becomes "more visible" (Larkin 2008, 245), thus making it easier for their close granular interrogation. Moments of conflict reveal systems, structures, and conventions working at their extremities and limits, especially when faced with anomalous and irreducible alterity.

The technologies of the internet are hardware and software, but more specifically they are also conventions, designs, affordances, and algorithmic systems that together create a technological infrastructure representing a complex assemblage of fixity and variability. Digitization makes media programmable (Manovich 2001) but only within the rules and constraints of possibilities enabled by the hardware and the software. As these overarching structures of conventions globalize and get taken up at distances far away from their sites of origin, they play a dual role of both facilitating and channeling but also shaping and nudging (Thaler and Sunstein 2008; Yeung 2017) user behavior. Situated within the lineage of philosophy of technology, this book interrogates their consequences to understand how the web's protocols, conventions, and standards assert a cultural force especially in the non-Western Global South. What are the technology's orientations and directionalities, and what are the ways in which social milieus at distant sites push back against them? What is the nature of the power this technology heralds, and how may we conceive of its operation through the networks and sinews that form the cultural and material architecture of the web? Answers to these questions can be at least partially arrived at through a close examination of the ways in which networked digital media make certain actions possible while constraining others. The novelty and opacity of this technological formation makes its interrogation difficult but must not deter us from examining the ways in which their seemingly democratic aspects are simultaneously circumscribed by an emerging form of power. The goal of this book is to decipher and unpack that power's global manifestation.

The Power of Conventions on Networks

In expanding on the idea of the web as a global technological infrastructure, it is important to emphasize its networked architectural core, which distinguishes it from other media technologies. Key theories help us apprehend the social dimensions of this design; network theory in particular has sought to deploy the abstract idea of a network to understand how it reveals a radically different ontology of the web when compared with other media technologies prior to it. Even though Bruno Latour's work on networked phenomenon long predates the internet, his thinking about the interdependence of natural phenomena and its challenge to the notion of self-contained events or actors (Latour 2011, 2005) presents us with a resonant metaphor to conceptualize the social dimension of the internet. The actor-network theory (ANT), which Latour summarizes as "an actor is nothing but a network, except that a network is nothing but actors" (Latour 2011, 800), makes a persuasive case for studying the redistribution of causes and consequences of actions through interconnected channels of associations. Emphasizing the interconnectedness of social life—for instance, in his claim that "there exists no place that can be said to be 'non-local'" (Latour 2005, 179)—Latour's work pushes us to always juxtapose the macro with the micro, the meta with the granular. In definitively asserting that "universality is now fully *localizable*" (Latour 2011, 802; italics in original), Latour implies that any abstract idea must materialize and manifest itself in a form that is necessarily local, and the web allows that process as never before. This ability to reveal hitherto invisible networks and interconnections is key to ANT's emphasis on redrawing networked life to reimagine sociality.

In pushing us to think deeply about the social dimensions of networked architectures, Latour's work provides a valuable opening to simultaneously interrogate the reciprocity of "power and freedom" (Benkler 2011, 724) within such horizontal structures. Their empowering dimension has convincingly been established by global events that leverage networked architectures' ability to enable simultaneous action, foster seamless communication across space and time, and bypass traditional modes of control and strictures. While acknowledging its enabling potential, this project responds to the equally vital imperative to interrogate their disciplinary dimensions of control, especially those manifested at the global scale. The deceptive gambit of any decentralized architecture is wagered on its seeming lack of a center, which is commonly conflated with an egalitarian ethos both because it is partly true (at least in its promise) and due to the challenge of identifying a unitary core or a protagonist that benefits from the structural inequities within networks.

Notably, this morphing of power was anticipated by scholars (Schmitt 1985; Hardt and Negri 2000) who predicted its gradual devolution from a unitary and centralized avatar to a decentralized web of global alliances and associations—a networked form strikingly similar to the internet. Carl Schmitt's (1985) schema of this devolution is historically described as a transition of power from a singular overarching transcendent entity to a diffused network of singularities that he describes as an immanent form of power. Therefore, the global emergence of digitally networked media is only the latest iteration of this gradual devolution that, for Schmitt, signals a shift in sovereignty from divinity through monarchy and the nation-state to networked structures. Extending this to show that "sovereignty has taken a new form," Hardt and Negri (2000, xii) famously anticipate a schema of global power that is diffused and decentralized but also immanent and omnipresent within its subjects and hence far more effective in concealing its modality of operation. Borrowing from Foucault's notion of biopower, Hardt and Negri describe immanence as operating and regulating social life from within and being reactivated in each instantiation of the network's assertion. Their claim that the diffused and decentralized form of sovereignty masks a centralized core operating under the premise of "universal values" (23) was prescient in its anticipation of how a networked global ecosystem of platforms and digital corporations pervade and shape the global web today. The internet, after all, is only one instance of the "rematerialization" of the abstract idea of a network but also starkly different from other kinds because digitization "has rendered collective existence . . . traceable in an entirely different way than before" (Latour 2011, 803).

Articulated during the early years of the web's emergence, these theories about the morphing structure of sovereignty lend credence to the central premise of this book: that cultural power today manifests itself through ostensibly decentralized and diffused digital infrastructures of control operating through the social web's design, conventions, and affordances, which perform the dual function of shaping social behavior even as they facilitate global interaction. This premise is advanced by closely attending to the specificities of the medium to claim that, akin to other instances of how the medium shapes social interaction (e.g., the constitutive power of language and communication), the conduits and conventions that compose the hardware and the software of the digital network shape and channel global interaction, thus engendering a form of control unprecedented in its scale and reach. By focusing on the role of the in between—i.e., the medium that constitutes the digital network—this analysis seeks to interrogate how decentralization can often be a seductive ruse under which centralized power can operate far more effectively (Galloway 2006), and understanding how that process works is key to appreciating the web's global effects.

The imperative of this argument moves through unmasking and making visible the unobtrusive ways in which decentralized architectures exercise a coercive effect. They present a double-edged arrangement where the obvious advantages of access arrive alongside the costs of constraining standards and opaque algorithmic regulation. Access to large numbers of people (nodes) in a network invariably requires rules and standards that facilitate coordination and communication while also limiting pathways and choices. This paradoxical duality of access and constraint, of possibilities and prohibitions, of freedom and control, given that they are hardwired within its design, are presented to users as inextricable parts of the same package that we can accept or reject in its entirety. This all-or-nothing binary is evident in our limited ability to customize our digital ecosystem, as in the case of the settings of social media platforms, where the only choices available are from a list predetermined for us. These restrictions on adapting the settings according to our needs and desires concretizes a key mechanism (the predetermined rules and conventions) through which control operates within networked digital sociality. Given that their conventions and protocols are choices that platforms and websites arrive at by excluding other possible options (and that are presented as a fait accompli to users), the process has invariable cultural, political, and hence ideological consequences.

Conventions, after all, are only "certain versions of local practices, routines, and symbols" (Grewal 2008, 4) that erase alternatives by creating "path dependence" (Busch 2011, 60) and, as in the case of the web, assert what scholars have called "network power" (Grewal 2008; Castells 2013; Galloway 2006) due to their scale of adoption. These homogenizing effects of conventions and standards (both emerging and preexisting) are especially accentuated when faced with irreducible heterogeneity where radical differences among a network's various participants impose a larger burden of change on those furthest from the dominant standard. The phenomenon of globalization, which is arguably one of the earliest and most successful instances of networked human association at a global scale, reveals the most prominent instance of the homogenizing power of conventions given their simultaneous dual roles in the process as conduits for global interaction while also instantiating the operation of network power.

The coercive effects of standards that facilitate globalization (which is a key example of a global network predating the digital era) in realms as distinct as trade, technology, sports, science, culture, and travel, among others, are evident in the ways they shape and advance particular ways of being, thinking, and communicating; the case of English as a global linguistic standard is a pertinent exemplar of this. And given that "standards are also political" (DeNardis 2011, ix), their gradual proliferation in a globalizing and interconnected era establishes their emergence as among "the most important manifestation of power relations . . . in our modern world" (Busch 2011, 28). Their anonymity is a key to this power, which accrues from "*the ability to set the rules that others must follow, or to set the range of categories from which they may choose* (28; italics in original). As those rules become immanent and immersed in social life even as they regulate and enfold it, they are everywhere and yet nowhere in particular, thus masking their origins and successfully "deflecting attention to the rule and away from the ruler" (29). The immanent nature of this modality of control in the digital domain ensures that we are both inside and outside of it, making each online user both a node on the network but also an enforcer of its protocols and standards. We become both the actor and the acted upon, the subject and the object of our own power. As we interrogate the pervasive power of standards and conventions on the web, it is important to acknowledge that the internationalization of our world is, in fact, also a story of their global adoption, a process arrived at often through politically contentious negotiations that were rarely about science or reason alone.

Global Conventions as Historical Sites of Contestation

The importance of protocols and standards as sites of contestations on digital networks today can be better contextualized when juxtaposed with the historical tussles over rules and conventions that were then spread and imposed globally through colonialism and trade (Busch 2011). Feuds over global conventions have been legion in areas as distinct as trade, science, law, culture, and technology, and in most such rivalries, the final determinations of global standards were arrived at not through some uncontested and scientifically determined consensus but often due to their suitability and convenience for the dominant political powers of the day. Deliberations over global standards were invariably enmeshed within geopolitical power games of the day wherein barely concealed nationalism was masked behind intellectual and scientific rationale. In a fascinating tale that instantiates this duplicity, Galison (2004) reveals how the very meaning of the word *convention*—understood today to mean both a get-together (conference) and a rule—was expanded during the contentious deliberations about the standardization of the meter for calculating distance and the prime meridian for calculating global time. The eventual adoption of the French meter as the standard for measuring distance was seen as a national triumph and met with "patriotic satisfaction" (Galison 2004, 90) in France. The victory was short-lived, however, because Britain and America soon challenged it and won during the next clash over standardizing time, thus ensuring that the prime meridian would pass through the English town of Greenwich and make Britain the epicenter of global time for perpetuity.

Within these deliberations about determining the prime meridian that played out at the turn of the nineteenth century, "shipping and imperial power trumped history, mysticism, celestial mechanics, and other nations' nationalism" (Galison 2004, 119). As he lists the arguments and counterarguments presented at the International Meridian Conference (1884) for determining the global standard of time, Galison finds they were rarely based on rational scientific foundations but invariably on nationalism, power, and hence geopolitics. Britain's global dominance of the shipping industry and trade routes meant that an overwhelming majority of the ships were already using Britain as the center of global time—a fact the English deployed when posing the question, "What will provide the greatest convenience to the world?" (149). Even as he acknowledged defeat in the battle for the standard of time, French delegate Albert Lefaivre's spirited response, excerpted below, serves as an enduring reminder about why conventions are deeply political and invariably non-neutral, thus propelling this book's argument about their power in the digital world: "Speaking for France, Lefaivre morosely assessed the debate as void of astronomy, geodesy, or navigation. Reminded of tonnages in the context of Anglo-American complacency, he allowed 'the only merit of the Greenwich meridian . . . is that there are grouped around it, interests to be respected, I will acknowledge it willingly, by their magnitude, their energy, and their power of increasing, but entirely devoid of any claim on the impartial solicitude of science.' No reason, neutrality, or impartiality—only commerce pure and simple. Lefaivre conceded that the Empire had won by commercial prowess, but on no other grounds" (151–52).

This ringing indictment of the underlying reasons for choosing the prime meridian in 1884, rooted no doubt in a (French) nationalistic lament of its own, underscores the immense political, economic, and cultural power accruing to the nation it passed through. Placing one country's national capital at "the symbolic center of every global map" (Galison 2004, 144) would ensure that "every clock and every longitude measurement in the world would refer back to the dead center of one country's transit instrument," (144) and become an enduring "symbol of the former English domination of the sea and the world" (Schmitt 2003, 88) for perpetuity. Even though science was invoked in the debate, it was only "as the humble vassal of the powers of the day to consecrate and crown their success" (Lefaivre, quoted in Galison 2004, 152). The French censure of the choice of location for the prime meridian underscores reminders from our network theorists that seemingly universal conventions, while essential for regulating interaction, also encapsulate invisible cultural and political particularities and are hence ideological and political. It pushes us to ask similar questions about the stakes involved in determining the rules and protocols that regulate digital sociality today. Where do they emerge from, and what political and cultural power accrues to their sites of origin?

These historical conflicts over conventions reveal that global standards have been deeply imbricated within the tussle for political and economic power among European nations during the heydays of their power. However, this phenomenon was just as prominently on display in the relationship between these European nations and their colonies. Colonialism showed the indispensability of procedures, laws, and protocols in consolidating the power of colonial nations and regions over colonized ones (Schmitt 2003; Busch 2011), thus establishing their hegemonic role beyond the limiting boundaries of nation, culture, and region. The era showed that "the grand universalizing project" (Busch 2011, 83) of the Enlightenment, so ardently challenged and critiqued by postcolonial theory (Chakrabarty 2007), relied on the homogenizing effects of conventions through which the ruling nations sought to conquer the "particularisms of the past" (Busch 2011, 83) in the colonies. The presentation of colonial rules, norms, and customs as reflecting some common human spirit, hence making them universally applicable, while concealing their contingent and culturally rooted origins was a powerful modality through which Western power was consolidated. The recurrence of that exact trope (of the common global good) today in discourses of global digital platforms (e.g., Google, Apple, Facebook, Amazon, and Microsoft [GAFAM]) as they claim to embody and speak for universal values, while masking their own interests behind those claims, is hard to ignore.

In fact, conventions and standards instituted and globalized during the colonial era continue to shape global power relations in today's postcolonial world. The global dominance of some languages over others, a clear legacy of colonialism, is a pertinent reminder of the endurance of these soft structures of power long after the physical occupation of the non-Western world receded. Even though they form the bedrock on which global interaction occurs today, dominant languages (e.g., English, French, Spanish, Hindi, Mandarin) exemplify global standards that influence cultural choices, human thought, and action simultaneously. While Lacanian psychoanalysis ascribes a constraining role to all languages, famously moving the register of human desire from the biological to the symbolic/linguistic realm (Fink 1997; Lacan 2006), critics have shown how the global dominance of particular languages over others also advances geopolitical power that accrues political and economic benefits (Phillipson 1992, 2008) to particular nations and regions at the expense of others. These instances of their role in geopolitics, colonialism, and globalization underscore the dual function of conventions, protocols, and standards as both enabling and regulating. Acknowledging their necessity in facilitating communication and collaboration must therefore simultaneously account for their cultural and political power—a process far too visible in other instances of globalization including international law.

The Nomos of the Digital

Among the most generative historical exemplars of this hegemonic role of conventions in enabling colonial appropriation is the case of international law, whose global spread is rooted in the colonial era and whose current iteration in the domestic legal systems spans countries around the world. German jurist Carl Schmitt's (2003) argument that the arrival of colonial modernity was premised on a reordering of the globe elaborates how colonial usurpation of non-European territories gained its justification from but also simultaneously imposed a norm or order over the colonized world in the guise of universal law. In *The Nomos of the Earth*, Schmitt (2003) describes how this spatial ordering brought both "undiscovered" lands and the borderless "*elemental* freedom of the sea" (175; italics in original) within a European legal framework that was expediently created and given a global writ. In explaining Nomos as "the *measure* by which the land in a particular order is divided and situated," Schmitt adds that "it is also the form of political, social, and religious order determined by this process" (70; italics in original). In his account, the attempt to order the world through the paternalistic classifying gaze of Europe ensured that "the term 'European' signified the normal status that set the standard for the non-European parts of the Earth. Civilization was synonymous with European civilization" (86). Notable for this project, which is focused on the role of conventions in the digital domain, codes and protocols of international law were key to enabling this spatial reordering of the world, as its newly ascertained spherical shape and the physical limits of the planet were being apprehended. Schmitt explains, "No sooner had the contours of the earth emerged as a real globe—not just sensed as myth, but apprehensible as fact and measurable as space—than there arose a wholly new and hitherto unimaginable problem: the spatial ordering of the earth in terms of international law. The new global image, resulting from the circumnavigation of the earth and the great discoveries of the 15th and 16th centuries, required a new spatial order. Thus began the epoch of modern international law that lasted until the 20th century" (86).

Colonialism provided the urgency for seafaring European conquerors to be given legal justification. Expediently relying on cartographic surveys by Europeans, so-called international law responded to this exigence by codifying the conditions and legal categories under which territorial expansion could occur. The legal concept of discovery, for instance, could apply only beyond the line where European public law ended and wherein lay "*free space* as an area open to European occupation and expansion" (Schmitt 2003, 87; italics in original). Moreover, the idea was "not a timeless, universal, and normative concept" (131) but applicable only during a particular historical moment, conveniently termed the "age of discovery," when the appropriation of distant lands could occur. These legal conventions' expedient definition of discoverers excluded categories of adventurers such as pirates, sea entrepreneurs, and others acting on their own who could not be legal occupiers of "free space."

European jurisprudence, functioning under the guise of universal international law and procedures, therefore emerged as an active enabler of the land appropriations that created the colonial empire. This geopolitical deployment of seemingly neutral and universally applicable legal conventions, even while barely concealing their parochial political ends, is vital to understanding how conventions can function similarly on the global web today. The interweaving of international law with colonialism, as delineated by Schmitt, provides a concrete instantiation of how norms, standards, and procedures can function as the handmaiden of global political and cultural power. This holds many lessons for our analysis of moments and sites of conflict in the digital ecosystem today where the conventions, rules, and affordances of the social web come into conflict with the irreducible local, cultural, and national particularities that resist them. As the dominant Western digital oligopolies scramble to enfold the next half of the world's population that is currently "beyond the line" (Schmitt 2003, 93) of the expanding web into their private enclosures, the parallels between the historical process Schmitt describes above and the ongoing ordering and carving of the digital sphere are hard to miss. Through aggressive and innovative machinations that include satellites, balloons, and drones, the oligopolies' goal to be the first to reach the unconnected half of humanity reveals a structuring process akin to an emerging nomos of the digital. It seeks to tame the unruly and contain the excess. In examining the oligopolies' machinations in the digital domain, this study is only extending into that realm well-established insights from other eras and global processes. Consequently, a similar analysis of the global terrain of the digital is timely.

Digital Conventions as Global Infrastructures of Control

What, then, are the digital equivalents of these historically contested standards for law, language, time, distance, and commerce (and other elements of global life)? The much-needed turn to the lens of infrastructuralism within media studies (Peters 2015; Plantin and Punathambekar 2019; Parks and Starosielski 2015; Larkin 2008) gives us a conceptually rich vantage point from which to consider how elements such as protocols, standards, design, and algorithmic regulation make up the architecture of the digital ecosystem and are enmeshed within relations of power that perform ideological functions online. The taken-for-granted role of physical infrastructures that in their most basic manifestations are "material forms that allow for exchange" (Larkin 2008, 5), such as aqueducts, highways, bridges, plumbing, electricity wires, and networks of cable (Appel, Anand, and Gupta 2018; Edwards et al. 2009), form the normalized backgrounds of our lives and provide a productive conceptual lens through which to study large sociotechnical systems. The current interest heralded by the infrastructural turn in key disciplines including media studies was presciently anticipated by Gilles Deleuze (1998), who underscored their constraining role within societies of control by citing the example of the highway on which "people can drive infinitely and 'freely' without being at all confined yet while still being perfectly controlled" (Deleuze 1998, 18). Transportation systems such as highways are the archetypical infrastructures of modernity, enabling exchange, facilitating movement, and regulating the distribution and flow of goods, people, and traffic.

In each such instantiation, the essential role of infrastructures as mediating symbolic and material goods and resources gives them the capacity to distribute progress and prosperity as well as hardships and death (Appel, Anand, and Gupta 2018), making them prized tools of power caught up within social and political contestations. The abundant material infrastructures around us that form the invisible (until they break down) background of our lives, however, should not keep us from examining the role of their "soft" counterparts (Aouragh and Chakravartty 2016). Those include the seemingly intangible ordering structures of life such as calendars, law, religion, websites, protocols (Peters 2015), culture, and aesthetics (Larkin 2008) as well as processes of knowledge production (Bowker 2018) that powerfully "shape the formation of social collectivities and the circulation of media objects, ideas and so on" (Punathambekar and Mohan 2019, 13) within social life. Through emphasizing the role of these soft infrastructures over the material and physical ones, this project is concerned with the cultural and ideological force of these seemingly "soft" elements, such as default settings, affordances, design elements, protocols, and algorithmic regulation, in shaping the sequence of actions, choices, and possibilities within the digital domain.

The Deleuzian reference to a highway as an archetypical instantiation of control points to the centrality of enduring sociotechnical structures of mediation and distribution within his schema. In fact, there could hardly be a better conceptual metaphor than the one invoked by infrastructures to help realize the eternal oscillation between constraints and freedom through which Deleuzian control operates. Since "controls are a *modulation*" (Deleuze 1992, 4; italics in original), the agility, pliancy, dynamism, and portability of the structures through which they operate are key to their effectiveness. And while physical and material infrastructures can embody the logic of control just as well, it is their "relentlessly recalibrating" (Cheney-Lippold 2018) soft counterparts where this alternating modality of power attains true culmination. In the endlessly customizable digital domain, therefore, "softness" is the sine qua non of control. In this terrain, the seemingly intangible settings, protocols, design, and algorithmic regulation that shape the directions of our digital journeys thus double up as *infrastructures of control.* They are the visible (as the user interface) and invisible (as the algorithmic viscera) structures of the digital ecosystem that shape, persuade, nudge, and regulate who we are, what we do, where we belong, and what we know, create, or consume online. They give in and resist by wagering a potent mix of variable rewards for desirable actions and penalties for undesirable ones, thus making the implicit bargain (e.g., attention for content, data for sociality) a pervasive ethos through which they operate. And given the global-by-default character of the web, soft infrastructures have an unprecedented ability to project their sway across time and space globally. As they do so, these global and seemingly intangible "amorphous networks of cultural exchange" (Aouragh and Chakravartty 2016, 564) also continuously open up sites of conflict over culture, knowledge, ideology, and political power.

Given the above, an infrastructural analysis of the global dimensions of digital media requires emphasizing the role of "pipelines and protocols of culture, not its products" (Vaidhyanathan 2012, 109), and when seen from such a geopolitical vantage point, their structuring role gives us an inkling into what some scholars have described as the emergence of "infrastructure imperialism" (109). The combination of the intangibility of soft infrastructures, their immanent form, their ability to reify cultural and political ideas, and their seeming invisibility gives them an enduring power as emphasized in the dictum that "software often outlasts hardware" (Peters 2015, 32). Their effects pervade deep into the nooks and crannies of global social life, but, equally importantly, they persevere and thrive long after physical and tangible structures have perished.

These digital infrastructures of control are the modern-day equivalents of the historically contested conventions and standards described in the prior sections that today form the "common rules for structuring information" (DeNardis 2011, vii) online as well as the "technoscientific rules and standards that govern relationships within networks" (Galloway and Thacker 2007, 28). They operate both in the invisible (to the user, as it is behind the interface) realm of codes, standards of interoperability, and algorithms as well as in the visible realm such as the design, affordances, and default settings of platforms. The former category has recently emerged as the subject of widespread critical enquiry (DeNardis 2011; Bucher 2018; Beer 2017; Willson 2017), given their prominent role in shaping online behavior and regulating relationships between users and content (among other things).

Growing critical scholarship on the power of algorithms, for instance, has focused on their role as gatekeepers of cultural content (Gillespie 2017; Bishop 2018; Kumar 2019), the opacity of their decision-making processes (Pasquale 2015), their ability to "nudge" human behavior at a computational scale (Yeung 2017), their role in regulating the emerging gig economy (Rosenblat 2018; Wood et al. 2019), their shaping of online culture by rewarding desirable and penalizing undesirable behaviors (Cotter 2019; Bucher 2012), as well as the inherent bias within their decision-making processes (Noble 2018; Eubanks 2018), thus raising worrying questions about their emergence as instruments of cultural and political power in the digital domain. Designing these blueprints of code, which mostly remain opaque to researchers and users (except in the visibility of their effect), is not merely a scientific and technical exercise but also a discursive one (Braman 2016) with little public input (Morris Jr. 2011) and hence invariably laden with cultural, social, and ideological values and biases (Cotter 2019) that are bound to seep into their design.

As digital systems pervade global social life, so do these opaque architectures alongside them, thus leading to a form of "protocol globalization" (DeNardis 2009, 26) that gradually enfolds global subjects within the clutch of a "a power they feel but whose nature they may not be able to articulate clearly" (Grewal 2008, 6). By associating certain combinations of actions and choices with predetermined cultural, political, or identity markers (Cheney-Lippold 2018), mirroring and amplifying oppressive social norms of othering and denigration (Noble 2018) as well as imposing particular interpretations of "valuations, meanings, and relationships to objects and actors" (Cotter 2019, 898), these algorithmic systems reify particular digital pathways of relating, being, communicating, and performing online subjectivities. The global ramifications of the cultural and political values that these digital infrastructures embody remain largely uninterrogated due to both their inaccessibility and their anonymity within the distributed network. If "*no one controls networks, but networks are controlled*" (Galloway and Thacker 2007, 39; italics in original), it becomes imperative for critical scholars of media and digital culture to unravel the locus and modality of that control. Far from resigning itself to the opaque machinations of this environmental form of power, this project takes up the challenge of understanding its operation and the enduring changes coming in their wake.

In addition to the invisible and opaque realm (e.g., codes and algorithms), soft infrastructures also operate at the visible (user interface) level, asserting a cultural and ideological force through an ever-expanding array of rules, settings, affordances, and design elements that users must navigate to get around the digital ecosystem. The conventions that regulate knowledge production on Wikipedia, for instance, help determine standards of proof, evidence, and fact but also advance particular notions of epistemology and truth that are arguably political and ideological. Similarly, nuances such as layout, design, and default settings of social media platforms that incentivize self-revelation and disclosure while penalizing reticence and privacy (Cirucci 2015) advance key cultural notions about what it means to be an ideal subject in the digital world. This power is also evident in the rules and protocols regulating speech, commerce, and subversion (among other factors) that push against laws of sovereign states and draw the digital domain into direct conflict with nations and states. Often posing a bigger challenge to the sovereignty of nations today than military, economic, or political power, these conventions—for instance, about allowable speech or online commerce—may align far better with certain nations' values than others (Mueller 2017). The global nature of the web ensures that these culturally and ideologically derived rules and standards arising from contingent geographical, historical, and cultural contexts become global and universal conventions, with regulatory power across national and cultural boundaries. Soft infrastructures of these kinds, which enable interactions while also regulating and shaping them, assert control through the paradox that "coordination is both liberating and entrapping: liberating because it offers greater access to others, and entrapping because it does so—often necessarily—in a way that privileges one mode of access rather than another" (Grewal 2008, 7). As subsequent chapters will show, the privileging of particular "modes of access" on the digital domain is also the simultaneous advancement of particular cultural, political, and ideological values that are corralled alongside the affordances and choices that enable association, communication, and creation. In the emergent global platform ecosystem, therefore, freedom is the wile of control.

An instance of such privileging (embedded at the invisible/opaque level as well as at the user interface level) can be the economic logics that often form an "intricate part of a site's philosophy" (van Dijck, Poell, and de Waal 2018, 11), especially those governing the collection and usage of data online. The emphasis on sharing and interactivity that propels the collection and monetization of user information (Couldry and Mejias 2019), as visible in the design of most dominant social media platforms across the web today, instantiates how seemingly neutral infrastructures can encapsulate ideologies such as capitalism and the profit motive. Designed to foster a kind of connectivity that has the business interests of particular and private web entities at its heart (van Dijck 2013; Vaidhyanathan 2012), the default settings and conventions of globally dominant platforms today function akin to the assembly lines of yore, collecting and channeling the raw material (data) that fuels and sustains the core businesses of these digital platforms. Interactivity, the very lifeblood of most social networking sites, is presented as satiating some universal human need, thus providing the ideological mask for what scholars have identified as a new form of data-driven "digital capitalism" (Fuchs and Mosco 2017; Pace 2018). Today's dominant platforms are the sites where these processes of digital capitalism play out, and their global spread accrues increasing economic, political, and cultural gains for particular corporations and in turn the nation-states where they are located. Dal Yong Jin (2015) has established how the meteoric rise of mobile devices to access the web, for instance, only further amplified the power of platform intermediaries such as Facebook and Google as well as mobile operating systems (e.g., Android, iOS), giving them increasingly greater ability to shape access and monopolize interactive data.

The Geopolitics of Digital Conventions

With the global spread of the web, collisions between the political, cultural, and ideological values embedded within what has been called its infrastructures of control and the national, regional, and local sites irreducible to those values around the world are creating a "geopolitical minefield" (van Dijck, Poell, and de Waal 2018, 4) that increasingly pits nations, regions, and cultures against the digital ecosystem and each other. Along with these conflicts, both real and potential, there are intensifying attempts to shape and align the web to each state's own cultural and political orientations (Mueller 2017). The resulting geopolitical struggle to control and mold digital networks has led to a contentious politics over internet governance (DeNardis 2014; Balleste 2015) that has involved nations and governments, thus emphasizing our rethink of claims about the acultural neutrality of digital conventions. Akin to the French complaint that the convention of the GMT passing through Greenwich was about political power rather than the "impartial solicitude of science" (Galison 2004, 152), positions taken by different countries on internet governance (Powers and Jablonski 2015;

DeNardis 2014) today are increasingly determined by national interest and fears about the loss of cultural and political sovereignty instead of by scientific and technological rationale.

Scholars, for instance, often point to how the discourse of openness, neutrality, and internet freedom is increasingly being called out as a ruse to advance specific goals of dominant global powers (the United States, for instance). These critiques often rely on the visible convergences of American political interests with those of the emerging dominant digital media platforms and corporations (e.g., the Big Five) that show how seemingly altruistic calls for freedom of information often mask the web's cultural baggage of values and ideals that are arguably Western. The infamous Google-China conflict of 2010 (as well as the recent US push for a "clean-network" and United States-Huawei conflict of 2019–20) exemplifies this tussle, wherein the difference between its portrayals in the United States as a clash between liberty and authoritarianism and in the Chinese press as a global geopolitical battle pointed to the loaded cultural and political stakes being masked by the discourse of openness and access. Powers and Jablonski (2015) also buttress this argument by claiming that Hillary Clinton's (2010) speech and its coverage in the Chinese media showed that while Clinton presented it as an issue of global rights, it was widely perceived as a hegemonic move veiled by the discourse of internet freedom to advance US foreign policy and economic interests.

In other similar instances (e.g., the use of Twitter in the Iranian protests of 2009), scholars have shown how Western power was enhanced through advancing a seductive and uncritical belief in the transformational effects of technology that bordered on a form of "cyber-utopianism" (Morozov 2012). Morozov's probing analysis of the active collusion of web platforms in furthering a political position, masked as the larger common good, during the protests against the Iranian government in summer 2009 reveals the geopolitical stakes in advancing a utopian view of technology. The protestors' active use of Twitter was called into question by governments opposed to the United States after it was accidentally revealed that the US State Department explicitly requested Twitter to "reschedule the previously planned—and now extremely ill-timed—maintenance of the site, so as not to disrupt the Iranian protests" (Morozov 2012, 9).

Even as Twitter complied with the request, the leaked email to the *New York Times* confirmed the suspicion that "Twitter is an instrument of Western power and that its ultimate end is to foster regime change in Iran"

(Morozov 2012, 10). While other nation-states latched on to the critique for their own political goals, this controversy nudges us to reconsider Twitter's own claims (van Dijck 2013) of functioning like the public sphere or a global town hall. Undoubtedly, the values of freedom, democracy, and free expression that Twitter ostensibly symbolized during the Iranian protests are worthy causes, especially in a context of extreme repression, but they are specific values nonetheless. As Siva Vaidhyanathan has argued, such calls to specific political values "carry strong assumptions that people everywhere have the same needs, values, and desires—even if they don't yet know it themselves" (Vaidhyanathan 2012, 109). Embedding these values within the web universalizes them and functions to erase their specific historical, cultural, and geographical origins that are being globalized through digital networks.

A cursory survey of the digital ecosystem (of platforms, corporations, media coverage, etc.) shows how these seductive narratives abound, presenting the web akin to a globally representative network that is shaped by the summative mean of all the nodes inhabiting it. For digital oligopolies such as Facebook, such a narrative manifests in the altruistic motive to connect the entire world (while also claiming to fiercely protect our privacy); for Google it is to help create order on the web and parse out the useful from the useless; while for a collaborative knowledge platform such as Wikipedia that seductive narrative manifests itself in the slogan to "create the sum of all human knowledge" (Slashdot 2004). Even though these powerful narratives have been shown to be selectively applied and to mask corporate agendas, they refuse to lose their potency (at least in the public realm) because when seen through a unidimensional lens that eschews questions of power and imagines a world made up of sovereign, equally strong cultures, they do seem to be correct.

Undoubtedly Facebook does connect us in some fundamentally newer ways, Google does help organize and sort through the web's information for us, and Wikipedia does provide access to a wealth of knowledge. What remains underinterrogated in these seemingly true narratives, however, are the ways in which other things get corralled as a part of the same package but are the obverse side of the dominant narrative of emancipation, liberation, and connection. To return to the Heideggerian question, these dominant narratives are seemingly correct but not true (Heidegger 1977; Ihde 1979), and understanding that necessitates that we expand the frame to get at the totality of their scale of operation. In providing a framework for interrogating this phenomenon across various sites of conflict that involve the dominant platforms on the web, this book seeks to unravel how sites and structures with preexisting cultural power (accumulated through the dominance of legacy industries) can deploy and merge with the networked infrastructural power of digital platforms to create a newer still-emerging form of global cultural power.

Chapter Overviews

This book makes its argument by weaving through four aspects of cultural life online to show the political, social, and ideological reordering underway in the global digital domain. Each of these aspects is captured in a chapter that uses recent case studies and conflicts to explicate its argument about the power of conventions, norms, and standards on the global web. Each chapter is driven by the insight that sites and moments of conflict reveal a breakdown of routine processes and procedures, thus providing rich case studies for analysis. Close study of conflicts, breakdowns, stalemates, and malfunction (Larkin 2008; Gillespie 2017; Kumar 2017; Burgess and Matamoros-Fernández 2016) have provided scholars with productive examples that suggest broader ramifications. As subsequent chapters will show, such conflicts also allow us to unravel the dialectic of culture and code, the universal and the particular, and the global and the local that animates the current global adoption of the web.

Chapter 2 of this book prepares the ground for the subsequent case studies in the book by focusing on the scramble to appropriate the undigitized regions of the world, led by the Western digital corporations (four out of the Big Five—Facebook, Google, Microsoft, and Amazon; the fifth is Apple). By showing how this scramble represents both the globalization and the usurpation of digital infrastructures, the second chapter forms the ground on which the subsequent operations of cultural power are shown to operate. In each of these attempts to connect the world, discourses of altruism and empowerment are being used to peddle companies' own versions of the internet, which, in some cases, grossly violate norms of network neutrality. The expanding digital empires of these digital corporations and the race to connect the world are strikingly similar to a prior history wherein a logic of spreading the benefits of "civilization" spurred European colonialism across the world. In showing parallels between the two, this chapter argues that just as the historical impulse to profit from the appropriation of land through force, deceit, and legal justifications created a division between the "civilized" and "uncivilized" lands that were separated by the colonial frontier, the current attempts to digitize the world expediently use the global digital divide to expand each corporation's private digital enclosure. This competitive rush to create private walled gardens (through schemes such as Facebook Basics) seeks to reorder the global web by locking up new netizens within private fenced-off enclosures, thus creating captive sources of data that will, through infrastructural nudges, generate and share behavioral information to be monetized by the dominant corporations. The offer of "free" internet services in the underdeveloped regions of the world (e.g., India and Africa) is a wager on the future rewards accruing from such a captive market as the next half of the world comes online. In showing how this is akin to a form of digital colonization, this chapter extends the concept from its historically territorial and physical dimension to a digital one.

The third chapter of this book analyses the epistemic realm by focusing on knowledge production online, with a specific emphasis on the collaborative encyclopedia Wikipedia. Inspired by the historically established relationship between knowledge and power (Foucault 1980; Said 1979; Chakrabarty 2007; Spivak 1999, 2013), the chapter on knowledge shows how that relationship continues in the online domain through hegemonic definitions of legitimate knowledge, visible at the sites of friction created from resistances to it. Chapter 3 begins with a broad analysis and critique of Wikipedia's organizational structures, rules, and policies that form its infrastructure of knowledge (Bowker 2018) and then focuses on how a disproportionate distribution of language, editors, content, and readers for the online encyclopedia align its content with Anglo-European definitions of knowledge. The consequences of its internal architecture as well as its skewed distribution of editors ensures that Wikipedia's goal to create "the sum of all human knowledge" (Slashdot 2004) remains severely compromised since certain dominant versions of knowledge come to count for global knowledge. The chapter establishes this by closely analyzing its processes of creating content, as revealed in its decade-long "edit war" about naming the Wikipedia page on the Indian Ganga/Ganges River, along with the overwhelming evidence about the skewed demography of its editors. The long edit war, archived in the talk pages of Wikipedia, shows how the conflict over neutrality, evidence, and local versus global versions of English masked what was equally an ideological and political conflict.

Chapter 3's analysis is informed by the backdrop of the global digital divide (Warschauer 2004; Straumann and Graham 2016) that limits internet access in large parts of the world, thus ensuring continuing inequities of participation in online knowledge production. The hegemony of certain languages over others, of certain histories over others, and of Eurocentric paradigms of knowledge production and legitimation pose sobering correctives to claims about the web's representative ethos. In bringing the insights of postcolonial theory to bear on knowledge production online, this chapter will add to prior scholarship that has investigated the asymmetries within linguistic and geographic distribution of knowledge online (Pimienta, Prado, and Blanco 2009; Kittur et al. 2007; Kittur and Kraut 2008; Flammia and Saunders 2007; Gerrand 2006, 2007) as well as recent studies that have questioned the collaborative and participatory claims of Wikipedia (Jemielniak 2014; Callahan 2014; Tkacz 2015). This chapter's argument corroborates other findings about online knowledge production such as UNESCO's inquiry into online linguistic diversity, which concluded that search engine results privilege particular cultural connotations pointing to significant Eurocentric biases in the ideas, terms, and values that dictate and influence online discourse.

The fourth chapter of the book focuses on the social dimension of the web to argue that the growth and global uptake of digital infrastructures of sociality are globalizing particular normative ideas of selfhood. The emergence of particular notions of the self as an aspirational ideal to be emulated is visible across the digital platforms that shape and regulate user behavior by rewarding particular performances of subjectivity and punishing others. The reward of visibility juxtaposed with the disincentive of irrelevance and invisibility on the social web functions to encourage particular kinds of behavior (e.g., self-expression, lifestreaming, and entrepreneurial management of one's online persona) while discouraging others such as reticence, privacy, and lack of sharing and self-revelation. This structure of rewards and sanctions is embedded within the affordances of the web wherein the design elements (e.g., placement of buttons as well as textual and symbolic cues) and algorithmic regulation nudge particular notions of a normative self whose examples are visible across all dimensions of the global web today.

Chapter 4 locates the particular cultural origins of this subjectivity within the churnings of Euro-Western capitalist modernity (Rose 1996, 1999) wherein new technologies, practices, and discourses about the ideal subject functioned to create an aspirational notion of the self. That ideal subject had key attributes such as radical individuality, an expressive and self-revealing personhood, and an entrepreneurial attitude of managing and crafting one's social identity. The chapter concludes by showing how each of those three attributes can be found within specific dominant practices of the global selfie culture, the culture of lifestreaming and vlogging, and the growth of the global influencer culture. In nudging the discrete disconnected self, in encouraging a practice of limitless self-revelation and in displaying an attitude of self-sufficient entrepreneurship, each of these three dominant cultural practices online showcases the main features of the aspirational subject that the chapter upholds as instances of the global reshaping of culture in the wake of the globalization of digital platforms.

The fifth chapter focuses on the nation-state's gradual recession in the face of network power—a phenomenon whose signs are visible within the political, cultural, and social sphere the world over. The effortless ease with which digital networks can transgress boundaries and bypass traditional controls on information flow (Mueller 2017; Morris and Waisbord 2001) has dialectical consequences because the same networked architecture that aids democratic forces by challenging the oppressive state can also be a tool for reactionary elements to undermine the nation-state's stated egalitarian and progressive ideals. Such struggles between the emerging and receding forms of power are clear in what has been called the global "war" for internet governance wherein nations compete over shaping the web's technical architecture, thus underscoring the idea that the internet's scaffoldings contain arrangements of cultural power (DeNardis 2014). Through analyzing several recent conflicts broadly categorized under the categories security, law, culture, and information, this chapter makes a case for differential sovereignty in the global domain. It closely interrogates controversies such as Google Earth's repeated confrontations with nation-states, states' difficulties in regulating malicious and hateful online content, and widespread fears about the erosion of national and cultural identities (such as Europe's ongoing tussles with digital platforms such as Google and Facebook). Through these analyses, this chapter argues that even though all nation-states are besieged by this new networked form of power that claims a deterritorialized status, their abilities to align the web to their values and ideals is directly proportional to their power in the off-line realm. This notion of differential power challenges claims about equality on the web to show that the stark differences in states' abilities to align the internet to their own priorities and values also points to a new era in the short history of the Westphalian nation-state wherein state power is enhanced in key areas of the national domain (e.g., surveillance and control) but significantly diminished in other areas (e.g., regulating flows of information, law enforcement, and national security).

The conclusion of the book evaluates a future wherein the operation of power delineated in this book continues to strengthen and thrive thus, further amplifying the continuing asymmetries and inequities in the global cultural realm. It envisages the consequences of a world that is far more connected and integrated but also one that is far more homogenous and less differentiated than the present world, thus showing how the current architecture of the web moves us in a direction contrary to the utopian ideals of true global representation. In taking note of this future, the conclusion also dares us to imagine an alternative one—ensuring a networked society that does not compromise on difference by requiring cultural change as a prerequisite to accessing and inhabiting the network while also not leading us toward a balkanized web. In thinking of this inclusive alternative, my goal is not to proffer some final solution to the imperatives raised within the book but to show the value of a relentlessly critical perspective inspired by an idealistic (even at times utopian) ethos. I wish to underscore the value of that perspective in thinking about and theorizing the emerging global web by cautioning against the complacent notion that we have already achieved the best possible global digital network. The conclusion is thus animated by my belief that the cumulative progression of history toward a more egalitarian future is one we must all actively shape.

2

FRONTIER

THIS CHAPTER ANALYZES THE GLOBAL EXPANSION OF PRIVATIZED digital enclosures on the web by studying the large-scale efforts, led by the dominant digital corporations, to connect the unconnected parts of the world's population to the internet. These ongoing efforts to connect the world through "free" internet schemes launched by Google, Facebook, Microsoft, and Amazon (which, incidentally, are four of the five oligopolies that form the acronym GAFAM [Smyrnaios 2018]) rely on the inadequate reach and resource scarcity of sovereign states' public institutions to maneuver a space for themselves as internet service providers (ISPs) globally. Large-scale investments in connectivity infrastructures, combined with the corporations' dominance as digital platforms, allow these digital oligopolies to control both hard and soft infrastructures in order to extend their spheres of influence. As they maneuver their way into pole position as ISPs in many parts of the world, they simultaneously also take on the role of public infrastructures and instantiate a new dimension of a process aptly called the "infrastructuralization" of platforms (Plantin et al. 2018).

Moreover, the companies' expanding role as gateways of connectivity is foundational to creating and delimiting the grounds on which their infrastructural power, exercised through the conventions, protocols, and algorithmic regulation outlined in the introductory chapter, operates globally. Deploying the power of standards and protocols to foster and encourage particular behaviors that enable the generation, extraction, collection, and monetization of user data is premised on expanding their private digital enclosures in the physical world where user loyalty is being bought through ostensibly "free" internet schemes. It is this chapter's goal to show how private corporations effectively deploy the ruse of charity and altruism—serving the interests of the unconnected—to expand their enclosures of control in a process that elides pertinent questions about parity, equality, and access, thus undermining the very goals proffered as reasons for increased digital access. This race to expand the territorial fold wherein their cultural power can operate and from which user data can be mined shares its expansionist impulse, its realization of dual and unequal systems, and its use of the discourse of humanitarianism with a prior colonial history of conquest and usurpation.

The common logic among discourses of "free" internet being offered by the dominant digital companies (Facebook, Google, Microsoft, and Amazon) and a prior colonial history of conquest and usurpation that similarly sought to carve out the "newly discovered" world among European powers shows us the similarities in the machinations occurring in these two moments. The aggressive private initiatives for global connectivity, especially within unconnected areas such as the "archipelago of disconnection" (Straumann and Graham 2016, 97), betray corporations' nervousness about losing out in the race to reach potential customers that are prospective long-term captive sources of monetizable data. The bargain of a "free" product or service in return for long-term loyalty is hardly a new strategy and in fact is a salient characteristic of multisided markets (Coyle 2018; Rieder and Sire 2013), which defines the business model of digital platforms wherein subsidizing one side of the business (e.g., free access to draw in users) ensures higher returns from the other side (through advertisements or product sales).

Presenting free connectivity as a charitable act conceals the value accruing to digital platforms from the positive network effects (Flew 2019) created by an increasing number of users that can then act as a magnet to draw in other content creators, services, sellers, and advertisers. As those benefits go uninterrogated, the presumption of philanthropic motives takes center stage, thus obfuscating the clear commercial imperatives and long-term corporate strategies driving these efforts. Their aggressive machinations to connect the world show that for these global web companies, the undigitized terrain is just as inviting and luring a territory as the undiscovered lands during the "age of discovery" wherein the "first partition and classification of space, for the primeval division and distribution" (Schmitt 2003, 67) took place. Then, fortifications, boundaries, and lines of division sought to create distinctions between the conquered and the unconquered that were often coterminous with European and non-European lands. Discourses of the "civilizing mission" and "manifest destiny" that created the grounds for appropriation of new territories by producing legal, moral, and ethical justification were just as crucial to that usurpation as the actual military conquests.

Similar discursive moves are visible within the ongoing high-voltage advertising and public relations campaigns as well as the largely favorable media coverage of these private internet connectivity schemes in the developing world today. The discourse emerging from corporations (interviews, advertisements, public relations exercises) positions these free connectivity schemes as philanthropic missions devoid of any pecuniary motives, and the typically glowing media coverage of these schemes rarely interrogates the reasons behind the free connectivity. Such framing by the media has helped construct a false binary between the status quo of no internet versus what is often a limited version of the internet (e.g., in the case of Facebook's Free Basics, currently offered in sixty five countries at the time of this writing; internet.org, n.d.) provided by these digital corporations. What remains craftily concealed in this framing within media discourses is the fact that by securing these large populations of emerging internet users as captive customers, these companies are ensuring their own long-term growth, reliant on a perpetual pipeline of data, and hence profit. The convergence of the position of the big internet companies and their favorable coverage in the media also instantiates the marketing power and economic strength of these oligopolies in ensuring favorable framing of these schemes.

Analyzing details of these connectivity schemes and their media coverage allows this chapter to extend the conceptual framework of "digital enclosure" (Andrejevic 2009) to a global context wherein its manifestation is akin to a form of digital colonialism (Vaidhyanathan 2018). The promise of access, emancipation, and lives transformed by connectivity helps companies such as Facebook, Microsoft, Amazon, and Google enfold large aspects of the offline life and the commons by creating "walled gardens" on the web. The notion of "free" but limited internet, which often limits access to certain sites and parts of the web, militates against the very spirit of equality, democracy, and plurality that supporters of net neutrality have hailed as crucial to the web's ethos. While it is a well-discussed issue within the Western world (particularly in the United States), the debate about net neutrality has been increasingly taking hold in non-Western settings due to these connectivity providers' predatory efforts to subvert it. The expansion of the corporations' private digital domains therefore shifts the ideology of colonial appropriation from the offline physical world to the online digital one. Just as the colonial discourses of the past saw unconquered lands as "the commons" (Locke 2003, 112) ready to be transformed into private property through human labor, the corporate and media discourses of the present, in providing justifications for these expansionist designs, construct the undigitized world purely as a market ready to be captured and appropriated by private enterprises.

This chapter's argument proceeds by navigating discourses from the peak of the colonial era to show how they created a mandate for usurpation and territorial expansion through presenting legal, religious, and civilizational justifications. The goal of this brief historical overview is to draw parallels between claims such as "manifest destiny" and the "civilizing mission" and contemporary arguments for global connectivity found in the corporate and media discourses this chapter analyzes. The chapter then moves to provide a broad overview of the global connectivity efforts being operationalized by the four big internet oligopolies (Google, Facebook, Microsoft, and Amazon). It enumerates specific details of their ambitious plans and the seriousness with which they are pursuing efforts to connect the world. The concrete details of these connectivity schemes help us closely analyze the role of media and corporate discourses and unravel three dominant frames through which the connectivity schemes are covered by the global press.

The role of discursive framing in advancing particular regimes of truth (Foucault 1980) and "authoritative accounts" (Friederici, Ojanperä, and Graham 2017) about private connectivity efforts underscores the suasive force of discursive formations in creating the mandate for specific maneuvers of power in the material world. Drawing out the convergences between these discursive logics deployed during two distinct temporal moments— one to appropriate land in an earlier era and the other to accumulate data and users from the unconnected half of the world's population—allows this chapter to show how the expanding zones of corporate influence in the digital domain enlarge the terrain of cultural power operating through the conventional and infrastructural nudges of digital culture. While the earlier conquests brought in spoils of natural resources, raw materials, land, and (often) people, expansion in the digital realm is a race to divide the global pie of user-generated interactional data, the extraction and monetization of which is inherently predatory and comes alongside particular behavioral modifications on the part of the users.

The Digital Frontier

The broader issue of the global digital divide is germane to understanding the aggressive campaigns to digitize and connect the unconnected parts of the world. Global digital penetration has risen sharply in the past two decades, from about 1 percent in 1995 to approximately 53 percent in 2019 (International Telecommunication Union 2019). The rate of growth has been exponential: the benchmark of the first billion internet users was reached in 2005, the second billion in 2010, and the third in 2014, making the growth almost tenfold since 1999. The world average of 53 percent, however, conceals stark variations between the developed countries (with 87 percent internet connectivity), developing countries (at 48 percent), and the least developed countries (at 19 percent).[1] Although almost half the global population has yet to come online, the increasingly accelerated rate of growth of connectivity means that the second half will gain access at a much faster rate than the first half did. However, the task of digitizing the next half of the global population presents both challenges and opportunities since it raises pertinent questions about the terms and conditions underlying access to the next half of the web's users. While the desirable goal to have the entire global population online is beyond question, this analysis seeks to focus on the geopolitical power plays and the resulting asymmetries within the private corporate-led designs to digitize the world.

In doing so, I find useful the concept of the "digital frontier," which can be understood as a demarcating line separating the digitized from the undigitized populations of the world. The metaphor of a dividing line (even though one cannot delineate such a straight line) helps invoke a prior colonial history whose lessons are insightful in understanding the aggressive efforts to connect the world to the web. The populations with and without access to the internet are geographically dispersed and coexist within cities, countries, and regions, and yet certain parts of the world have a disproportionately higher percentage of digital access than others by far. Even as connectivity expands, these global imbalances have continued. Estimates at the end of 2014, for example, showed that nearly 75 percent of the world's internet users resided in the top twenty countries (ordered by their extent of connectivity) with the remaining 25 percent distributed across the remaining 178 countries (Internet Live Stats, n.d., "Internet Users"). Iceland (100 percent online) and Eritrea (1.3 percent) occupy the two extremities of this list; the countries in between represent a diverse range of digital diffusion. More recent statistics show these disparities continuing as the geographic regions of Europe (86 percent) and North America (89 percent) have the highest percentage of their populations online, while Africa (39 percent) and Asia (51 percent) have the lowest. Latin America stands in between, with about 68 percent of their population online (Internet World Stats, n.d.).

This unequal distribution of digital connectivity means that the next wave of internet users will come from Asia and Africa (Arora 2019), which form the frontiers separating regions with high internet penetration from the regions still largely deprived of the internet. The notion of the frontier holds strong resonances within colonial discourses of the past as newer lands were being discovered, colonized, and "civilized." In the case of colonial America, the term *frontier* emerged as a metaphor to denote the seemingly limitless, ever expansive unconquered and uninhabited west. It signified "virgin" land where one escaped "history to live with nature" (Noble 1965, 13). The frontier denoted the complex and conflicted symbolism of adventure, risk, opportunity, anxiety, and reward, thus entrenching and legitimizing the mindset of outward expansion. By allowing individuals and societies to appropriate new lands and start anew, the frontier was associated with "perennial rebirth," since it formed "the outer edge of the wave, the meeting point between savagery and civilization" (Turner 1920, 12) beyond which "the wilderness masters the colonist" (13). Despite occurring in a different historical context, the colonial frontier that separated the conquered (or tamed) from the unconquered (or wild) holds notable conceptual similarities with the digital frontier separating the connected from the unconnected parts of the world today.

Just like the colonial frontier, the digital one works through a particular imaginary of what exists on the other side of the dividing line. In the case of the colonial frontier, the terrain beyond the line was seemingly open for exploration and settling, thus ensuring that America could defer social and class conflict by externalizing it. The frontier allowed the dispossessed and the disgruntled sections of society to free themselves from the historically entrenched structures of power and oppression and begin anew in a process that Turner describes evocatively: "For a moment at the frontier the bonds of custom are broken, and unrestraint is triumphant. There is not *tabula rasa* . . . each frontier did indeed furnish a new field of opportunity, a gate of escape from the bondage of the past; and freshness, and confidence, and scorn of older society, impatience of its restraints and its ideas, and indifference to its lessons" (Turner 1920, 42). The digital frontier invokes similar tropes for the undigitized parts of the world, which are seen as waiting to enter the wondrous world of digital connectivity, wherein lies the solution to all their social problems. These tropes of digital emancipation accompanied by a missionary zeal, common in the corporate discourses of the oligopolies (discussed below), barely conceal an ambition to bring new users into their private enclosures before they are lost to other tech companies and platforms. They function similarly to arguments such as the idea of manifest destiny (Mountjoy 2009), which suggested a divine sanction to conquer and predicted an ordained victory of ideas such as "liberty and federated self-government" (O'Sullivan, quoted in Mountjoy 2009, 10) over the preexisting cultures and civilizations of North America.

Analyzing similarities in these usurpative logics, despite their temporal distance, is important because they allow us to observe that particular discursive formations (Foucault 1982; Foucault and Hurly 1990) are wedded to institutions of power and create and advance specific realities. They highlight and make real certain meanings and interpretations of events while glossing over competing versions and parallel histories. Both these urges of expansion, though temporally separate, rationalized their ambitions by conflating their own pecuniary self-interests with those of the populations being colonized and connected. The counternarrative from the vantage point of those being subjected or digitized is erased in the case of colonialism and provided as the justification for expansion in the mission of connecting the world. Just as critiques of the discourses of frontier and manifest destiny have sought to reveal the violence of the act of usurpation, the task here is to show that despite impassioned claims to the contrary, the interests of the undigitized populations are not at the center of efforts to bridge the digital divide led by private corporations.

The "walled garden" that these digital oligopolies seek to create by expanding their private enclosures (Andrejevic 2009) functions analogously to physical barriers in the offline world in controlling and regulating human behavior for achieving efficiency and profit. But unlike the coercive logic of physical control that functioned in the case of colonialism, control in the digital realm works through the power of conventions, protocols, and algorithmic manipulation (Willson 2017) and relies on habit, convenience, and the routinized inertia of users (Duhigg 2012) to keep them confined within their enclosure. The oligopolies' larger goal of becoming the "gateway drug" (Morozov 2012) of internet experience for millions seeks to foster and encourage online behaviors that allow for the collection of behavioral data. By staking the first claim to the undigitized half of the world's population before publicly accountable state institutions do so, the corporations seek to leverage the "winner-takes-all" (Barwise and Watkins 2018) nature of digital markets through a phenomenon described variously as the network effect (Vaidhyanathan 2012) or network power (Grewal 2008) that makes it very difficult (if not impossible) to dislodge digital platforms with large networks of users.

The Race to Divide the Global Internet Pie

What, then, are the concrete ways in which this race is being played out? To win the competition to connect the world and gain the largest share of the digital pie composed of the second half of the world's population, each of the four big digital oligopolies has dedicated, ambitious connectivity projects backed by significant resources. Google, Facebook, Microsoft, and Amazon are all trying to outdo one another, thus expanding their roles beyond software and web technology firms to emerge in their alternative avatars as global ISPs. This dual role, by concentrating the soft (content, services) and hard (material) infrastructures in the same hands, raises troubling questions about fairness, equity, network neutrality, and asymmetrical corporate power, the answers to which will hold significant consequences for how the future of the web will unfold in large parts of the world. In order to appreciate the chapter's argument about the mechanics of how the discourse of the "frontier" operates in this process, it is important to get an overview of the schemes through which the dominant Western internet companies are seeking to digitize and connect the world. While not an exhaustive list of all connectivity projects they have launched, the summary below attends to the most prominent ones led by each corporation to show their significant investments of manpower, capital, and technological infrastructure. These commitments underscore the ambition of plans that range from buying drone manufacturing companies to laying fiber optic cables under the sea, exploring connectivity through satellite, employing television white space technology, collaborating with telecommunication companies, and sending balloons into the stratosphere. None of these investment strategies accrues immediate profits for these companies, thus pointing to the long-term designs driving these connectivity projects.

Google leads the charge of providing internet connectivity globally through various schemes such as Project Loon, Project Fi, Google Fiber, TV White

Spaces, and country-specific programs such as Google Station in India. Space constraints prevent a detailed description of each scheme, but an overview will help us understand the ambition and scale that take the company far beyond its core competency of search and web products to make it an ISP with global ambitions. Project Loon is Google's most ambitious moon shot; its aim is to provide global connectivity through a network of solar-powered balloons floating at heights of up to twenty kilometers—an audacious attempt at providing internet to areas that are still out of reach through the regular connectivity mechanisms.

As the Project Loon website (X—The Moonshot Factory, n.d.) states, Google has taken "the most essential components of a cell tower and redesigned them to be light enough and durable enough to be carried by a balloon 20 km up in the stratosphere" (Loon.com, n.d.). Despite posing technological challenges, it is easy to understand the advantages of such a scheme, as connectivity through floating balloons allows one to provide the needed service with a relatively light footprint on the ground, obviating the need for permanent structures or navigating bureaucratic procedures and government regulations. As it is run by Company X, Google's secretive research and development wing, the exact details of the project, including the countries targeted, the costs incurred, and future expansion plans, remain closely guarded. However, news about the project continues to emerge through occasional media write-ups and incidents such as the crash-landing of its balloons in places including Sri Lanka, New Zealand, Peru, and South Africa. While Google's plan to provide connectivity through drones was quietly shelved (Burgess 2017), Project Loon continues to ride on recent successes that use the company's engineering knowledge in other areas to increase efficiency and feasibility. By incorporating lessons from machine learning, Google's engineers have managed to decrease the number of balloons required to provide connectivity from the expected three hundred to four hundred to only ten to twenty per region, thus bringing the project far closer to profitability (Metz 2017).

While Project Loon remains its most ambitious and global scheme, Google has aggressively diversified its approaches to providing internet access through a variety of mechanisms by striking deals with local institutions and stakeholders. With over half a billion of its population yet to be brought on to the web, India is a key site for a slew of such projects, which include teaming up with the government-owned RailTel through a plan called Google Station (n.d.), where the company partners with local institutions and businesses (e.g., cafes, bus stations, hotels) and organizations that provide online literacy to rural women. Now also available in Indonesia and Mexico, Google Station is aggressively pursuing providing Wi-Fi connectivity (in partnership with RailTel) in places without access. It started with a goal to provide Wi-Fi at 400 train stations in India (RailTel, n.d.) and was already providing access to two million people every day in 2016 (Condliffe, 2016). By 2019, the number of connected stations had jumped to 1,600 (*Economic Times* 2019), with ambitions to connect all stations in the country (nearly 8,500 in all) by the end of the year, which one media report called "overtly optimistic" (*Business Today* 2018). The scheme converts a wired network into a wireless one for any location willing to share its revenue with Google, as explained in this news excerpt describing Google's connectivity efforts: "The search giant then launched Station, wifi for any venue—bus station, hotel, or café—as long as the place has wired internet connectivity. Google will provide the wifi equipment, and work out a shared-revenue model" (Sen 2016).

These technological solutions to provide connectivity are supplemented by Google's educational and training programs, such as Internet Saathi, which trains women in rural India to use the internet and has targeted half of India's villages to bring them online. Other schemes such as launching local language keyboards and "lite" versions of its websites and apps (so it can be accessed with lower data usage) show the importance of connectivity in Google's future strategy. With almost 70 percent of its population untapped and relatively lax regulatory and privacy laws, India gets particular attention as it represents "the largest open internet market in the world" (Kuchler 2016). The country has emerged as a crucial site of raging competition among the big web companies, and a recent Bloomberg article rightly described the process as Western web companies "flocking to India to amass their next billion users" (Rai 2016) as markets in the West reach saturation. So intense is the competition between the digital giants in India that media reports frequently speculate about who is winning the race (Doshi 2016; Condliffe 2016).

Google's efforts to connect the world are closely followed by Facebook's as it aggressively seeks to carve out its own share of the global pie of the unconnected through schemes that range from utilizing drones and collaborations with telecom companies to country-specific programs (similar to Google) that involve local governments and stakeholders. The most ambitious plan within Facebook's portfolio of global connectivity efforts is its

Free Basics scheme (previously called internet.org), which was successfully running in sixty-five countries as of September 2020 (internet.org, n.d.), with plans to expand to many more. In each of these locations (which comprise twenty-six countries in Africa, twelve in Asia-Pacific, and twenty-five in Latin America), Facebook has teamed up with a local mobile company to offer "a set of free basic services that will serve as an onramp" to the internet. While India's regulatory body barred this plan in January 2015 after allegations that it violated norms of network neutrality, it has thrived and grown in other parts of the world (primarily in Asia, Africa, and Latin America) and has already provided connectivity to over a billion people (Facebook for Developers, n.d.). As the list of the countries where it has been launched shows, Facebook is primarily targeting nations in the developing world that lack resources and technical infrastructures to prioritize internet connectivity for their citizens. As will be shown below, Facebook's campaign to peddle this scheme leverages this lack of connectivity and technical infrastructure to present its efforts as a charitable mission with no financial motives. Its framing of this scheme as a philanthropic enterprise stands in contrast to what critics have argued is its highly selective criteria used to pick websites (Morozov 2015), which violates norms of net neutrality and makes Facebook the adjudicator and gatekeeper of content on the web.

The rejection of Free Basics in India after accusations of violating net neutrality, while a setback, has not deterred Facebook from seeking its share of the digital pie in that country, as exemplified by Express Wi-Fi (Express Wi-Fi by Facebook, n.d.), a new plan that it first offered only in India (Baraniuk 2016) and has since expanded to a handful of other countries. Having learned from its mistakes with the Free Basics debacle, Facebook remains guarded about the new scheme, but it is described on its website as empowering "local entrepreneurs to help provide quality internet access to their neighbors and make a steady income." The website goes to explain that the plan provides technology and software for local entrepreneurs to work with "local internet service providers or mobile operators . . . to connect their communities" (Express Wi-Fi by Facebook, n.d.). Media reports have indicated that while it will not be entirely free (like Free Basics), Express Wi-Fi will be "affordable" (*Economic Times* 2016), thus hinting that Facebook would address a major barrier to connectivity in India: the cost of access.

While Google has shelved its drone program in favor of Project Loon, solar-powered drones form a key part of Facebook's strategy to connect the world. Through acquisitions and in-house research, the social media giant has consolidated expertise in the field of solar-powered drones with its first test flight in June 2016, which made global news (Metz 2016). Called Aquila, the plan is to have these drones fly in the stratosphere for up to sixty to ninety days (Glaser, 2016) and beam down a signal that can be received through tiny antennas to provide connectivity. Facebook's foray into the area of drone technology has been enabled by the 2014 acquisitions of drone makers Titan Aerospace for $60 million (Solomon 2014) and UK-based Ascenta for $20 million (Garside, 2014). Despite these efforts, however, the technology of providing sustainable connectivity through drones "is still years from completion" (Metz 2016) and faces innumerable challenges that need to be addressed. Given these challenges, Facebook's drone project remains far behind Google's Project Loon, which has already begun beaming down internet and is at a far advanced stage of trial. After their first test flight suffered a "structural failure" while landing, Facebook's technology blog (Cox 2016) listed the challenges that yet remain to be solved, such as collecting enough solar energy for power as well as issues with the batteries, size, speed, and cost of the technology. These expensive acquisitions and technological forays belie claims that the goal of connectivity has an entirely philanthropic purpose—a point on which I elaborate in the subsequent sections.

The importance of global connectivity for Facebook can be understood by the fact that it has set up an entire unit called the connectivity lab (Maguire 2015), primarily to solve the challenge of connectivity in remote areas of the world. The lab is pursuing an array of technologies such as satellites, free space optics, and ground-based solutions that add to its programs such as Free Basics, Express Wi-Fi, and drones to significantly expand and diversify the bouquet of schemes that Facebook is pursuing for connectivity. As the head of the lab, Yael Maguire (2015), explains in a blog post, each of these solutions is meant to bypass the "traditional model of connectivity" that invariably requires acquiring rights to land, building extensive infrastructure on the ground, and obtaining access to power to provide the energy for the system. By operating from the stratosphere and beyond, companies such as Facebook and Google can simulate a borderless world where they can pursue their commercial imperatives unhindered by other sovereign entities.

Even as Google and Facebook take giant strides in connectivity, the other major players, Microsoft and Amazon, are now serious competitors through their own innovations by using a mix of available options including providing connectivity through satellites and utilizing unused (and lapsed) frequencies called white spaces within the spectrum allotted to broadcast television. Known as dynamic spectrum access (DSA), this is Microsoft's preferred connectivity method because it can be operationalized without significant investment in physical structures such as towers or broadcast stations. Microsoft claims to have worked on the technology "for over a decade," undertaking innumerable field trials and pilot projects to deliver broadband access using the method. Also called White Space or White-Fi, the technology is one example of the broader type of access technology that Microsoft calls Networking over White Spaces (or KNOWS), which delivers internet connectivity over unused frequencies between those allotted for specific purposes (such as television, mobile phones, radio, or local Wi-Fi). These unused frequencies, as well as those that have been freed up with the move from analog television to digital, are deliberately left empty within the spectrum to act as a buffer, ensuring noninterference between signals from adjacent wireless channels. Since it uses these specific unused frequencies within the spectrum, connectivity through this technology requires approval from the national regulatory bodies that control the distribution and use of particular bandwidths to ensure equity and noninterference. The Federal Communications Commission (n.d.) in the United States approved the use of "broadcast television spectrum (TV bands)" by "low power unlicensed wireless devices" in 2011, and nine companies, including Microsoft and Google, received permission. Microsoft claims to currently offer the scheme in eight different countries (Microsoft Whitespaces Database, n.d.) including Jamaica, Namibia, the Philippines, Colombia, the United Kingdom, the United States, Tanzania, and Taiwan and is aggressively pursuing the scheme in India, where the Indian government has proceeded cautiously on connectivity offers from Western digital companies after its experience with Facebook Basics. While other companies, including Google, also use TV white spaces for providing connectivity in various parts of the world, Microsoft has pursued the option most aggressively both globally and in India, where it awaits regulatory clearance from the government to begin connectivity. Even as it waits, however, it has pursued connectivity through the White Space technology in other parts of the world. In Africa, for instance, its 4Afrika program, launched in 2013 (Microsoft 4Afrika, n.d., "Improving Quality of Life"), is pursuing a slew of initiatives including "delivering affordable access to the internet, developing skilled workforces and investing in local technology solutions" (Microsoft 4Afrika, n.d., "Our Story"). It claims to have successfully run fifteen pilot projects and brought over half a million small and medium enterprises (SMEs) online.

Amazon is the latest entrant to this race with its Project Kuiper—an audacious plan announced in early 2019 to provide "low-latency, high-speed broadband connectivity" (Amazon Jobs, n.d.) through a network of more than three thousand low earth-orbit satellites. The capital-intensive project is likely to cost billions over the coming years—a scale of investment that underscores the corporation's desire to join the race of large digital corporations doubling up as ISPs for the "unserved and underserved communities around the world" (Sheetz 2019). Amazon's entry is significant as it comes alongside the launch of its AWS Ground Station (Amazon Web Services 2019), a network of receiving stations on the ground for communicating with and processing information received from satellites it recently made available for general commercial use. Despite its delayed entry, these complementing forays signal the serious intent behind Amazon's ambitions to catch up with the other three corporations in the race to connect the world.

While this is a broad and cursory overview of ongoing connectivity efforts, the descriptions give us enough of an inkling into the designs of large digital corporations who seek to double up as ISPs. That these dominant companies, each with well-entrenched global businesses in niche areas of digital culture and commerce, should want to connect the world should be of immense interest to critical media scholars. What drives these expensive, capital-intensive global projects? How seriously can we take the corporate narratives that present these free connectivity schemes only as attempts to do good for the world? While questioning their narratives, it is also vital to pay attention to their discursive power in shaping public opinion and global policy. By creating the mandate for these connectivity efforts, the corporate discourse as well as the media coverage of these plans are just as important enablers of those schemes as the technology or the capital investments behind them. These supporting discursive formations aided the ambitious plans of companies that, despite being global leaders in arenas of e-commerce, software services, social networking, and search (among others), seek to also become users' primary gateway to the internet in large parts of the world. These corporate designs point to the high stakes in controlling the global infrastructures of digital connectivity and access. Ownership of the mediating channels of connectivity allows corporations to shape the terms of access wherein at some sites, infrastructures enact "differential provisioning" (Appel, Anand, and Gupta 2018, 3) by offering limited versions of the internet. Arguably, these ambitious designs give us insights into the corporations' unacknowledged plans to dominate all aspects of digital life globally.

The Corporate "Mission" to Connect the World

Not surprisingly, the launch of and advocacy for each of the schemes being pursued by Facebook, Google, Microsoft, and Amazon have been accompanied by lofty discourses of altruism that focus on the global common good but simultaneously seek to conceal the companies' own commercial interests in connecting the world. These discourses—comprising speeches of and interviews with their CEOs, promotional videos on their sites (internet.org and x.company/loon) as well as advertising campaigns—present persuasive arguments packed with facts and anecdotes about how the scheme would be singularly effective in transforming lives by bringing the internet to the unconnected. By the same yardstick, these narratives label any opposition to their plans as coming from obstructionists who use an unrealistic perfect version of the global internet to stonewall a realistic (albeit imperfect) internet from coming into being.

This discursive strategy is premised on presenting global connectivity as an urgent need that would bring benefits such as Facebook CEO Mark Zuckerberg's claims of helping "a chicken farmer in Zambia using free internet access to sell way more of his stock" or "a student using Wikipedia for free to study for her exams" (see the download "Full Video with Hindi Subtitles" at Facebook Newsroom 2015). These evocative images are accompanied by statistics such as "more than 20 percent of gross domestic product growth is driven by the Internet" in developing countries and "if we connected a billion more people to the internet, 100 million more jobs would be created, and more than that would be lifted out of poverty" (Chang and Frier 2015). These numerical descriptions about the benefits of connectivity are made real by invoking the implicit metaphor of the dividing line that starkly contrasts the connected with the unconnected. Numbers such as "two thirds" and "more than four billion" yet to be connected create a visual imagery of two contrasting worlds divided by a line that, akin to the colonial frontier, separates the online and the off-line worlds. Numbers about the benefits of the web presented along with the contrasting imagery about two different worlds presented by these corporations seek to create a compelling argument that internet connectivity is a panacea to common social problems afflicting the developing world. More importantly, they help frame these connectivity efforts as philanthropic acts with no obvious commercial motive.

Facebook's CEO, Mark Zuckerberg, for instance, often points to the three impediments to connectivity—access, affordability, and people's lack of knowledge about things to do online—while also claiming that the last of these leaves tremendous scope for corporations such as Facebook to "educate" people about the benefits of the web. Notably, this last reason (lack of knowledge to explain low connectivity) is presented as a strong argument for providing limited internet—a scheme that his Facebook Basics has been accused of—since a taste of the web would help draw in users by showing them its potential future uses. Some argue that if only people's ignorance about the internet could be removed, they would flock to it, echoing tropes of cyber-utopianism that have frequently accompanied discourses about the web. Critics have shown that the line between cyber-utopianism and a form of cybernaivete is often "a blurry one" and especially so when it is tantamount to the "unthinking acceptance of conventional wisdom" (Morozov 2012, 21) about the internet's cure-all potential for social problems. Undoubtedly, it is in Facebook's interest to advance this narrative and present the corporation as akin to a charitable enterprise devoid of any pecuniary interests of its own. Not surprisingly, the trope of working for the larger common good repeats itself in various conflicts involving new media entities globally, including Google's defense during the controversy about Google Earth (Kumar 2010), Twitter's defense during the Iran elections of 2009 (Morozov 2012), and Google's reasons for quitting China (Jin 2015). In each instance new media platforms have presented themselves as disinterested, decentralized entities working only in the common global interest.

In fact, Zuckerberg directly engaged with the contradiction between Facebook's so-called altruistic motives and it being a profit-making company: "If we were primarily focused on profits, the reasonable thing for us to do would really just be to focus on the first billion people using our products. The world isn't set up equally, and the first billion people using Facebook have way more money than the rest of the world combined. So from a biz perspective, it doesn't make a whole lot of sense for us to put the emphasis into this that we are right now" (Chang and Frier 2015). This deceptive explanation distracts from the main critique by presenting a naive corporate strategy (as a plausible one) wherein corporations must ideally only focus on their existing customer base and not inculcate or foster consumer loyalty beyond that to ensure future profits. By presenting an implausible and unimaginably shortsighted strategy as a straw figure and then showing how, by not following it, Facebook was actually being altruistic, he treats his audience as naive enough to believe that Facebook is an inept corporation that does not seek growth through new users who would increase its advertising revenue. Zuckerberg betrayed his subterfuge in the same interview, admitting that Facebook could perhaps gain in "a 10-20-30 year time" (Chang and Frier 2015), but that was not the primary motive given the larger, more urgent task at hand. This philanthropic trope is echoed by another senior Facebook executive, Chris Daniels, who was the vice president of internet.org (now Free Basics), who explains, "I don't think the question is necessarily what Facebook gains, but what the world gains. And what the world gains is more people have better opportunities in their lives, more people have the opportunity to express themselves, the communication tools" (Yahoo Finance 2015).

Facebook leadership's incredulous claims about altruism find striking resonance in the media interviews of other corporations. In answering questions regarding whether their connectivity efforts were driven by altruism, Microsoft's India chairman, Bhaskar Pramanik, answered in the affirmative but acknowledged that there may be some benefits to Microsoft down the line. He then explained, "But am I being altruistic? The answer is absolutely. This was a promise made by Satya (Microsoft CEO Satya Nadella) and I committed to make it happen. There's no revenue attached to it whatsoever. I'm just trying to help the government solve the last-mile problem. Somewhere in that value chain there will be some piece that'll be valuable for Microsoft but it may be equally valuable to Google or any other provider" (Aggarwal 2018).

This theme reverberates in the discourse of the other two companies as well. In explaining Project Kuiper, Amazon's CEO, Jeff Bezos, dabbled in a similar language of philanthropy by claiming that the scheme helps the company in "servicing the whole world" and especially those "people who are 'under-bandwidthed.' Very rural areas, remote areas. And I think you can see going forward that internet, access to broadband is going to be very close to being a fundamental human need as we move forward" (Boyle 2019). Framing a business enterprise as being driven by the desire to serve a fundamental human need rather than the pursuit of profit de-emphasizes its commercial motives and defuses critical interrogations of the terms and conditions on which said need is being fulfilled. Google, the fourth big corporation racing to connect the world, is no different when talking about its purpose in terms of a mission—a phenomenon that Ken Auletta (2009) deciphers in Google CEO Eric Schmitt's discourse when he "sometimes lapses into speaking of Google as a 'moral force,' as if its purpose were to save the world, not make money" (66). So deep is this self-belief about being a different kind of company that in a Q&A as a part of Google's Prospectus, its cofounder Sergei Brin claims Google's purpose is to "ameliorate a number of the world's problems and ultimately to make the world a better place" (594).

This is similar to Zuckerberg's interviews wherein he presents Facebook as uniquely positioned to play a special role above and beyond its pecuniary interests. In stating unambiguously that "Facebook is here on this planet" on a "mission . . . to help connect the world" (Chang and Frier 2015), he echoes this higher purpose that runs through the discourse of these large digital behemoths. Such claims go alongside assertions that any benefit the company may accrue in the process is purely incidental and secondary because "if you do good things, then some of that comes back to you" (Chang and Frier 2015). In the case of Google, these allusions to a higher purpose go beyond specific utterances to run through their entire corporate philosophy itself. In describing how Google achieved a consecrated status in our culture, Hillis, Petit, and Jarrett (2013) argue that the company's self-description often invokes theological allusions (e.g., "don't be evil") and reflects a "hubristic messianism" about " its ability to provide access to, if not to actually be, the divine" (176). Cutting across the four companies, this notion of being driven by a higher calling beyond mere profit serves the useful deception of them operating in a stratified zone above parochial selfish interests that drive other earthly corporations. The success of this discursive framing of being driven by the larger global good is evident in its resonance in media coverage of these schemes, as will be shown below.

Connectivity as a Human Right

The quasireligious missionary zeal and theological resonances in their discourse, no doubt used because of their persuasive import, position these corporations well to make the claim that internet connectivity is a human right that these connectivity schemes are advancing. Values such as human rights and fundamental human needs recur in the corporations' interviews and promotional materials and also find echo in the global media coverage about free internet schemes they peddle. Zuckerberg's (n.d.) assertion that "I believe connectivity is a human right" was most clearly made in the ten-page white paper on the launch of internet.org (now called Free Basics)—a point he reiterated evocatively in his address to the United Nations in September 2015, where he claimed that "just as denying people of their fundamental rights robs them of their full dignity and liberty, ensuring access is essential to ensuring global justice and opportunity" (United Nations News 2015).

Google, too, has deployed the language of human rights in key conflicts including, most ardently, in its tussle with China in 2010. Right after Google had decided to pull out of China, its executives asked the US government in testimony before a congressional panel to intervene in disputes about the internet because "censorship had become more than a human rights issue" (Hernandez 2010). Presenting connectivity to the internet as a universal human right, as opposed to a privileged luxury for the few, undoubtedly signals a turning point in the global evolution of the Information Age but also showcases the expedient deployment of the human rights trope to advance corporate and geopolitical interests. One prominent instance of the latter was made in the now famous speech by the then US Secretary of State Hillary Clinton (US Department of State 2019), where she called for countries to remove "electronic barriers" that "contravene the Universal Declaration on Human Rights, which tells us that all people have the right 'to seek, receive and impart information and ideas through any media and regardless of frontiers.'" This linkage, immediately criticized by countries she was subtly targeting (e.g., China), nevertheless sought to make a claim for the global good while concealing its conflation with American foreign policy (Powers and Jablonski 2015; Jin 2015).

Given its politicization, the invocation of human rights by private corporations leading global connectivity efforts must be contextualized within a history where the discourse of human rights remains centrally "mired in superpower politics" (Black 2009, 49). Despite the United Nations Declaration of Human Rights, the issue has been used as a lightning rod that often divides the world along competing articulations such as the north's demands for political rights versus the Global South's emphasis on economic rights, or between universal values versus culturally determined rights as well as between individual versus collective rights. Those deploying discourses of human rights have often been criticized for applying it selectively only when it conveniently aligns with their own geopolitical interests

(Senarclens 2003; Evans 2005). During the Cold War, for instance, the call for particular kinds of rights—such as the political rights to freedom of speech, assembly, and so on—was deployed by the West against socialist nations that countered with their own versions of human rights (e.g., economic rights). Therefore, the big corporations' articulation of internet connectivity with human rights, while seeking to tap in to a globally resonant idea, also betrays an attempt to use the ideology to advance their interests. Their repeated use of the term isolates a particular notion of human rights while glossing over other kinds of rights that may be more important and that access to the internet may be contingent on.

Whither Network Neutrality?

Web corporations' persuasive articulation of the internet's benefits and the conflation of connectivity with human rights nevertheless leaves unaddressed the incriminating charge of violating net neutrality levied against the limited version of the internet that Facebook's Free Basics provides. The cause of net neutrality that has justifiably galvanized civil society in the West (MacKinnon 2013) has resonated increasingly in non-Western locations where curtailed versions of the internet are being peddled as a compromise solution to lack of access. Facebook has responded to these charges by arguing that some internet, while not desirable, is better than none and that its criticisms invariably originate from privileged elites who are compromising a good enough version of the Internet for some perfect idea of the web. This distinction between the good and the perfect is rearticulated by Zuckerberg as "reasonable" versus "extreme" definitions of net neutrality; he claimed in a web video launching internet.org that "it is not an equal internet if a majority of the people cannot participate" (see the download "Full Video with Hindi Subtitles" at Facebook Newsroom 2015). In a talk at the Indian Institute of Technology (IIT), Delhi, Zuckerberg reiterated the charge of elitism against those initiating online petitions in support of net neutrality by claiming (to applause): "people who are not online cannot sign an online petition for increased access to the web" (NDTV 2015). This move of speaking for the voiceless on the web and pitching his advocacy of a limited internet as being in the interests of those unable to advocate for themselves allows Zuckerberg to pit the idea of universal access in opposition to calls for equity of content on the web. The equation of Facebook's interests with those of the voiceless global citizens barely conceals the irony of the world's biggest online social network repeatedly being accused of tracking, surveillance, and exploiting personal data for generating its multibillion-dollar profit as well as conducting manipulative social experiments (Kramer, Guillory, and Hancock 2014) on its users.

Making the difficult case that internet.org (now called Free Basics) supported net neutrality despite providing only a limited version of the web required complicated rhetorical jugglery and hairsplitting about definitions and legalities that raised more questions than they satisfied. "Net neutrality is an important principle and we do a lot to support it," stated Zuckerberg at IIT Delhi, but in that very talk he conceded that given the costs, "You cannot provide the whole internet for free," but "any developer that meets the definition for free basics will be zero-rated" (NDTV 2015). He defined the criteria for inclusion, but the fact that Facebook remains the arbiter of who gets to participate in Free Basics goes against the very notion of an all-inclusive web that treats all content equally. Zuckerberg invariably responds to charges of violating net neutrality by presenting the false binary of no internet versus limited internet, which he resolves in the favor of the latter. He does so by presenting contrasting images of those with internet and those without it, as in a response to a question at IIT Delhi: "If you are a student who is getting free access to the internet to do her homework and she is not getting it . . . who is getting hurt by that?" (NDTV 2015). Presenting the problem as a binary with an obvious and commonsensical resolution allows him to further advance Facebook's role as a savior fighting for a just cause that the entire world should rally behind.

The binary also allows him to conflate his company's interests with those without digital connectivity and delve into the technicalities of the debate on net neutrality on his own terms. In emphasizing the public utility aspect of Free Basics, Zuckerberg argues that the program provides the bare essentials, akin to the internet's version of 911, the emergency number dialed when needing urgent help in the United States. He elaborates, "So even if you haven't paid for a phone plan, you can always dial 911, and if there is a crime or a health emergency or a fire, you get basic help, and we think there should be an equivalent of this for the Internet as well—where even if you haven't paid for a data plan, you can get access to basic health information or education or job tools or basic communication tools, and it will vary, country by country" (Chang and Frier 2015).

Undoubtedly a noble sentiment, the equation of Facebook's Free Basics with public services like the police or the fire department that are paid for by tax money and are equally accessible to everyone betrays the eventual goal of the social media company of becoming an indispensable public utility (Kumar 2019). Its goal to achieve "ubiquity and taken-for-grantedness" by "embedding itself in our daily existence" (Plantin et al. 2018, 304) signals the platform's goal to become infrastructural. What remains unsaid in Zuckerberg's quote here is the fact that this public utility would be owned by a profit-driven private corporation working within an oligopolistic ecosystem with no accountability to its users while also dabbling as the second-largest advertising company on the web. The invitation to enter Facebook's digital enclosure relies on a ruse of convenience and utility to redefine the public/private distinction in the digital realm wherein the latter gradually encroaches on the former. This redefinition inverts the balance between the commons and the private realm for the digital world. The line distinguishing public spaces and services (parks, libraries, highways, police and fire services) from privately owned property and businesses in modern liberal societies is premised on creating a balance between competing ideologies of social life. The balance acknowledges the roles performed by both while also protecting key aspects of life from the vagaries of capital and the usurpative tendencies of the profit motive.

Even in the United States, preserving the public commons despite historical challenges to it signals their value as the invisible infrastructure on which private enterprise thrives and whose very function is undermined if subsumed by the logic of capitalism and profit. The FCC's 2017 reversal of rules protecting network neutrality ignored a federal appeals court's (Kang 2016) definition of internet broadband connectivity as a utility, thus opening the gates to regulate it in the public interest. That momentary victory of the court's decision, however, was expectedly overturned by the new administration and likely to be challenged in and decided by the Supreme Court. These ongoing conflicts represent a long-running tussle between differing opinions about definitions of the public and the private spheres on the web. Facebook's discursive construction of itself as the commons and efforts by private companies to peddle their versions of internet globally, while remaining beholden to their bottom line and shareholders, undercuts this debate by categorizing the internet infrastructure as privately owned and hence outside the purview of government regulation and public accountability.

Facebook's scheme to offer limited internet, while violating the norms of net neutrality, makes sense from the vantage point of its financial interests that benefit from keeping current and future users enclosed within its platform. But increased connectivity also benefits the other oligopolies competing to bring the internet to the world, which explains their aggressive efforts. As opposed to Facebook's business model, platforms such as Google and Amazon have their tentacles spread throughout the global web, the former with its advertising service AdSense (Google AdSense, n.d.; Rieder and Sire 2013) and the latter, which has used its position as the preeminent e-commerce platform to launch a slew of businesses,[2] cutting across all aspects of digital life and culture. Transgressing national boundaries, many of these businesses are nearing monopoly status in the countries where they operate. In comparing the difference between Facebook and Google, analyst Roger Entner of Recon Analytics told the *E-Commerce Times*, "Google makes money on the entire Internet with its advertising empire. Facebook just makes money on Facebook" (Suciu 2016). Similarly, in explaining Amazon's business interests in Project Kuiper, a story on CNBC quoted analyst Sam Korus as saying, "If you get everyone access to the internet then you've just doubled your total addressable market for e-commerce, cloud, internet and any other business Amazon wants to do" (Sheetz 2019). This view is endorsed by other analysts quoted in the same story, for example, Chad Anderson, the CEO of venture capital firm Space Angels, who cuts through the altruistic discourse: "You can see the clear profit motive here for Amazon: 4 billion new customers" (Sheetz 2019). These business interests unmask and get to the real motives behind connectivity schemes, purported to be philanthropic endeavors but in fact strategic and smart business investments into their own future.

Global Media's Celebratory Framing of Free Internet Schemes

While the attempt at the discursive construction of private corporations as altruistic entities on a charitable mission is revealing and problematic, the echoing of those themes within the media coverage of these schemes peddling "free internet" shows the success of their articulations in portraying themselves as being on a philanthropic mission rather than on a commercial business venture. A study of the global media coverage of these schemes within the countries where they are being aggressively offered shows widespread celebratory and uncritical coverage of the issue. Schemes by each of these companies have received animated support in the media, which often repeats the deceptive and false binary being advanced by the corporations: no internet versus limited internet. A close study of the newspaper coverage of these schemes in ten countries where they are at various stages of introduction (Kenya, Bangladesh, Tanzania, Nigeria, Thailand, Pakistan, Philippines, South Africa, Sri Lanka, and New Zealand) brought up negligible critical reportage. This study focused on the mainstream newspapers in each of these countries sourced through the LexisNexis database, and their analysis shows the predominance of three broad categories—namely, an emphasis on "free" internet, an elaborate delineation of the schemes' benefits, and the process of collaboration around the schemes. These themes are notable because they repeatedly emphasized the how and the what of the free internet schemes without delving into why they were being offered for free. Laden with anticipatory quotes from company spokespersons, industry insiders, experts, and prospective users, the discursive regime of truth (Foucault 1982) created by these supportive accounts in the news media across different countries provides compelling evidence for the global success of these schemes and the resonance of the arguments made for them.

That media coverage did so by framing the issue of free internet schemes through the lens of the above-mentioned categories while eschewing (with some rare exceptions) any critical analyses of the terms and conditions on which these schemes are being offered. The continuing global success of these private connectivity schemes can be ascribed in no small part to their favorable coverage, which points to the widely accepted power of discursive regimes (such as media coverage) in shaping public opinion and especially among the decision-makers and elites of a society. In his now classical definition of how frames work within media coverage, Entman (1993, 52; italics in original) argues that framing "involves *selection* and *salience*." He goes to explain that "to frame is *to select some aspects of a perceived reality and make them more salient in a communicating text, in such a way as to promote a particular problem definition, causal interpretation, moral evaluation, and/or treatment recommendation* for the item described" (52; italics in original). By highlighting particular aspects and dimensions of multifaceted and complex events (Entman 2010), frames encourage specific interpretations and readings at the expense of other equally valid interpretations. This implicit "metacommunicative" message to read facts, events, actions, or messages in particular ways shows that the process of framing "gives the receiver instructions or aids in his attempt to understand the messages included within the particular frame" (Bateson 2006, 323).

This implicit messaging to interpret free connectivity schemes in particular ways was evident within the media coverage analyzed below, which encouraged particular interpretations of the process while discouraging others. A frame performs the dual function of not just including and emphasizing but also excluding (Bateson 2006) and hence "is always partly constituted by what it is not" (Tkacz 2015, 76), since every act of selection is also an act of deselection. In specifically applying frames to study the relationship between politics and the media, Chong and Druckman (2007), for instance, show framing as "the process by which people develop a particular conceptualization of an issue [or individual] or reorient their thinking about an issue" (104). Since frames channel and shape dominant versions of reality, they are also ideologically laden and invariably function to reduce complex multidimensional issues into simplified tropes and concepts. As media framed free connectivity schemes by emphasizing the emancipatory consequences of the web through associating the internet with a better, often utopian future, they presented connectivity's benefits as self-evident despite there being little scholarly or empirical support for it (Friederici, Ojanperä, and Graham 2017). In their analysis of policy documents and reports on digital connectivity from organizations, Friederici, Ojanperä, and Graham (2017) found that utopian claims about the consequences of digital connectivity were "at least overblown, if not misleading" (2). Such claims recur in my findings from analyzing the coverage of connectivity schemes wherein the dominant frames of altruism, cyber-utopianism, and collaboration all focus on the benefits of connectivity while completely eliding any questions about motives, equity, or the oligopolistic nature of the Western corporations providing the connectivity.

Newspaper headlines played a key role in this process of framing by frequently making adulatory claims such as that Facebook's scheme was a "gift to the entire world" (*News Today* 2013; Bangladesh, August 23), thus echoing the position of the corporations. In the case of Facebook Basics, a majority of the headlines implied Zuckerberg's effort was driven entirely by the desire to connect the world instead of gaining new customers to boost advertising revenue. This dominant framing is reflected in a sample of headlines such as "Facebook Ready to Spend Billions to Bring Whole World Online" (*Pak Banker* 2014; Pakistan, September 8), "Facebook's Zuckerberg in India to Get 'Next Billion Online'" (*Pakistan Today* 2015; October 28), "Facebook Chief in Bid to Widen Global Internet Access" (*Bangkok Post* 2013; August 22), "Linking Up World's Unconnected Two-Thirds" (*Nation* 2014; Thailand, October 28), "Facebook Boss Wants to Get the World Online" (*Nation* 2013a; Thailand, August 25), Facebook Ready to Beam Free

Internet in Kenya" (*Daily Nation* 2015; Kenya, October 5), "Facebook Aims to Get World Online" (*Sowetan* 2013; South Africa, August 23), and "Zuckerberg on the Hunt for 5 Billion New Friends" (Vincent 2013; *Independent on Saturday*, South Africa, August 24). One headline even had the tantalizing and anticipatory tone of an advertising teaser: "Coming Soon: Free Internet to Rural Areas" (Ochieng 2015; *Daily Nation*, Kenya, November 16). Ranging across countries as diverse as Bangladesh, Pakistan, Thailand, and South Africa, these headlines constructed a narrative of empowerment and progress as opposed to commercial exploitation or an expedient business strategy; closer examination of the headlines would reveal these schemes as the latter.

This dominant framing also extended to Google's free internet scheme, Project Loon, which has received glowing coverage in headlines such as "Google to Cover Lanka with 3G Floating Balloons" (*Daily News* 2015a; Sri Lanka, July 29), "Loon Project Brings the Web to Millions" (*New Zealand Herald* 2013b; July 16), "Internet Balloons to Benefit Small Firms: Google" (*Nation*, 2013b; Thailand, June 13), and "Google to Deliver Internet Service to Indonesia via Balloons" (*Waterloo Region Record* 2015; October 29). For both schemes, headlines also went beyond mentioning the plans to describing specific details of the story such as "Get Information at Your Fingertips Anytime, Anywhere Even without WiFi" (Canoy and Lacan 2015a; *Philippine Daily Inquirer*, April 10) and "Facebook's Internet.org Has More Pros than Cons" (Fonternel 2015; *Cape Times*, South Africa, July 13). The broad support reflected in these headlines often echoes the very positions and thematics visible in the companies' own discourses and public relations material, thus instantiating a convergence of frames between media coverage and corporate discourse. These headlines and the stories analyzed below hold clues to why these schemes have mostly had an unimpeded sway around the world (with the recent exception of India, where Facebook Basics was barred). The resonance between corporate and media discourses found in the headlines continues within the copy of the stories, which frame the issue through three dominant recurring themes: emphasizing the free service (altruism), descriptive details about the specific benefits of the scheme (cyber-utopianism), and motifs of collaboration and cooperation between the private companies and local governments. Having already been operationalized in over sixty countries, Facebook's Free Basics receives the dominant share of media coverage, but the reportage on the other schemes is not too different.

It's "Free"

The fact that there are no data charges associated with the schemes (thus making them "free") was mentioned as the lead in most stories about them and remained implicit throughout the text. A quote in *This Day*, published out of Lagos, Nigeria, from an official in a telecom company partnering with Facebook describes the scheme as one that allows customers to "for the first time, access Facebook through their handsets without incurring any data charges" (*This Day* 2014). Another story in a Pakistani newspaper begins with "after Facebook CEO Mark Zuckerberg unveiled his free content access service Internet.org in Pakistan" (*Daily Pakistan Today* 2015) and then goes on to describe specific details of the scheme. These representative snapshots emphasize the fact that critically interrogating the reason for "free" schemes was not a primary concern in these stories. This emphasis on the free nature of the service continues in the coverage of Google's Project Loon, as exemplified in this description (in Sri Lanka's *Daily News*) of the scheme as "an experimental program to provide free internet access to people in remote rural areas, using high-altitude balloons floating in the stratosphere 19 Km up in the sky" (*Daily News* 2015b). By emphasizing this early on in the lead paragraph, making it the most important aspect, these stories frame these schemes as philanthropic, charitable acts, thus buying wholesale into the discourse of the corporations. What goes uninterrogated in these news reports is the immense value that each user brings to the business models of these digital platforms, which are usually functioning in a "multi-sided market" (Flew 2019; Barwise and Watkins 2018; Coyle 2018). Such businesses (e.g., social networking, search, or e-commerce sites) bring different types of needs together on a platform and benefit from "indirect network effects" where the increased number of one type (e.g., users on a social networking platform or a search engine) increases the likelihood of other types (e.g., advertisers or content producers) flocking in. Once a platform reaches a critical mass (of number of users, for instance), "these network effects become self-sustaining as users on each side help generate users on the other" (Barwise and Watkins 2018, 27), thus making it extremely difficult, if not impossible, to dislodge them. Therefore, free connectivity to lure users is hardly incidental or philanthropic but quite central to the long-term business strategies of these dominant platform businesses.

The media coverage of these schemes, however, far from analyzing the reasons behind them being free, go a step further in the opposite direction to often position free internet schemes along with other charitable

announcements by these companies, leaving no doubts about their philanthropic nature. A story on Facebook's Free Basics in Thailand's *Nation* (2013a;
August 25) headlined "Facebook Boss Wants to Get the World Online" ends
by listing his other "humanitarian" deeds: "The billionaire CEO made his
first charitable splash in 2010, two years before his company went public,
when he donated $100 million in Facebook Inc. stock to schools in Newark,
New Jersey. He later gave another $500 million to a Silicon Valley charity
with the aim of funding health and education issues. Earlier this year, he
launched Fwd.us, a political group aimed at changing immigration policy,
boosting education and encouraging investment in scientific research."

The equation of Free Basics with Zuckerberg's donation to schools is
a telling articulation primarily because the donation itself was made in
the run-up to and to mitigate the negative publicity from the release of
the movie *The Social Network*, whose unflattering portrayal of Zuckerberg
had led to significant anxiety within the company. The uncritical deployment of tropes of charity and altruism within the coverage of "free" internet schemes also calls attention to the erasure of the built-in inequities
and ambitions driving them. The role these positive frames play in shaping
favorable public opinion and policy, thus leading to the success of these
free internet schemes in developing countries, cannot be overstated. The
lack of internet penetration in most countries where these schemes were
introduced undoubtedly made free internet an enticing offer, and the media discourse reflected a notion of gratitude for a service that poorly connected and resource-scarce countries could not afford to set the terms and
conditions to access. When a Pakistani businessman placed a giant billboard in Karachi thanking Mark Zuckerberg for bringing Free Basics to
his country, newspapers covered it prominently including interviews with
the businessman and reprinting images of the billboard with the message
"thank you Mark Zuckerberg and Facebook for giving free Facebook to the
entire country of Pakistan" (*Daily Pakistan Today* 2015; Ashraf 2015). A list
of the websites accessible for free through the scheme is included with the
fawning excerpts from the interview in the *Express Tribune* (Ashraf 2015).
The counterintuitive idea of a free service or product is presented in these
stories as a matter of fact without interrogating the hidden costs of "free."

Cyber-utopianism

The second broad frame through which the stories covered these schemes
of free internet consisted of detailed explanations of their technological

and beneficial aspects, often listing the websites one could access and their benefits for the users. This recurring frame of accruing benefits, which appeared in stories across newspapers in ten countries, was portrayed in a descriptive and explanatory tone as stories tried to break down the technological and service details for lay readers. The stories' implicit emphasis was on the transformative future awaiting each country as a result of free connectivity, as in this excerpt from Nigeria's *Daily Independent* (2015): "The Free Basic Services will provide access to services like health, educations, jobs, communication and local content at no additional cost. They include providing free health, education and finance-related information to people in developing countries so that they can make informed choices and decisions to improve their lives."

This exact motif of painstaking details about the benefits of the scheme was repeated across different newspapers with striking similarities in each iteration. A daily from the Philippines, for instance, described the scheme as a "game changer" through which "online activities like job hunting, buying and selling, or reading news, which typically would require the use of desktop computers five to seven years ago, are now made available for free access on mobile phones" (Canoy and Lacano 2015; *Philippine Daily Inquirer,* April 10). The story goes beyond just cataloguing the websites accessible through the scheme to actually naming the real-life problems solved through them, an idea endlessly repeated by the CEOs and the public relations machinery of the corporations. Another story in Kenya's *Daily Nation* describes the benefits of Facebook Basics by elaborating that "the portal will provide information on health, education and finance to enable them to make informed decisions that will improve their lives" (Ochieng 2015). By framing the coverage of the schemes as solutions to particular life problems (job hunting, education, health care), these news stories made key facts about the schemes salient while suppressing others (Entman 1993), thus playing the metacommunicative role of shaping the opinions of readers and policy makers. They framed the contours of the conversation not as a critical interrogation of motives and interests but as a description of the immense benefits of connectivity and its ability to offer deliverance from debilitating hindrances that constrain life and limit opportunities in developing countries.

These solutions are underscored along with the notion that the widespread introduction and usage of the web would take societies toward a utopian future (without presenting much evidence for the fact). This juxtaposition is evident in the following description of Project Loon by the *New Zealand Herald* (2013a; June 15): "If successful, the technology might allow countries to leapfrog the expense of laying fiber cable, dramatically increasing Internet usage in places such as Africa and Southeast Asia." The project leader is quoted as describing the Internet as the "most transformative technologies of our time." Similarly, a Nigerian daily quotes a telecommunication executive benefitting from its alliance with Facebook as saying, "The new service will open new frontiers to Tanzanians and to other Swahili speakers by offering them new business, educational and other socioeconomic opportunities across the world" (*This Day* 2014; Lagos, April 27). This emancipatory discourse is presented along with compelling statistics, as in this quote from the Telecommunications and Digital Infrastructure minister of Sri Lanka: "a 10% increase in internet penetration has the potential to drive a 1.2 increase in GDP" (*Daily News* 2016b; Sri Lanka, April 11); one is left guessing about the source of the data. There are strong resonances between these definitive axiomatic accounts asserting the benefits of connectivity and findings by other scholars from similar analyses of discourses about the internet. Friederici, Ojanperä, and Graham's (2017) study of ICT policy documents from seven African countries found that benefits of connectivity were often presented "as self-evident truths, as passive truths without specifying a source ('it has been acknowledged'), or as based on unspecified evidence ('evidence shows')" (11). Just as the media coverage of free internet schemes analyzed here presented their benefits as unquestionable and obvious, these scholars found that "not a single case was found where specific evidence, such as a published study or paper, was cited" (11).

In addition to presenting the benefits of connectivity as an uncontested fact, the framing of the stories is also revealed by the voices they quote and the portraits they bring into the stories. Favorable quotes and anecdotes of common people excited by the possibilities opened up by free internet schemes support the media frame of technological utopianism. A student at Dhaka University in Bangladesh, Sarmin Sultana Toma, is quoted as predicting that Free Basics "will be an Internet revolution for the nation" (*Financial Express* 2015). Another story in the *Philippine Daily Inquirer* (2015a) presents a glowing portraiture (evocatively titled "Mai-Mai's World") about an "island girl" who is a fisherman's wife and whose "phone became a classroom" because of free internet and helped her finish her college degree. The story goes on to describe how she featured in a promotional video for internet.org and cites Zuckerberg's frequent mention of her as an example in talks around the world. Evoking the emotions Mai Mai felt on learning she was being mentioned by Zuckerberg, the story deifies the Facebook CEO as a benefactor on a philanthropic mission. The emphasis on the details and the utopian narrative within which the details of the schemes are framed supports claims of social transformation made by the digital corporations, thus allowing their free internet schemes to be introduced without critical debate and interrogation. This framing, along with the emphasis on cooperation and collaboration between internet giants and local governments and corporations, which is analyzed below, obviates any need for critical analysis of these free schemes.

Collaboration

Plans for providing free internet schemes around the world requires partnerships between the internet companies, local governments, and telecommunication companies. In the case of Facebook's Free Basics, terms of these associations are tilted against norms of net neutrality and in favor of Facebook as it brings in the technology and the capital that is used to subsidize and set the conditions for the partnership. Media coverage of these schemes invariably frames these associations as equal partnerships between the parties, even going to the extent of describing them as favors being granted by the internet giants to the countries where the schemes were being introduced. This idea is emphasized through the commonly recurring tropes of partnership, alliance, and cooperation that repeat within different contexts in their stories. Positioning these schemes as equal partnerships or favors preempts any substantial discussion about the advantages accruing to the internet giants while bolstering the earlier themes of altruism and cyberutopianism within the media coverage. Coverage of Free Basics often describes details of the arrangements that Facebook entered into with telecom companies to offer its bouquet of "free" websites. Emphasizing the notion of collaboration presents telecom companies and state governments as equal partners of the global social media giant while erasing any asymmetries that may undergird the relationship. A newspaper in the Philippines emphasized this collaborative theme by introducing the scheme thus: "Internet.org is an initiative by Facebook—in close collaboration with top tech firms, mobile networks and content providers—that aims to make mobile Internet services available to two-thirds of the world who are not yet connected. In May, the internet.org official website noted that it has brought more than 9 million people online and introduced them to the incredible value of the Internet" (*Philippine Daily Inquirer* 2015b; July 8). Thailand's *Nation* (2013a; August 25) wrote in the same vein that "Facebook CEO Mark Zuckerberg wants to get all of the world's 7 billion people online through a partnership with some of the largest mobile technology companies. He says the Net is an essential part of life, and everyone deserves to be connected, whether they live in Norway, Nicaragua or Namibia." Another story about Indonesia in the same newspaper said, "Facebook, Ericsson and XL Axiata are working together to improve network performance for better app coverage and experience in Indonesia, the fourth largest Facebook user base in the world" (*Nation* 2014) The repetitive invoking of alliances, collaborations, and partnerships portrays Facebook as a well-meaning ally of these countries and a joint partner in the endeavor of increasing connectivity and access.

This notion of partnership continues in the coverage of Google's Project Loon, wherein the company's partnerships are presented as an innovative firm bringing cutting-edge technology to recipient countries. In describing the launch of Project Loon, the Sri Lankan newspaper *Daily News* (2015a; July 29) wrote, "The Information and Communication Technology Agency of Sri Lanka (ICTA) has partnered with Google to cover the entire country with 3G internet under the 'Google Loon project.'" While expecting an analysis of Google's motives may be unrealistic given the emphasis on reportage in a news story, opinion pieces are similarly adulatory in describing the scheme as "a great partnership" that is "highly commendable" (*Daily News* 2015b; August 1). This editorial piece goes on to laud Google for choosing Sri Lanka as the first country to start Project Loon, portraying it as a sign of global confidence in the country's economy and investment climate. The *New Zealand Herald*, in writing about the difficulties of providing access to remote, mountainous locations, fetes Google by saying, "Google's ignored all that and is now working with Vodafone in New Zealand and Telstra in Australia to set up a ring of mass-produced stratospheric balloons around the Southern Hemisphere for uninterrupted connectivity" (2015; April 22). Such an adulatory description, written with an awe-stricken tone, marvels at the technological genius that is Google given that it overcame the challenges of terrain and distance.

As in the case of the coverage of Free Basics, the media reporting on Project Loon presented the scheme in highly animated tones that often bordered on outright fealty to the internet company providing it. A case in point is the *Daily News* (2016a; Sri Lanka, February 2), which quoted the Sri Lankan minister of telecommunications to make its point: "Fernando said this is the first time this project is launched in the world and it's an honour that the global search engine giant Google has selected Sri Lanka." The sense of gratitude and pride invoked by describing the scheme as an "honor" is diametrically opposed to the categorization of these free internet schemes as exploitative ventures tailored for profit or to accumulate more users. In deploying these themes, the media coverage entirely buys the self-serving notion, advanced by these companies, that they are a moral force on a mission to change the world and ordained by destiny to provide global internet connectivity. The lack of critical questions alluded to the widely held notion that these companies have little commercial or business interests of their own and therefore can do no wrong.

Walled Gardens and the Colonization of the Digital

The detailed analyses of the corporate discourse and media coverage of these internet schemes being peddled by the dominant Western digital empires is important given how they reveal glimpses of and critique the unfolding shape of the future web. They help us answer the following questions: Will the next half of the world have access to the totality of the internet in just as open and free a manner as the first half? How central will users' interests be in determining the conditions that shape their internet experience? The corporate rush to gain captive users in the developing and yet-to-be-connected world poses sobering reminders, especially when seen in the light of a prior expansionist history of usurpation by the dominant colonial powers. These reminders take on a renewed importance when juxtaposed with the list of countries (internet.org, n.d.) being offered services such as Free Basics, which consists predominantly of developing and formerly colonized countries. Continuing to probe these similarities between the corporate and media discourses analyzed above show us at least three points of resonance between these expansionist impulses that are elaborated in sequential paragraphs below. The first lies in the common motive of usurpation, which in the case of colonialism led to the appropriation of land and in its digital avatar seeks to expand a private enclosure to lock in sources of user data. Secondly, they share the convenient application of dual rules and yardsticks in different parts of the world with accompanying justifications for the duality. Third, each is advanced through humanitarian/

philanthropic discourse that conceals its commercial designs of profiting from the acquired territory/user base.

The import of the web's current direction hits home when juxtaposed against John Barlow's (1996) prescient forebodings about its usurpation by the state and "information industries." In likening resistances to them to the anticolonial movements of the past, he berates "these increasingly hostile and *colonial* measures" (my italics) put in place to control the emerging technologies. His early caution anticipates the ongoing political and corporate machinations to control the medium, as visible in today's competition to carve up undigitized areas among the dominant internet companies. This corporate race to provide "free" internet has a logic analogous to what has been termed the "scramble for Africa" (Brantlinger 1985, 192), as epitomized by the Berlin Conference (1884–85), which witnessed a similar competition to carve out the newly "discovered" lands. The technological and capital investments, the aggressive publicity campaigns, and the political lobbying undertaken by web companies to expand their market shares underscore this common logic of appropriation shared with the colonial past.

In addition to their expansionist impulses, these processes also share the second commonality: a duplicity of yardsticks that expediently uses the underdeveloped physical infrastructure, limited economic resources, and lack of cultural and technical knowledge about the web (just like colonialism used lack of development and the absence of "civilization") in large parts of the world to peddle privatized and often limited internet as a better option than the status quo. This adoption of dual standards to become the primary gatekeepers of Internet connectivity in large parts of the world in order to appropriate user data on asymmetrical terms risks creating a two-tiered digital ecosystem among the digitized populations of the world. This dual schema distinguishes those with access to the full web from those able to access only limited portions of it, thus begging the question of whether the global internet giants such as Facebook would offer a limited version of the internet to locations in the developed western world. If not, then their current schemes that do so (Free Basics, for example) reveal a bifocal and hierarchical view of the world with historical parallels that instantiate a form of "digital imperialism" (Vaidhyanathan 2018, 112).

As they imposed their imperial writ around the globe, colonial distinctions between the old world and new, between Europe and non-Europe, as well as the land and the sea, were similarly underpinned by a duality. Lines marked where "Europe ended and the 'New World' began," and "beyond the line was an 'overseas' zone in which, for want of any legal limits to war, only the law of the stronger applied" (Schmitt 2003, 93–94). These convenient distinctions between regions and the declaration of open territory, beyond the lines where "force could be used freely and ruthlessly" (Schmitt 2003, 94), could be rationalized only under the guise of a compelling need such as the "civilizing function" (Bolton 1917, 57) that emerges as the third similarity between the historical phenomenon of colonial usurpation and the present corporate machinations to expand digital enclosures. Just as pronouncements from the digital corporations today emphasize their philanthropic purpose and the greater common good as the driving motives behind connectivity schemes, the historical territorial usurpation was justified by the desire to make the subject "disciplined in the rudiments of civilized life" (47). Such mandates had to speak in a "forked tongue" (Bhabha 1984, 122) wherein the overt expressions of humanitarianism concealed the covert goals of imperialism. As Brantlinger (1985, 167) has noted, "Humanitarianism applied to Africa, however, did point insistently toward imperialism."

Today the digital divide reveals a design akin to the "age of discovery" to appropriate the digital commons before others get to it. In the undigitized parts of the world, markets and zones of influence are still undefined, territories of dominance are yet to be fully marked out, and a large number of users are yet to be brought under the sway of the private digital oligopolies. The aggressive scramble to bring connectivity to the world therefore betrays a desire to have the first mover's advantage in these areas, a phenomenon that is far more rewarding in businesses wherein networked platforms operate as multisided markets where scale determines success. In such markets, platforms that are the earliest to reach a tipping point of users (Coyle 2018) enter into an upward spiral of growth given that the mere existence of a large number of preexisting users is reason for others to join a network. Given the stakes involved, it is not surprising that areas of the world where issues of access and connectivity are settled are viewed very differently from those where connectivity is still an open question, where rules are yet to be fully formulated, and where users are yet to develop loyalties. John Locke's ringing words "thus in the beginning all the world was America" (Locke 2003, 121)—ready to be conquered, civilized, and owned—are as true for the undigitized realm today as they were for the yet-to-be-"discovered" world during the peak of colonialism. Each new connection expands the realm of influence, thus increasing a platform's share of the digital pie, just as every inch of territory conquered and occupied during the "age of discovery" locked in for perpetuity the zone where the "superior" and "civilized" cultural values could prevail.

Consequences of Dual Internet

Early consequences of this emerging dual structure created by differing versions of the internet are visible around the world as consumers introduced to the web through these free (but often limited) schemes frequently fail to distinguish between the internet and the "walled garden" version of it they inhabit. Surveys of users, especially in countries with low connectivity, often point to their inability to distinguish between the entire internet and the specific platforms and services on it, thus conflating the latter with the former (Silver and Smith 2019; Milani 2015; Mims 2012). A recent report published by the Pew Research Center, for instance, claimed that significant percentages of people in countries with low connectivity were "unaware that the platforms themselves are part of the broader internet" (Silver and Smith 2019). These percentages include a worrying 25 percent of the users in Kenya, 19 percent in South Africa, 17 percent in the Philippines, and 11 percent and 8 percent in Tunisia and India respectively (Silver and Smith 2019). This recent survey corroborates earlier findings, thus revealing a long-term pattern. A 2015 survey commissioned by Quartz (Mirani 2015) in Indonesia and Nigeria had found that 11 percent of Indonesians and 9 percent of Nigerians said they used Facebook but not the internet. More worryingly, mentioned in the same report and another poll by Quartz (Mirani 2015), the percentage of users agreeing with the statement "Facebook is the Internet" ranged from 65 percent in Nigeria, 61 percent in Indonesia, 58 percent in India, and 55 percent in Brazil. Both the 2019 Pew Report and the 2015 Quartz study replicate a pattern first seen in a 2012 study conducted by LIRNEasia in Myanmar, Indonesia, the Philippines, and Thailand where "more people said they were Facebook users than Internet users" (Woollaston 2015).

When large digital entities become primary gatekeepers of the web, they exponentially increase their ability to concentrate online activity within their own walled gardens because of the "winner takes all" (Barwise and Watkins 2018, 24) nature of the business of social media platforms. Since their business model relies on "*matching customers with complementary needs*" (26; italics in original), they invariably function like multisided markets where dominance in one aspect (e.g., bringing in a large number of users) indirectly leads to dominance in another (bringing in advertisers, content creators, app developers, etc.). Milani summarizes this phenomenon well: "If the majority of the world's online population spends time on Facebook, then policymakers, businesses, startups, developers, nonprofits, publishers, and anyone else interested in communicating with them will also, if they are to be effective, go to Facebook. That means they, too, must then play by the rules of one company. And that has implications for us all" (Milani 2015). Once they take the premier position, multisided businesses (such as networked and social media platforms) benefit from a self-sustaining upward spiral, making them difficult to dislodge.

Consequences of such dominance are visible around the global web where the cultural, political, and economic heft of the dominant platforms (e.g., the Big Five) has allowed them to shape the digital ecology around them. The mechanism by which a monopoly can allow a company to shape the aesthetics and design of the web is best illustrated by the ways in which Google's dominance of the search function on the web allows it to dictate terms to websites. The drive to optimize one's site to rank higher in Google's search results has spawned an entire industry around search engine optimization (SEO) that formats websites using Google's public guidelines to achieve higher rankings. Given the role a site's ranking within Google plays in its visibility and survival on the web, following Google's guidelines becomes an imperative and not a choice. Similar phenomena are visible on other platforms, such as in the case of Google-owned YouTube's recent restructuring after the adpocalypse (Kumar 2019), wherein content creators had no choice but to operate in a new advertiser-centered content ecosystem. A platform's unchallenged dominance in a niche area of the web makes it the digital gatekeeper but also the repository of cultural, political, and ideological power since it can dictate the terms and conditions of access to its users.

Given the cultural and political consequences of platform dominance, their conflation with the web by users in large parts of the world, as shown by different surveys, makes these large web companies the "gateway drug" (Morozov 2014) that functions to gradually ensnare the unconnected parts of the world within the privatized digital fold with freebies (e.g., free Internet and zero-rated websites). The strategy to gradually entice users to make them accustomed to a product or service before charging them a cost, a time-tested marketing strategy, has been compared by critic Evgeny Morozov (2014) to providing free "digital showers" in the hope that consumers will eventually pay for the "digital bath." What, then, are the benefits accruing to these internet companies through new users that they gain through the expansion of their digital enclosures? While control over territories brought spoils of labor, material goods, and political and military influence, the carving out of the digital sphere brings a reward that is just as valuable, if not more. The expanding spheres of influence of the big web companies and their dominant positions through the "winner takes all" model of networked markets brings an ever-growing volume of interactive data within their dragnet to be mined, analyzed, and monetized.

In an emergent data economy, where information has been called "the new raw material" (Castells 2000, 70) or the "new oil" (Andrejevic and Burdon 2015, 20) that enables new modes of production and end products, delimiting new enclosure of users for extracting data (Couldry and Mejias 2019) is akin to owning physical territory of yore that were sources of fuel and raw material in the industrial economies. As opposed to the humanitarian values they espouse publicly, signing on large territories of new users moves the web companies toward an oligopoly status and expands their field of operation to harvest "standing reserves of data for marketing purposes" (Andrejevic 2011, 84). The finished good on the other end of the assembly line is the packaged and tailored demographic, created by data gleaned through the profiles, browsing activity, and nudged self-expressive behaviors that are then peddled to advertisers desperately seeking to pierce through the clutter and target consumers that would yield to sales. A version of this packaging is "behavioral targeting" (Turow 2011, 177), which enables advertisers to sift through (in one case) up to eight hundred characteristics to choose user profiles most likely to be their potential customers.

The political consequences of this kind of targeting has already caused widespread alarm with the unraveling of the linkages between Facebook and Cambridge Analytica in 2018, but fears about how the mining of user data from social networks could be used to create "psychographic profiles" (Davies 2015) for targeted political ads were already being raised early in the US presidential campaign of 2016. Connecting the appropriative logic for new users—as seen in web companies' designs to provide internet connectivity to the undigitized parts of the world—back to the business and political goals of marketing tailored and packaged demographics of users to political and commercial advertisers allows us to show the vertical integration that transforms users on one end of the assembly line into profits at the other. This value chain, conspicuous by its absence within the discourse emerging from corporations as well as within the media coverage of these schemes, further underscores the congruence between the colonizing impulse of the past and present corporate designs in the unconnected parts of the world.

An enhanced ability to turn users into products is a key motive driving digital platforms to go beyond their role of providers of content to owners and controllers of conduits in their role as ISPs. This dual role not only makes them owners of soft infrastructures (e.g., search, social media, web service, and operating systems) but also their hard counterparts (satellites, towers, drones, and balloons). By emerging as prominent gateways of internet connectivity in large parts of the world, these large digital corporations are able to shepherd users far more easily into their digital enclosures, thus further strengthening and expanding the reach of the cultural, ideological, and behavioral nudges exercised by what I have called the infrastructures of control. They hold this asymmetrical power far more extensively in certain parts of the world where they increasingly seek to control both hard and soft infrastructures by leveraging the lack in resources to provide equal connectivity for all. Even in cases where they provide the full internet (as Google's Project Loon does), their dual power of owning both conduit and content makes it a different and more unequal digital ecosystem than in places where connectivity and content rest with separate entities.

In their productive exploration of the expanding role of Google and Facebook in our lives, Plantin et al. (2018) ascribe the splintering of public infrastructures as the primary reason for the "'platformization' of infrastructures and an 'infrastructuralization' of platforms" (298). This chapter extends and builds on their rich schema to show that in large parts of the world, the public infrastructures for internet connectivity barely gained any ground and established themselves only to be splintered or replaced. What we see in these parts is a preemptive usurpation of the commons relying on the logic that some or private internet (even when it risks ceding content and connectivity with the same digital oligopolies) is better than publicly supported or no connectivity. As users get on board the digital bandwagon, invited by promises of jobs, education, and prosperity, they are enter a digital assembly line sharing their data and navigating a labyrinth of affordances, designs, rules, and algorithmic modulation wherein "control operates a plurality of effects multiplied on, in, and across networks" (Guins 2009, 5).

As will be shown in the chapter on selfhood, users experience the modulating nature of dispersed control through a system of rewards (for desirable behaviors) and penalties (for undesirable ones) that nudge profitable actions and constrain unprofitable ones. Aided by a profusion of networked devices on and around us as well as an increasing well-entrenched "sensor society" (Andrejevic and Burdon 2015) that leaves no social space unwatched, this modality moves along with us and follows us exercising "continuous control and instant communication" (Deleuze 1995, 174). Societies of control come to fruition in the platform society given their "intensification and generalization of the normalizing apparatus of disciplinarity that internally animate our common and daily practices" (Hardt and Negri 2000, 23). The emergence of this change within Western societies and its convergence with neoliberal governmentality has been established through wide-ranging scholarship (Rose 1990), and the analysis within this chapter has pointed to its global expansion through an overarching privatized and "free" digital network.

Conclusions

The goal of this chapter has been to show that the internet would look very different for a significant part of the half of the global population that still remains off-line. Its analysis proceeds by making the claim that while internet connectivity was regulated by, if not remaining entirely within, the purview of the public institutions (for the most part) for the first half of netizens, connectivity for the next half of the global population (especially those living in the most deprived regions of the world) is increasingly within the purview of private, for-profit companies seeking users as part of their future business strategies. This difference is key as it enables the subversion of the founding ideals of the web that sought to create a networked media entity far from a commercialized media network beholden to the bottom lines of private corporations. While the incapacity and lack of resources of public institutions has created an opening for these corporations, the terms and conditions on which they are providing connectivity must continue to be rigorously scrutinized and evaluated. In analyzing the motives behind these efforts and drawing comparisons between the impulses and the discursive justifications of colonialism and present connectivity efforts, this chapter's analysis provides a cautionary note for critical scholars and policy makers alike. In its claim about the appropriation and colonization of digital territories, this chapter anticipates the specific ways in which the power of conventions and protocols works within the specific domains of knowledge, subjectivity, and sovereignty that the subsequent chapters focus on.

If the end goal of the early visionaries of the web was a plural and globally representative web, the next half of the web's population must be given the same choices to shape their internet experience as the first half did. By enfolding users within their digital enclosures and becoming gatekeepers of their online experiences, the big internet corporations undercut the inspiring vision that the web started out with. When dominant digital platforms also double up as ISPs for the next half of the world's population, it significantly compromises norms of neutrality, plurality, and transparency within digital culture. While significantly increasing their power, this process simultaneously undermines states' sovereignty and their ability to negotiate with these private corporations on equal terms. By transferring power away from public institutions to private entities, "free" internet schemes compromise democracy, political freedom, and cultural plurality. The process compromises the truism that in the realm of information, a plurality of voices, perspectives, and knowledge systems is far more desirable and amenable to achieve the ends of global democracy and self-governance. By allowing the vertical integration of pipes and products and limiting the gatekeeping function to a few instead of opening it up to many, schemes peddling "free" internet therefore compromise some of the key promises of cultural sovereignty and freedom of the postcolonial era.

Notes

1. The categories of *developed* and *developing* have been divided using the United Nations' M49 method as explained by International Telecommunication Union (2019).
2. Buzzfeed has attempted a partial list of Amazon-owned businesses in Miranda (2019).

3

KNOWLEDGE

THE USURPATION OF THE DIGITAL COMMONS ANALYZED IN the previous chapter positions us well to look at concrete ways in which private domains of influence can become arenas where specific cultural and ideological values predominate over others. This chapter locates its analysis in the domain of online knowledge production to interrogate the ways in which the conventions, standards, and rules that form the "knowledge infrastructures" (Bowker 2018, 205) in the digital domain reproduce and amplify the preexisting asymmetries in knowledge in the off-line world. While the latter has been closely scrutinized as a key mechanism through which global power has and continues to operate (Connell 2007, 2014), its iteration in the online world poses a sobering reminder against narratives of emancipation and empowerment accompanying the rise of the web. In critiquing the production and consumption of knowledge on the web, the goal here is to evaluate how the internet's democratic ethos and egalitarian ideals play out in the realm of online knowledge production.

The analysis in this chapter focuses on the rules, conventions, and protocols that regulate the collaborative production of knowledge on platforms such as Wikipedia. Its goal is to understand how these infrastructures of control privilege particular epistemologies, notions of what counts as proof, and modes of argumentation over others, thus making the creation and documentation of knowledge on the web far from a globally representative and inclusive exercise. Given the historically salient relationship between knowledge and power (Foucault 1980), the analysis of knowledge production and circulation online allows us to understand how global digital networks reflect but also reshape global power dynamics. While claims about the value-free and apolitical nature of knowledge have been critiqued from varied vantage points (Spivak 1999; Kuhn 1962; Foucault 1972, 1980), this chapter zooms in on the invisible ways that knowledge infrastructures and dominant political institutions regulate the boundaries of sayable truths in collaborative knowledge production on the web. Comparing the current state of knowledge on the web against its egalitarian founding ideals by posing questions about power, voice, and global representation is crucial to interrogating the extent to which those ideals remain fulfilled.

In focusing on Wikipedia, this chapter analyzes the largest and most successful attempt at collaborative knowledge production on the web. With over forty-nine million articles (as of December 2018; see Wikimedia 2019) in 304 different languages (Wikimedia, n.d., "List of Wikipedias"), the collaborative encyclopedia has emerged as the de facto representative of the web's potential to crowdsource knowledge. Given its global ambitions and readership, the pages of Wikipedia can be scrutinized to gauge the representation of diverse epistemologies and perspectives on it. This chapter attempts such an analysis through delving into the mechanisms and procedures by which deliberations proceed and decisions about content are made; in doing so, it critiques Wikipedia's self-proclaimed claims of being a globally representative attempt to collate the "sum of all human knowledge" (Slashdot 2004).

While versions of Wikipedia in different languages have been shown to have clear biases (e.g., the linguistic point of view discussed by Rogers 2013 and Callahan 2014), the critique of its English-language version gains particular significance because of both the growth of English as the global lingua franca and the significant global traffic (cutting across language and country) attracted by this version of the site. Versions of Wikipedia in other languages frequently use the English one as their reference point, often translating English pages into their own languages. A global survey of Wikipedia editors in 2011 (Wikimedia 2011, *Editor Survey Report*) found that while English was the first language of only 52 percent of the editors, as many as 76 percent of the global editors edited and contributed to the English-language Wikipedia. It thus gains from contributions from a linguistic, cultural, and nationally diverse community, making it "a kind of global version of the online encyclopedia" (Rogers 2013, 171). Given its global readership and contributor base, articles on the English Wikipedia frequently eschew their situated locational perspective to claim to represent a universal and global one, thus making it a useful object for considering the kind of questions raised in this book.

This chapter conducts a close analysis of Wikipedia's design, its rules and policies, its editor demographics, and the content of its articles to unravel the inherent contradiction between the encyclopedia's global ambitions and the ideological and cultural underpinnings that shape its contents. Moments of conflict, as are expected within any global collaborative effort bringing together diverse perspectives and cultural viewpoints, are particularly crucial to this analysis, as they magnify the weak links within the operation and interpretation of rules and policies. Hence this chapter conducts a close analysis of a decade-long edit war about the naming of Wikipedia's page on the Indian Ganga/Ganges River. Analyzing the debates and the modes of argumentation within the long-running conflict reveals how hegemonic tropes are repeatedly deployed to persuade others and to prevail over opposing arguments within the debate. Specifically, these debates show how Wikipedia's emphasis on published and verifiable evidence, rational argumentation, editorial consensus, and neutrality masks the domination of certain epistemologies, ideologies of knowledge, and histories over others.

Long-running edit wars on Wikipedia (such as the Ganga/Ganges debate) hold a particular significance when placed within a broader history of epistemic contestations and the privileging of key perspectives that symbolize what scholars have argued to be Eurocentric universalism. More importantly, edit wars reveal the central role of Wikipedia's demographic distribution as a key determinant in adjudicating over its content during deliberations where opposing positions may be equally valid. Despite its well-known discouragement of voting, deliberations over its contentious issues function akin to voting (Jemielniak 2014), where editors more familiar with rules and procedures invariably prevail, often at the cost of better arguments or counter evidence. The intertwining of knowledge with politics, culture, and location that these edit wars reveal instantiates in a digital avatar the mutually reciprocal relationship between knowledge, truth, and power that has historically regulated the boundaries of knowledge.

Knowledge and Power

The relationship between knowledge, truth, and power is germane to understanding the historically salient affinities between regimes of power and systems of legitimizing true knowledge. If the web privileges certain epistemologies, then understanding the cultural and historical underpinnings of those dominant modes of knowledge production allows us to make visible the seemingly invisible hegemonic foundations of the web. This detour also contextualizes the critique of Wikipedia's rules and procedures that have been instituted with the goal of producing a version of neutral, apolitical knowledge free from individual, cultural, or nationalistic biases. This endeavor for value-free knowledge must be seen alongside historical critiques of knowledge production (Foucault 1980; Kuhn 1970; Mignolo 2011) that have shown it to be invariably intertwined with dominant social, political, and cultural institutions.

The institutional regulation of boundaries that form the invisible edifice of knowledge have not merely policed the dividing line between knowledge and its Other but also shaped the definition of sayable truths. Foucault's unraveling of the social effect produced by discursive structures is prescient for understanding how "one cannot speak of anything at any time; it is not easy to say something new" (Foucault 1972, 44). This ability to regulate the distinctions between what is sayable and unsayable, between reason and folly, truth and falsehood, has historically privileged certain discourses and modes of knowing over others. Foucault shows its operation through entire systems, fellowships, and disciplines that emerge and present themselves as legitimate truth procedures, thus obviating alternatives. Through regulating the boundaries of knowledge, this "economy of discourses of truth" (Foucault 1980, 93) is key to facilitating the exercise of political power and establishing an unequivocal relationship between knowledge and power.

The role that Foucault ascribes to structures that distinguish between legitimate and illegitimate knowledge are very similar to what other scholars such as Bowker (2018) conceive of as "knowledge infrastructures" (203) that are institutionalized "ways of knowing" (207) that channel scholarly labor and productivity along predetermined grooves and pathways. Bowker shows how these ways of knowing—such as the classification of knowledge into disciplines and the distinctions between the soft and hard sciences as well as the humanities and sciences—"order the possibility of discourse" (206) but are also "vestigial or anachronistic activity persisting through an inertial scholarly infrastructure" (206). The gradual hardening of those pathways emerging from the churnings of the European Enlightenment and realized in Baconian empiricism has turned knowledge production into a "factory system" (210) comprising three vital components: specialized areas and fields, disciplinary journals and academic fora for communicating field-specific knowledge, and a scholarly community to vet, read, and deliberate knowledge production.

Given this lineage, definitions of legitimate and true knowledge that the web universalizes and that are enshrined in Wikipedia's rules can be arguably said to have Eurocentric origins that were born out of the

Enlightenment's (Mignolo 2011; Spivak 1999) disavowal of its imagined antithesis and Other. They were a consequence of an attempt to move away from magic, superstition, and myth toward a system of self-interrogating reason born from a radical reimagining of what counted as truth claims. Driven by the goals of calculability, utility, and mathematical efficiency, these notions of knowledge abstracted experience into neutral (and hence calculable) signs but simultaneously emptied knowledge of meaning (Adorno 2007). In showing the unstable opposition created during the Enlightenment between science on the one side and magic and superstition on the other, Adorno (2007) argues that what began as a radical challenge to pre-Enlightenment epistemologies "eradicated the last remnant of its own self-awareness" (2). Adorno critiques this erasure by showing how it denies space to the Enlightenment's Other, thus turning dominant epistemologies of modernity into a solipsistic echo chamber.

Critics have argued that this epistemic turn has historically served as the handmaiden of certain forms of power such as patriarchy and colonialism. Feminist theory has critiqued the elevation of reason and rationality and the simultaneous de-emphasis on experience and emotion as the "indispensable faculty for acquiring knowledge" (Jaggar 1989, 151). This ordering, driven by the goal of dispassionate investigation, summarily equates emotions with irrationality, unreason, the natural, and the female while privileging masculinist modes of cold, dispassionate rationality as the preferred approaches toward knowledge. Jaggar goes on to argue that "the perspective on reality available from the standpoint of the subordinated, which in part at least is the standpoint of women, is a perspective that offers a less partial and distorted and therefore more reliable view (Jaggar 1983: chap 11)" (Jaggar 1989, 168). Feminist postcolonial theory (Jacobs 2003) has similarly called out the denigration of native/colonized/Aboriginal knowledges as undeserving of the same status as those that uphold the desirable colonial attributes. Rules such as the active discouraging of points of view (POV) in order to attain a neutral point of view (NPOV) within Wikipedia's articles therefore feed into this historical quest for an abstract universalism that knowledge was supposed to attain.

Notably, the culturally unique and historically contingent claims to neutrality did not arise until the Enlightenment, when prejudice and bias acquired negative connotations (Gadamer 2004). Gadamer's pertinent reminder, therefore, that "the fundamental prejudice of the Enlightenment is the prejudice against prejudice itself" (Gadamer 2004, 273) echoes with multiple critiques of neutral and dispassionate knowledge from different vantage points. The concept of situated knowing arising from feminist epistemology similarly argues that one's social location both shapes and limits one's knowing as opposed to neutrality's ideal of the "view-from-nowhere" (Grasswick 2011, xvi) that encapsulates a masculine bias. In emphasizing the collaborations between the colonial project and key disciplines such as anthropology, ethnology (Obeyesekere 1997), English (Viswanathan 1997), and history (Chakrabarty 2007; Guha 2002), among others, postcolonial theory (Said 1979; Mignolo 2003; Spivak 1999; Guha 2002; Shome and Hegde 2002) has sought to unmask the invisible ways in which the dominant disciplinary formations arising from the Enlightenment created the mandate for and colluded in the cultural and territorial expansion during colonialism.

Key principles and works that constitute the Western canon advanced their postulations and propositions by creating the imagined non-European Other that was inaccessible and impenetrable through its categories. Spivak (1999) critiques notions such as the Kantian sublime, Hegelian historiography, and Marxist political economy for constructing and drawing sweeping conclusions about the non-European Other, thus not only ignoring the ongoing conquests of non-European lands but articulating the grounds for it. Continuing this critique, Connell (2007) expands on how the sociological method worked to create "bold abstractions" in the form of social and cultural laws and thus shows how it was premised on "a one-way flow of information, a capacity to examine a range of societies from the outside, and an ability to move freely from one society to another" (12). The resulting "imperial gaze" (Connell 2007, 12) led to broad and totalizing claims that created a relationship of dependence between the colony and the empire and, in the name of justifying progress, often constituted the mandate for colonialism. These collusions between knowledge and political-military power corroborate charges that the former has historically served as the modus for domination, conquest, and control. A dialectical understanding of the key premises that make up the pillars of Wikipedia wherein their contributions toward advancing knowledge is juxtaposed with their exclusionary tendencies allows us to understand how epistemic power operates within collaborative knowledge production in the online domain.

The Importance of Wikipedia

As the fruition of an endeavor to create a crowdsourced global online encyclopedia, Wikipedia is a spectacular achievement. Launched in 2001, its staggering forty-nine million articles (December 2018) in 304 languages make it the ninth most visited website in the world (Alexa, n.d., "Top 500 Sites") and the "biggest nonmarket, peer produced platform in the ecosystem of connective media" (van Dijck 2013, 133). Even though the active number of editors is far smaller than the two million "Wikipedians" listed by the site, the sheer amount of unpaid labor that has gone into creating and maintaining the global storehouse of knowledge is a testament to the altruistic ethos of the early web and the free/open source movement that spawned Wikipedia. Even though its English-language version remains the largest, with 5.6 million articles in April 2018, its attempts to be globally representative are borne out by its 304 language versions. The growth and stabilization of Wikipedia has defied several predictions of its demise (Simonite 2013; Carr 2006) as well as legitimate questions about its quality and veracity over the years.

This commendable achievement is unimaginable without the networking across space and time enabled by the web, but in particular it can be credited to the development of key software such as the wiki that made it possible to edit and save a document simultaneously across space and time. Thanks to the wiki and over a decade and a half of its development, Wikipedia has evolved key mechanisms to ensure smooth collaboration among editors working with a common goal but from distant global locations and who are unlikely to ever meet in the off-line world. Rules such as NPOV (neutral point of view), verifiability, and no original research, among others, have evolved over time and form the bedrock on which conflicts and discussions about issues (such as content and article names and deletions) play out within the talk pages of Wikipedia. Despite the consternation it elicits among scholars and academics, Wikipedia's global reach and influence are beyond debate today. It is a long way from achieving the lofty dream of accumulating the "sum of all human knowledge," but its appearance in the top ten visited sites in countries from Afghanistan to India and Sri Lanka to Kuwait (in addition to all Western countries), close to two hundred billion page visits in 2017, and close to three hundred thousand new registered users each month (Wikimedia, n.d., "Wikimedia Statistics: Monthly Overview") is a mark of its reach and presence on the global web today.

The growing scholarly analyses of Wikipedia, which have included key recent books (Tkacz 2015; Jemielniak 2014; Fichman and Hara 2014; Reagle 2010; Dalby 2009; Leitch 2014; O'Sullivan 2009; Tkacz and Lovink 2011), reflects its growing importance. Its emergence as a global reference tool that has increasingly become the first (and often only) point of consultation for knowledge about most things—including current events, historical facts/personalities, and ideas—and whose content has become part of "conventional wisdom" (Kildall and Stern, 2011, 167) necessitates a continuous critical engagement to interrogate its role within the broader dynamics of the global web. Studies have sought to address varied dimensions of that dynamic including its processes of decision-making, conflicts over content, and its global and linguistic representativeness as well as its role within the global knowledge and educational ecosystem. In particular its global prominence and ambitions make it imperative to interrogate the state of knowledge production and consumption by using it as a case study of networked global collaboration and hold it up to the egalitarian and participatory promises that the web was founded on (Hillis, Petit, and Jarrett 2013). Driven by the ideal of a globally representative internet and the related pursuit of deciphering the nature of cultural power on the web, this analysis seeks to establish how the rules and procedures that determine what can be written, what counts for evidence, the role of existing editors, and the entry pathways for new editors, while serving certain purposes of collaborative knowledge production, also hinder it in other crucial ways. The effects of these enabling constraints are visible within the content of the online encyclopedia that this chapter uses as a key example to illustrate its point.

How Representative Is Wikipedia? Gender, Language, and Region

Despite its laudable and utopian vision of creating a globally inclusive collaborative encyclopedia, Wikipedia's global growth remains stymied from constraints of access, language, and economic and technological barriers that point to why key aspects of the World Wide Web remain Eurocentric in their content and orientation. Posing the question of representativeness to a site that seeks to create value free and neutral knowledge juxtaposes knowledge production alongside democratization to wonder if the former must remain the purview of elites. In fact, one of the most salient critiques of Wikipedia comes from its former cofounder Larry Sanger, who cites its "anti-elitism" and the fact that "*anybody* can contribute and that there are no traditional review processes" (Sanger 2004) as the reason for its perceived unreliability.

A closer look at the encyclopedia, its editors, its articles, and its global representativeness, however, goes against the basic premise of Sanger's critique. Several analyses, recent and past, have shown that "anybody" cannot contribute to Wikipedia (Carr 2006; Halfaker et al. 2013; Herring 2011). Contributing to and editing Wikipedia have been made increasingly difficult through barriers to entry for newcomers that are stiff enough for scholars to compare it to a "cabal" (Jemielniak 2014) run and policed by a few. The number of new editors has been declining since 2007, when it hit its peak, and many ascribe this drop to the strict rules put in place as well as the cliquish nature of the existing editors and administrators on Wikipedia (Halfaker et al. 2013). Running for an administrative post on Wikipedia is a contentious process akin to a "bloodbath" (Jemielniak 2014, 41) that scars newcomers since the odds are heavily stacked in favor of the well-entrenched editors who can leverage their associations in a process of quid pro quo. Jemielniak quotes a Wikipedian: "Administrators will stand up for administrators, no matter what, because they want the others to stand up for them when they decide to protect their 'owned' article(s) from some newcomer trying to improve or change them" (Peters 2007, quoted in Jemielniak 2014, 51). Their ability to converse with each other on a secret, nonpublic email list, their higher status on account of having made more edits on the website, and their general familiarity with the rules (or "frames" for making argument, as Tkacz [2015] puts it) and procedures have ameliorated the effects of Wikipedia's "do not bite" rule that specifically urges existing editors to make the site a friendly place for new editors and contributors. The rule (abbreviated as WP:DNB) asks existing editors to be gracious and welcoming and listen actively to newcomers because "all of us were new editors at Wikipedia once" (Wikipedia, n.d., "Wikipedia: Please Do Not Bite"). However, the diminishing effect of the rule is visible in the reduced number of editors, from a high of fifty-six thousand in 2007 to about forty-one thousand in October 2020 (Wikimedia, n.d., "Wikimedia Statistics: Active Editors"). This reduction in the number of editors even as Wikipedia grows in size (though at a smaller rate than before) and popularity is in fact an ironic side effect of its own growth (Halfaker et al. 2013; Vergano 2013).

Steps the site has taken for quality control—such as quick reversion of edits made by newcomers, its strict deletion policy, and the use of algorithmic tools (such as bots) to carry out much of the editing and cleaning up that was earlier done manually—has introduced a new culture that is different from the past, when "'unwanted' but not intentionally damaging contributions may have been handled differently" (Halfaker et al. 2013, 678).

These changes, while perhaps necessary to manage Wikipedia's growing size, have nevertheless helped foster a culture where only a newcomer "who understands the norms, socializes himself or herself, dodges the impersonal wall of semi-automated rejection, and still wants to voluntarily contribute his or her time and energy can edit" (683). This claim is further supported by Wikipedia's own survey of editors (2011) that found that as many as 24 percent had faced some form of harassment during the editing/contributing process. The fact that "anyone" cannot edit Wikipedia anymore is a crucial reminder about the contradictions between its starting ideals and the logistical realities of running a global collaborative project.

Moreover, the system of checks and balances ostensibly put in place to improve quality and prevent vandalism do not function to allow in the experts and keep out laymen (as Sanger wished above) but have created a system where investment of time and persistence distinguishes those who stay from those who leave the collaborative platform. While any attempt to create a labor-intensive online global community would require an investment of time and effort, Wikipedia's editing process as it currently stands, far from skewing the incentives toward contributors with expertise and knowledge, does so toward those who are willing to invest time and interest and who display overall tenacity. This structural feature has consequences for the site's content and its representativeness because global economic relations predispose certain sections of society to have more free time than others. The gendered nature of this consequence is particularly important given that women have historically been found to have lesser free time (Sayer 2005; Mattingly and Blanchi 2003) as they join the workforce and are overburdened with the dual labor of home and work. Hence communities that depend on voluntary time remain invariably underrepresented by women, and in the case of Wikipedia that fact is borne out by several surveys of their editors (Bayer 2015), including those conducted by Wikipedia itself.

The percentage count of women editors on Wikipedia (from 6 percent in a 2006 survey to 22 percent of new users in 2013—see table 3.1) varies depending on the instrument and sample used but had remain unchanged until 2017, according to its founder Jimmy Wales (Simonton 2018; Ní Aodha 2017). Predictably, the percentage of women editors tended to be lower for regions outside North America and Europe, owing to the continuing "digital gender gap" (International Telecommunications Union 2019) that manifests in significantly lower (a more than 10 percent gap) access to the

Table 3.1 Percentage of women editors each year according to various editor surveys

Survey year	Conducted by	Population surveyed	% of female editors
2005	University of Wurzburg	Contributors to German Wikipedia (n=106)	10%
2006	Oded (2007)	English Wikipedia Editors (n=151)	7.3%
2008	United Nations University; Wikimedia Foundation	Occasional/regular contributors to Wikipedia (n=53,888)	13%
2011 (April)	Wikimedia Foundation	Logged in Wikipedia users with at least one edit (n=4,930)	9%
2012	Wikimedia Foundation	Logged in Wikipedia users (n=8716)	10%
2013	Wikimedia Foundation (Gender microsurvey)	Newly registered users on English Wikipedia (n=32,199)	22%
2014	Wikimedia Foundation (Global South user survey)	Wikipedia users in 11 Global South countries (n=10,061)	20%

SOURCE: Data for this table is from Bayer (2015).

internet for women than men in the least developed countries [International Telecommunication Union 2019]). These disparities have led to wide-ranging debates (Eckert and Steiner 2013) including one in which many commentators weighed in on the issue in the opinion pages of the *New York Times* (Herring 2011). The continuing imbalance has also led to an acknowledgment and commitment toward increasing gender diversity from the Wikimedia Foundation (which runs Wikipedia). From this book's vantage point, it is especially pertinent to note the correlations (Cohen 2011) between the low percentage of women editors and Wikipedia's content. Several scholars (Kohs 2011; Reagle 2010) have found striking differences between Wikipedia biographies about men as compared with those of women. Some (Lam et al. 2011) have shown that articles that had a higher percentage of women editors tended to be shorter (the scholars took an article's length to be a predictor of its quality) than those that drew more male editors. They analyzed this disparity in article lengths about film genres to argue that films of more interest to men had longer articles on Wikipedia about them as compared with films of more interest to women.

These findings about disparities between content, focused on women versus men on Wikipedia, undermine its claims about producing value-free, apolitical, and neutral knowledge. Gendered disparity in content supports arguments that have historically tied the processes of knowledge production to subject positions of scholars (Grasswick 2011) as well as the cultural and locational contingencies that shape the very nature of knowledge. Going beyond numerical underrepresentation to analyze the inbuilt biases within processes of editing and determining significance of content is insightful in understanding how certain gendered norms and values are privileged. Sue Gardner, the former executive director and currently a special advisor to the Wikimedia Foundation has collated various reasons—from lack of time to the hostile environment—as explanations for the low percentage of women editors. She found that the invariably contentious nature of discourse on the talk pages, where persuading others requires taking on masculinist attitudes of antagonism and confrontation, plays a key role in deterring women editors.

As opposed to the dominant mode of discourse on Wikipedia, "women in contrast, tend to be more polite and supportive, as well as less assertive," claimed a contributor cited by Gardner (2011). Others added that editing on Wikipedia is akin to "getting into fights with dudes," with one contributor comparing it to "stomping on someone's foot when they get in your face, which a lot of women, myself included, find difficult" (Gardner 2011). Susan Herring (2011), who has studied the role of gender in online communication, ascribes the difference in the percentage of editors to gendered differences in the style of communicating. Not only is Wikipedia not as welcoming toward a "non-assertive style preferred by many women" but also some of its key pillars, such as NPOV (neutral point of view), "favors a more masculine style of communication—just the facts, ma'am" (Herring 2011).

These findings about the dominance of a masculinist ethos and its correlation with Wikipedia's content resonate with feminist critiques (Fraser 1990; Landes 1988) of seemingly open "public" spaces where the garb of "deliberation can serve as a mask of domination" (Fraser 1990, 119). Nancy Fraser's critique of the Habermasian public sphere challenges its participatory ethos to show how certain forms of talk have historically been devalued in the public sphere as "effeminate" and how the emphasis on rational deliberation was only a move from a "repressive mode of domination to a hegemonic one, from rule based primarily on acquiescence to superior force to rule based primarily on consent supplemented with some measure of repression" (117). The fact that women editors find seemingly open discussions on Wikipedia hostile and unwelcome connects with a longer history of the devaluing of certain modes of talking and forms of experiences associated with women (Landes 1988). The continuing detrimental effects of those enduring attitudes on the encyclopedia's content undermine claims about Wikipedia's representativeness.

Gender, however, is not the only axis along which Wikipedia remains woefully underrepresented. The global and linguistic distribution of its editors is predictably skewed toward the Western world (the anglophone United States and Europe). According to Wikipedia's own editor survey (2011), more than 50 percent of its editors live in the top ten countries, with only one non-US and non-European country figuring in the top ten (India at 3 percent). According to a presentation made by Asaf Bartov (Wikimania 2013), head of grants and Global South Partnerships at Wikimedia Foundation, only about 21 percent of the total Wikipedians reside in the Global South, and about 20 percent of the edits originate there. By its own admission, this is radically disproportionate to the global population, more than 80 percent of which resides in the Global South. The linguistic distribution shows a worse scenario, as more than 90 percent of Wikipedia editors identify their primary languages as European; 52 percent of them are primary speakers of English.

Despite Wikipedia's attempts to launch various language editions, the significant growth in readership of the English Wikipedia across non-Western locations shows the primacy of the English version of the encyclopedia, making it the most widely read and authoritative source around the world (even in countries that do not identify English as a primary language). Notably, as many as 93 percent of all editors surveyed (2011) claimed to read the English Wikipedia even though it was the primary language for only 52 percent of them. This traffic to the English version is also due to the fact that 76 percent of all editors (irrespective of their primary languages) edit the English Wikipedia, thus ensuring that it gains from global expertise as opposed to from only those who claim English as their primary language.

The English version, with an article count of 5.7 million (December 2018), is significantly ahead of its competitors (see table 3.2), such as the Swedish (3.8 million), Dutch (1.9 million), German (2.2 million), and French (2 million approximately) versions. The number of articles in combination with article "depth" (a measure of the edits on an article and hence its quality) gives us a sense of robustness of the particular language edition.[1] The authority of the English Wikipedia is underscored by the fact that it remains the most widely read/visited language edition of Wikipedia by a large margin, with more than 5.3 million page views per hour in February 2018, which is eight to ten times the number of page views for its closest

Table 3.2 List of top ten language Wikipedias by article numbers

Language	No. of articles	Edits	Admins	Depth
English	5,600,052	828,793,582	1,225	901.59
Cebuano	5,383,065	21,731,837	5	1.07
Swedish	3,783,833	42,581,228	65	5.81
German	2,167,696	174,662,583	194	94.24
French	1,969,541	146,515,691	164	220.58
Dutch	1,927,221	51,227,990	43	14.26
Russian	1,462,865	91,485,933	90	131.38
Italian	1,427,248	95,516,175	114	131.2
Spanish	1,399,724	106,211,640	70	205.56
Polish	1,272,278	52,863,352	106	27.81

SOURCE: Data for this table has been obtained from Wikipedia (n.d., "List of Wikipedias"). *Note*: While the other columns in the table are self-explanatory, the Depth column is a reliable measure of the *quality* of each language Wikipedia. It is arrived at by (Edits / Articles × Nonarticles / Articles × [1–Stub-ratio]). *Nonarticles* refers to user pages, images, talk pages, "project" pages, categories, and templates. Depth is an indicator of how frequently the articles are updated. It does not refer to academic quality. A few anomalies in this list also need to be explained: The appearance of Swedish and Cebuano (Philippines) editions of Wikipedia on this list can be credited to bots (software programs) created by the Swedish physicist Sverker Johansson (S. Tomlinson 2014; Guldbrandsson 2013).

rival Wikipedias—Russian, German, Spanish, and Japanese—which have 500,000–700,000 page views per hour each (Wikimedia 2018a). Additionally, the English Wikipedia has more than thirty thousand active editors (those making more than five edits in a month), which is almost six times the German version, with the second highest number of active editors. This relative global dominance of the English Wikipedia is a useful background against which to analyze its content.

While the Wikimedia Foundation's acknowledgment of these skewed linguistic representations is commendable, this disproportionate representation, just as in the case of gender, nevertheless manifests itself in the content of the encyclopedia and has yet to be studied more fully. The predominantly Western location of its editorship gives Wikipedia's content an invariable Eurocentric bias since editors are most likely to contribute to and edit articles that are of interest and familiar to them. Just as in the case of gender, the global disparity in the distribution of editors is visible in articles on areas such as popular culture and geography but also in categories of knowledge that make universal claims, such as history and culture (e.g., pages for terms such as *art* and *culture*). Given that the English version of Wikipedia has come to stand in for a global version of the encyclopedia, these disparities in its content function to conflate "the sum of all human knowledge" with predominantly Western knowledge.

O'Sullivan's (2009) critique about the disparity in "the geography and history of the United States as compared with that of, say, Africa or China" (81) on Wikipedia, or his observations about its coverage of popular culture wherein he claims that "there are long articles on each of the 144 episodes of the American television series *Buffy the Vampire Slayer*" (81), continues to accurately describe the picture years later. Various independent findings about Wikipedia bear out this critique. The list of most edited articles of all time have an unmistakably US/European stamp to them. The top three most edited pages on Wikipedia, for instance, are about the World Wrestling Entertainment (fifty-two thousand edits), George Bush (forty-seven thousand edits) and the United States (forty-one thousand edits; see Wikipedia n.d., "Wikipedia: Pages with the Most"; Griffin 2015), which points not only to a US focus but also to a privileging of recent events over more historical ones. Out of a total of twenty-six individual biographies in the top hundred edited articles on Wikipedia, twenty-one are of men and only five are of women. Out of the same list of twenty-six biographies, one (male or female) features a non-Westerner (three if you include pages on Jesus and Muhammad): Vijay, an actor from Southern India. The number of edits is an indication of strong interest more from a niche group of editors than in the wider readership, but they are nevertheless one key parameter (among others) by which the importance of Wikipedia's articles can be gauged.

Wikipedia's own list of its top twenty-five pages, ranked by the number of visitors each week, is another notable criterion that shows the correlation between the demography of its editors, page visits, and content. Its weekly list of top visited pages is expectedly skewed toward current events and more a reflection of the weekly zeitgeist of the global Wikipedians than a marker of the enduring importance of those particular articles and issues. The lists reflect the latest events and ongoing changes in the world of news (primarily politics, sports, and popular culture); the only overlaps across weeks are the items that have continued to remain in the news. As with the most edited articles discussed above, the most visited pages each week have a predominantly Western/American flavor, with non-Western news events making it to the list only if covered in the Western press.

Analyzing the list for three consecutive weeks in March 2018,[2] for instance, showed that Western news events and news about Hollywood movies topped the list in the weeks of March 4–10 (the film *The Shape of Water*), March 11–17, and March 18–24 (Stephen Hawking). Only one non-Western-focused page made it to the top twenty-five for the week of March 11–17, that of the Korean pop band Exo, who performed at the 2018 Winter Olympics, a globally watched event hosted in South Korea. Analyzing the last of those three weeks (March 18–24) as a representative period, one finds there were six pages about non-Western events or personalities among the twenty-five most visited, and each could be explained with justifiable rationale. Two out of those six, however, were about Vladimir Putin (ranked fourth out of twenty-five) and the Russian presidential elections (ranked twenty-first out of twenty-five) respectively, which had received significant coverage in the Western press; a third, the Japanese geochemist Katsuko Saruhashi, whose page was the second most visited, achieved that feat only because a Google Doodle announced her ninety-eighth birthday. A Bollywood movie (*Raid*) made it to number eighteen, the page of the India-born spiritual guru Rajneesh was at number fourteen (thanks to the release of a much anticipated Netflix documentary on his life), and the page for the Persian New Year was the last (twenty-fifth) on the list. Insightful asymmetries emerge when this list is juxtaposed with traffic to Wikipedia—a case in point being India, which is the source of the sixth largest amount of traffic (Wikimedia, n.d., "Wikimedia Statistics") to Wikipedia and the only non-Western country among the top ten sources of Wikipedia's traffic; only one page associated with it appeared on the list of the top twenty-five visited pages across the three weeks analyzed.

These revealing insights about the global zeitgeist bear out a larger pattern that this chapter takes as a symptom worthy of interrogation. The fact that the content of the English Wikipedia remains primarily Euro-American despite its global readership and contributions is symptomatic of the larger web, whose key ethos and values, embedded within their protocols, conventions, and structural designs (van Dijck, Poell, and De Waal 2018), are yet to fully extend their participatory ethos to the world. The manifestation of those values within collaborative processes (especially when adjudicating on contentious conflicts such as Wikipedia's edit wars) reveals how its founding and predominant location in the West (not numerically in terms of users but in terms of its cultural and technical infrastructure and key domains/sites) imbues its material and cultural architecture with cultural and ideological orientations. Abdicating this critique risks allowing an erasure by which online culture and knowledge disproportionately represent already dominant knowledge systems and epistemologies over others. The rise of Eurocentric modernity was arguably premised on precisely such an erasure (Mignolo 2011; Spivak 1999), and, far from correcting that imbalance, the current state of the web amplifies it. Commendable as Wikipedia's efforts toward reaching out and gaining readership across the world are, those efforts to expand can only partly address the problem without a simultaneous critical analysis of the dominant epistemic paradigms that determine and shape Wikipedia's content.

Infrastructures of Knowledge on Wikipedia

The processes by which articles are created, their content is debated, and their arguments are considered valid are rife with conditions and mechanisms that, while facilitating the creation of "true" knowledge, also shape it toward particular ends by excluding alternatives. Cases in point are Wikipedia's rule of verifiability, the related rule of "no original research" (Wikipedia, n.d., "Wikipedia: No Original Research"), and the determination of what counts as a valid "source" that can be cited as evidence for establishing repute and being featured in the encyclopedia. Wikipedia's rules are similar to any academic journal in that they emphasize corroborative evidence for claims that are reputable, traceable, and verifiable. These requirements are detailed in its pages on the rules of "verifiability" (n.d., "Wikipedia: Verifiability") and "third party sources" (n.d., "Wikipedia: Independent Sources"). Wikipedia explains that its content is "determined by previously published information," which, in addition to its rule of not allowing any unpublished original research, ensures that facts and events that may otherwise be true in the real world cannot find place on Wikipedia. Its rules define "published" to mean that the material should be "made available to the public in some form" (n.d., "Wikipedia: Verifiability"). The best kind of sources that can be presented as proof for claims are what the encyclopedia calls independent "third party" sources that are independent of the subject being covered (n.d., "Wikipedia: Independent Sources"). Additionally, its criteria of notability require that the topic, event, or person being written about in the article should have received "significant coverage in reliable sources that are independent of the subject" (n.d., "Wikipedia: Independent Sources"). Unless they meet these conditions, articles are recommended for speedy deletion that is typically carried out by bots, with little human intervention (Tkacz 2015; Niederer and van Dijck 2010). In its own words, these conditions ensure avoidance of conflict of interest and prevent Wikipedia from becoming a "dumping ground for facts" (Wikipedia, n.d., "Deletionism and Inclusionism").

But given that Wikipedia features many topics other than academic and scholarly ones, including those about events, people, issues, and controversies, the requirement of published sources presumes a well-established publishing and media structure at the site/region of the event's occurrence that can track and record noteworthy events and issues, which can then be used as supporting evidence on the online encyclopedia. This requirement of a published source ensures that content representation from those regions within any country with a well-established media system will remain much higher than the relatively lesser-covered regions of a country or the world. Within any country, then, Wikipedia is bound to have a bias toward the metropolitan centers with dense and highly developed media and publishing networks and toward well-known mainstream issues that get far more coverage. Since media coverage (which fulfills Wikipedia's criteria of third-party sources) is key to determining "notability" (Wikipedia, n.d., "Notability"), the online encyclopedia reproduces in the digital realm the disparities of media coverage in the off-line real world.

In the global context, this bias invariably skews toward parts of the world with more developed publishing and media systems than others. The list of countries ranked by the number of books (which function as a key published source on Wikipedia) published per capita (released by the International Publishers Association each year; see Ingenta 2014) is unsurprisingly populated by the developed world, as book-publishing rates correspond with global literacy figures. Moreover, as will be shown in the analysis of the edit war on the Ganga/Ganges page, articles need to be published in the same language as that of the version of Wikipedia for which it is used as a source. This makes it difficult (if not virtually impossible) for articles from regions of the world without an English-language media and publishing industry to appear on the English Wikipedia. The encyclopedia therefore not only reproduces the off-line global disparity in knowledge production in the online world but further amplifies it because while unpublished forms of knowledge cannot make it online, even published knowledge from the non-anglophone world cannot be used as credible sources to support articles. Wikipedia's rigorous "deletionist policy" continuously ensures that pages not meeting its criteria for significance and notability are deleted (often by mechanized bots). Deletions that are contested undergo a contentious discussion about proof, significance, and evidence similar to those discussed above.

Undoubtedly, the global digital divide and the continuing lag in internet access around the world are crucial explanations for the imbalances within Wikipedia in the decade and a half of its existence. But the structural reasons beyond the digital divide, such as specific requirements for proof/evidence and notability that require well-established publishing and media industries, modes and styles of argumentation within the talk pages, the cliquish nature of its editorial community (Jemielniak 2014), and the predominant Western location of its editors and administrators are also key hindrances to its becoming a truly representative global encyclopedia. The analysis of the impediments to realizing Wikipedia's goals of being globally representative prepares us to closely scrutinize these elements in practice through the exploration of a specific conflict. This chapter's analysis focuses on one of the longest running edit wars on the online encyclopedia, about whether the name for the Wikipedia page about an Indian river should carry its local Indian name, Ganga, or the anglicized British name Ganges.

While all edit wars or irresolvable conflicts over content on Wikipedia are different, they also represent the common phenomenon of infrastructural breakdown wherein the routine procedures and processes for achieving an end goal (that is, to create content) fail. The ongoing (since 2006) Ganga/Ganges edit war represents a test case wherein established rules and procedures for adjudicating edit wars have failed to resolve the conflict, thus bringing the dispute repeatedly to a vote, despite Wikipedia's caution that disputes over content "are almost never subject to polling" (Wikipedia, n.d., "Polling Is Not a Substitute"). Because these stalemates, caused due to the inadequacy of rules and procedures in anticipating an anomalous situation, reveal the limits and outer boundaries of those norms, they represent fertile test cases where the underlying infrastructure "comes out of the woodwork" (Peters 2015, 52) and becomes "more visible" (Larkin 2008, 245). Since they increase our "awareness of infrastructure" (Bowker 2018, 212), "glitches can be as fruitful intellectually as they are frustrating practically" (Peters 2015, 52). Despite repeated calls to vote on the issue, an uneasy truce prevails, and—much to the chagrin of those supporting a name change—the page has held on to the name Ganges, "a name more familiar to Western speakers of English" (Jemielniak 2014, 76). Editors and contributors continue to contest its current name, as they consider it to be a colonial relic and hence of "huge symbolic and emotional importance" (76) to them. In analyzing the conflict, the larger goal is to understand the invisible cultural and political valences embedded within the reified infrastructures of knowledge that manifest on online collaborative platforms such as Wikipedia.

My analysis of the conflict over the name of the page is inspired by other scholars (Tkacz 2015; Jemielniak 2014; Rogers 2013) who have similarly studied other conflicts over content on Wikipedia to understand the broader anatomy of contention on the platform. Rogers's (2013) analysis of the variations between different language versions of the Wikipedia pages on the Srebrenica genocide, Tkacz's (2015) analysis of the debates about deleting a Wikipedia page (Wikipedia Art) and the inclusion of an image of the Islamic prophet Muhammad in a Wikipedia page and Jemielniak's (2014) study of the long-running feud about the naming of the Polish city Gdansk/Danzig conducted similar analyses of ongoing conflicts. Even though the vantage points of their analyses of conflicts were different from mine, the questions they posed about the processes of knowledge production and adjudication of disputes form key precursors and hold important lessons that drive my analysis of the Ganga/Ganges dispute that follows. While being inspired by those prior studies, the following section seeks to use the debate generated by them to better understand how the broader systemic features and designs privilege certain forms of arguments and epistemologies over others, leading to the content disparity shown above. While most disputes are not prolonged for a decade the way the Ganga/Ganges debate has been, analyzing extreme cases such as this can be instructive (Jemielniak 2014) for understanding the multidimensional nature of debate and deliberation on the web.

Epistemic Conflicts in the Ganga/Ganges Edit War

The choice of this debate for analysis is determined by the appearance within it of the key themes that make up the argument of this chapter. Locally known as Ganga but called the Ganges by the British, the river has enduring cultural symbolism in India, thus making the title of its Wikipedia page the focus of a charged and often vitriolic debate between those arguing for one name over another. This debate is imbricated within a historic relationship between the East and the West, the colony and the metropole, and the role of English in our globalizing world. It also presents revealing insights about competing definitions of proof that reveal power dynamics between the editors and their role in interpreting the rules of Wikipedia. Despite several attempts to change the page's name through voting (the last as recent as February 2015) and evidence-based arguments and counterarguments, the name of the page continues to be "Ganges" for now. Created as a stub in 2001, the page has evolved to include various subsections and faced its first suggestion to change its name to "Ganga" in 2006. In the past decade more than fifteen different threads of conversation (each running for several months and totaling more than fifty thousand words) have been initiated specifically on the name change alone, many of them ending in a vote count—a process that Wikipedia discourages and considers a last resort to solve disputes.

Despite each side repeatedly bringing forth the same arguments embellished with their versions of "proof," the numbers during voting have continuously remained on the side of "Ganges." The debate's significance has been noticed by the powers that be at Wikipedia (Valby 2011), who have used it to show the encyclopedia's skewed demographics and disproportionately Western representation. Sue Gardner, the executive director of the Wikimedia Foundation, has argued that the Ganga/Ganges debate is "interesting because there's this tiny number of Indians who care a lot and are correct and have all kinds of citations and evidence to support their view, and then there's this group who just are rebuffing them because the numbers are on their side" (Valby 2011). While her comment focuses on the numbers, I seek to show that this long-running debate allows us to analyze the ways in which Wikipedia's rules, its privileging of certain kinds of evidence over others, and the larger structure of the web of which the collaborative site is a part move it away from its stated goals of being a globally representative encyclopedia containing "the sum of all human knowledge." My analysis of this decade-long debate identifies four themes emerging within it that, I argue, are key to understanding how the arguments unfolded within the debate. The four themes are (i) the nature of evidence and what counts as a reliable source, (ii) the political status and role of English in our world, (iii) colonial legacy and the postcolonial politics of naming, and (v) the role of voting versus consensus on Wikipedia. While specific to the Ganga/Ganges debate, these emergent themes are also a symptom of the broader intractable issue of online collaborative knowledge production that requires juxtaposing multiple perspectives, cultural backgrounds, and historical and geographic perspectives on a common platform. Similar to Rogers's (2013) analysis of how linguistic points of view challenge the very nature of reality across different language versions of the Srebrenica Massacre, the Ganga/Ganges debate shows us how knowledge, history, and competing versions of reality/truth are inherently tied to location, culture, politics, and eventually power.

In presenting how each of these themes played out in the debate, I present each side's contention and its significance for the larger questions driving the analysis. The goal of this analysis is not to privilege some form of neutral knowledge but, in fact, to show how the very goal of neutrality masks the varied ways in which culture, politics, and location (Kuhn 1970; Foucault 1980) determine what counts as knowledge. It underscores how the seemingly noble goal of rational, evidence-based argumentation is fated to exclude and hence erase what is presented as its Other with consequential aftereffects on the relationship between power and knowledge on the web.

Contestations about Evidence and Obvious "Facts"

Deliberations about the quantity and nature of evidence on either side formed a significant part of the back-and-forth arguments about changing the name of the page about the river. These arguments had to be qualified and filtered through Wikipedia's own policies and particularly its rule called "identifying reliable sources" (henceforth Wikipedia:Rs) that each side interpreted in its own favor. The rule is clear in stating that "Wikipedia articles should be based on reliable, published sources" (Wikipedia, n.d., "Wikipedia: Reliable Sources"). Discussions about the meaning of "reliable" and "published," when a significant amount of evidence presented by both sides was culled from what already exists on the web, led to some meaningful discussions about the value and representativeness of online sources.

However, they also demonstrated that the knowledge base of Wikipedia is fated to replicate and reproduce the status quo of knowledge distribution on the wider internet in a process of echoing and amplification. This emphasis on the published written linear text as the privileged means of production and dissemination is key to the modern infrastructures of knowledge that Bowker (2018) calls vestigial and anachronistic in an age of rapid technological change that is transforming knowledge production. Wikipedia's own nervousness about expanding its conceptions of knowledge and proof, while understandable given its limited access to institutional procedures of vetting new forms of evidence, nevertheless shows how the resistance to "acknowledge and reward emergent ways of knowing" (Bowker 2018, 207) can skew its content toward regions of the world with already established track records of publishing in privileged avenues and formats.

When presenting published evidence such as books and journal articles, the participants invariably submitted what they had found through search engine results such as Google Books, Google Scholar, and Google News. While both sides presented online evidence, it also led to questions (within the larger debate of name change) about the value of search engine results, especially given Wikipedia's own caution about how to read them (Wikipedia, n.d., "Wikipedia: Search Engine Test"). Those asking for a name change to "Ganga" (from the page's existing name of "Ganges") would have to prove that their preferred name was more "commonly used (as determined by its prevalence in reliable English language sources) as such names will be the most recognizable and the most natural" (n.d., "Wikipedia: Article Titles").[3] This sub-rule of commonly recognizable names is covered under Wikipedia's rule on article titles (n.d., "Wikipedia: Article Titles") and has been a continuing bone of contention between the two sides of the debate, especially as supporters of Ganga present another conflicting sub-rule that argues for using national varieties of English in titles. These conflicting rules and sub-rules, part of the now infamous bureaucratic structure of Wikipedia, ensure that opposing sides in a debate can pit them against each other, thus leaving a final vote count as the only way out of an intractable dispute.

As is evident in the archived discussions of the Ganga/Ganges debate, the quest to prove common usage of its name led each side to show search results from the web as evidence of its preferred name being more commonly used. Different results from Google (search engine, scholar, and books) were presented and then critiqued by opposing sides using various conflicting rules from Wikipedia. A supporter for the move to "Ganga," for instance, presented three different searches conducted through Google, even hyperlinking to the results in the comment to show that "Ganga is the more common title in scholarly publications (see #Google scholar above), It is the more common title in contemporary books (see #Google books above), It is the more commonly used term in recent news coverage, by a factor of 3:2" (JN466, November 28, 2010). This was immediately countered by an opposing user who presented a different set of search results to argue that "'Ganges' and/or 'Ganges river' wins over 'Ganga' and/or 'Ganga river' in Scholar and Books while losing in News (but the factor isn't 3:2)" (Flamarande, November 29, 2010). The first user then returns to make a case for focusing on Google Scholar instead of other kinds of searches as the former gives results that are "small enough to be countable" (JN466, November 29,

2010). This user then showed that a search for *Ganga* received 3,037 results in Google Scholar whereas *Ganges* receives only 2,561, thus implying that the numbers in Google Scholar favor the name change to "Ganga." These snippets from the debate that run into long paragraphs of back-and-forth arguments continuously return to the indeterminate question of which side had more evidence. This recursive back-and-forth invariably led to openly expressed frustration from each side and eventually a stalemate from which voting seemed the best way out.

The presentation of search engine results as proof for or against the name change was further complicated by Wikipedia's own advisory against their use as evidence within such debates. Search results can be a good place for "a first-pass heuristic or 'rule of thumb'" but cannot "guarantee the results are reliable or 'true,'" says the relevant Wikipedia rule (n.d., "Wikipedia: Search Engine Test"). The advisory further reminds users that search results may return fictitious results, and their numerical count is at best a "very crude measure of importance" and in fact "an extremely errone-ous tool for measuring notability." In presenting this caution, Wikipedia distinguishes itself from Google to claim that the latter does not "aim for a neutral point of view" whereas "Wikipedia does." Critiques of Google's bias (Pasquale 2015; Edelman 2014; Rieder and Sire 2013; Hillis, Petit, and Jar-rett 2013) have made similar arguments about the conflicting interests that compromise Google's page rank algorithm to privilege popularity, com-mercial interests, utilitarianism, prior search history, and locational data.

The predominant reliance on Google results to prove that one name was more commonly used than another therefore positions Google as an oracle-like neutral arbiter of knowledge, thus betraying an unrequited trust in the search engine. More importantly, this reliance points to the self-referential nature of an online encyclopedia that invariably recirculates and cites sources on the web as evidence while excluding the knowledge that may exist in the off-line world in nondigital or undigitizable forms. The overall imbalance in online content production and knowledge due to the global digital divide and the related inequities in resources and techno-logical capacities ensures that debates about notability, common usage, and relative importance on Wikipedia go beyond maintaining the status quo to in fact distort and amplify the existing knowledge inequities that have been a cause of much concern in the off-line world.

The fact that page titles in the English Wikipedia must be based on "reliable English-language sources" (Wikipedia, n.d., "Wikipedia: Article

Titles") was brought up by supporters of "Ganges" to reject attempts to move. In responding to the discussion on sources, one of them surmised that the supporters of Ganga must choose the Hindi version of Wikipedia to make their case: "Actually, the sources are on the 'Ganges' side. That's established English. 'Ganga' is not. We write in English. If you want Hindi, edit WP-hi" (kwami, July 21, 2011). Another asked the supporters of Ganga to return the gaze on themselves by reminding them, "You wouldn't like it either if a bunch of Hindi learners in London decided on what proper Hindi grammar and usage is either" (Akerbeltz, October 23, 2010). This linguistic emphasis in Wikipedia's rules, reiterated by the users, reflects a logistical challenge for any encyclopedia seeking collaboration from a globally dispersed group of editors. This challenge is moored around the dual position occupied by English wherein its gradual adoption as the global lingua franca (through colonialism, trade, wars, and cultural/epistemic imperialism) and the consequent changes and hybridization of the language conflict with its specificities that tie it to the anglophone west.

The global rise of English, often at the expense of local languages, has been justifiably critiqued, most directly by the theory of linguistic imperialism (Phillipson 2008, 2009). In the absence of either a more multilingual editor demographic or suitably adept translation services that could translate non-English sources, the English Wikipedia remains distorted in favor of anglophone knowledge and hence a Eurocentric worldview. Despite the supporters of Ganga producing an overwhelming amount of sources in English to show its common usage in English-language sources, it remained unconvincing for the Ganges side of the debate, which continued to insist that the English Wikipedia must reflect the anglophone view whereas the Indian view could be expressed only in the Hindi Wikipedia.

In supporting this argument, they presented yet another snippet from Wikipedia's (n.d., "Article Titles") rules on article titles that suggests the use of "other encyclopedias" as reference points to determine what titles are frequently used. One of the supporters of Ganges presented evidence to claim that "as for encyclopedia and dictionaries, as of today, some 63,000 use 'Ganges,' whereas approximately 18,000 use 'Ganga'" (Fowler&fowler, April 23, 2014). Yet another user showed that the "admittedly US-based Merriam-Webster's Geographical dictionary" (Pfly, October 24, 2010) did include both names—but a supporter of Ganges swiftly countered this to claim that "my dictionaries (OED, MWC, RH) don't include 'Ganga'" (kwami, June 29, 2011). The preponderance of Ganges in the encyclopedias presented by the supporters of Ganges remained far from fully countered by the Ganga side of the argument. This was because the lack of any reputable encyclopedias or dictionaries published in the English language in India combined with the inadmissibility of non-English dictionaries and encyclopedias weighed the evidence in favor of the Ganges side of the argument. While an uncountable number of tomes, poems, and hymns referring to the river as Ganga exist in local Indian languages, the requirement that the references on Wikipedia be from published English sources meant that they could not be brought in as evidence in the debate. For instance in describing his choice to use Ganga over Ganges in the English translation of one such source—the Sanskrit poem *Ganga Lahari* (*The Waves of Ganga*)—Cort (2007, 21) explains that the "tender softness" of *Ganga* better aligned with the feminine iconography of the river within Indian discourses in comparison to the "harsh diphthongs" of *Ganges*. This poem, like several other cultural and literary references that circulate in the textual and oral history about the river, would be inadmissible in a Wikipedia debate.

These contestations about evidence and in particular the overreliance on numerical proof betray an unquestionable faith in the "perfect quantification" of knowledge (Hillis, Petit, and Jarrett 2013, 59) wherein knowledge production takes "facts" to be beyond interpretation and hence unquestionable (Poovey 1998). Undoubtedly, this approach is encouraged by Wikipedia's rules, which, for instance, imply common usage to mean something that is numerically quantifiable, thus making it a numbers game. That the very definition of what *proof* means was up for debate and that its resolution could rely only on Wikipedia's own definition of the word (each side citing Wikipedia's own page on proof) showed the self-referential nature of knowledge production on Wikipedia. The paradox is evident in this sarcasm-laden exchange between two users:

> You're being ridiculous. I've already responded to your "proofs" (you may wish to look up what that word means). (kwami, November 15, 2010)

> In the dialect I am using proof has the meaning provided in this article Proof. (Yogesh Khandke, November 16, 2010)

> Ah, okay. I only know the term as what that article calls "formal proof." For you, "proof" only means "argument"? I accept that you've provided arguments. (kwami, November 16, 2010)

> A definition of proof is *sufficient evidence or argument for the truth of a proposition*, that it is sufficient is my opinion, if others agree, it will be our opinion. *I only know* perhaps does not constitute the boundaries of human knowledge. (Yogesh Khandke, November 16, 2010)

The distinction between argument and proof emerging in this exchange reveals two distinct and conflicting epistemological positions that will recur in the themes below. The emphasis on proof (implicitly equated here with facts or factual proof) and its conflation with empirical and objective knowledge at the cost of alternative epistemes (e.g., narrative, experiential, affective knowledge that could be differently interpreted) reified a phenomenon associated with the rise of Euro-Western modernity (Adorno 2007; Gadamer 2004). This scientization and quantification of knowledge (taken to an extreme with certain versions of logical positivism) must be dialectically understood as also being premised on erasures and exclusions that function just as dogmatically as the so-called premodern knowledge systems that the birth of reason and rationality sought to replace.

Wikipedia's overt reliance on restrictive notions of proof reifies preexisting and narrow definitions of knowledge that arguably comprise "vestigial or anachronistic activity persisting through an inertial scholarly infrastructure" (Bowker 2018, 206). Not only do such insistences erase alternative epistemologies, but they also fail to acknowledge the reality of how the digital divide creates glaring disparities in the amount of digital content from the well-connected versus the lesser-connected parts of the world. The extended discussions about proof versus arguments, the emphasis on quantifiable evidence, and the privileging of Western and English-based sources as evidence over non-Western and non-English ones all represent implicit hierarchies among competing knowledge systems of the world. This ordering places certain forms of knowledge and certain ways of knowing as more desirable than others and is key to understanding the exclusionary effect of Wikipedia's rules and processes of deliberation.

My English versus Your English

The globally dominant status of English and the resulting growth of hybrid language systems as a result of colonialism/imperialism, globalization, and trade emerged as a key thematic within the Ganga/Ganges debate. The debate shone light on prominent questions about the status of language and power in a globalizing world: Should the global prominence of English, which is invariably premised on the simultaneous decline of minority languages (Phillipson 2008), lead to a single standardized English or multiple versions of it? How can the emergence of English as the global lingua franca be juxtaposed with its creative adaptations through its encounter with local languages around the world? The polarizing debate saw entrenched positions on either side of this debate, with supporters of Ganges arguing for the use of standard English (which was equated with the British and American versions) and the supporters of Ganga making a case for regional variations based on cultural and geographical adaptations of the language.

Once again, conflicting aspects of the policy on naming article titles were proffered in support of their positions by the warring sides, thus rendering the rules inadequate in resolving this intractable dispute. In opposition to the advice on common usage for article titles cited by the supporters of Ganges, the supporters of Ganga presented a sub-rule within it (called national varieties of English; Wikipedia, n.d., "Wikipedia: Article Titles") that advises that "the title of an article on a topic that has strong ties to a particular English-speaking nation should use the variety of English appropriate for that nation." The use of this seemingly powerful supporting caveat (within the broader rule) in favor of Ganga was, however, subverted by the rule's own example of an exception (since removed) that cited the Ganges page debate as an instance when this particular rule could not be applied because of "its greater intelligibility to English-speaking readers worldwide (e.g., Ganges rather than 'Ganga')."[4] This self-contradictory proviso that qualified that section's call for allowing national and cultural variations of standard Western English in a case of strong ties was viewed with understandable suspicion by the supporters of Ganga. They claimed it went against the spirit of that section within the broader rule but more importantly had been inserted only as an exception in February 2011, when the contentious Ganga/Ganges debate was well underway and had already undergone several unsuccessful votes for a name change. They could prove this as well as provide the date of insertion of the exception due to Wikipedia's own practice of documenting and archiving every single edit made within an article.

During early discussions of this sub-rule on national variations, a user wondered if India counted as an "English speaking nation" because an "awful lot of Indians speak English, but very few natively" (Trovatore, October 22, 2010). This was promptly corrected by supporters of Ganga who presented statistics (Wikipedia, n.d., "Countries by English-Speaking Population") showing that India ranked second among the English-speaking countries of the world. Their claim for allowing variations for national and cultural versions of English within the globally dominant standard version of English relied on arguments such as India having the world's largest read English newspaper in the world (*Times of India*) as well as the gradual inclusion of several words from India and Indian languages within standard English. One user presented the list of non-English Indian words already used in the Ganges article, such as *ghats, kumbh mela, abhishek,* and *prayashchit* (Zuggernaut, November 19, 2010) to claim that the article would remain woefully incomplete without the inclusion of words culturally and linguistically unique to India and hence untranslatable into another language. The recurring claim for an Indian version of English was also supported by a list of comparative words, such as *petrol* instead of *gas,* and words with uniquely Indian meanings, such as *hotel, tiffin, strike,* and *picnic,* to show how Indian English had a distinct flavor. Notably, claims for an Indian version of English finds support from an increasing body of literary work from postcolonial sites that play creatively with dominant colonial languages to expand their oeuvre and scope. In the case of India, globally renowned English novelists and poets such as Salman Rushdie (1981) and Nissim Ezekiel (2006) have creatively infused the language with a world of meanings and cultural sensibilities,[5] thus making it hybrid and Indian.

The global phenomenon of national and cultural variations in English, however, was not a sufficient enough argument for its usage on Wikipedia, and those supporting the Ganges name raised fears of balkanization of the language if a change of the article's title to "Ganga" were allowed. The following exchange between two users on opposing sides of the debate is telling of the stalemate:

> In other words: you are in favor of "balkanizing" the English wiki along cultural/linguistic lines in order to satisfy national POV's/feeling. At least that is how I see your reasoning and I'm certainly free to disagree. (Flamarande, December 9, 2010)

> You are welcome to disagree with me; it is through disagreement and debate that we all learn. I would certainly prefer what you call "balkanization" to monolithic dominance of Wikipedia by American and British English. Wikipedia was not set up in that spirit; it was set up to be a free encyclopedia for the world. (JN466, December 9, 2010)

The fear of a chaotic and balkanized English Wikipedia that would pose hindrances to a general readership and limit the site to specific regions of the world reveal the paradox emerging with the global rise of English. Undoubtedly, common standards (such as a global language) are essential for any network whose primary purpose is to mediate between multiple nodes and users on it. A language, which is perhaps the earliest example of a standardized network, similarly requires the adoption of common grammar conventions and rules (as the supporters of Ganges repeatedly suggested) for its smooth and frictionless operation. As David Grewal (2008) argues about language, it "is perhaps the most obvious example of a mediating standard: to join the network of English speakers you must learn English" (22). Learning and following the conventions of a large network provides each member access to all other members of that network, and hence the larger a network already is, the more incentives new users have to learn and play by its rules in order to participate in it. Even as it draws more users and members, this "network power" (Castells 2013; Grewal 2008), accruing from the size of an existing network, simultaneously creates sites of conflict, as evidenced in the case of English.

As colonialism and globalization have given rise to multiple versions of English, attempts to assert the predominance of one version over others (even in the garb of authenticity or the standard version) on global platforms such as Wikipedia are bound to generate cultural fears and anxieties about erasure, loss, and linguistic hegemony. This is because even as dominant standards and conventions solve the problem of incommunicability and provide coordination among members, they do so by "by elevating one solution above others and threatening the elimination of alternative solutions to the same problem" (Grewal 2008, 5). Evident here is a double bind of networks wherein their enabling and facilitating aspects are also premised on the erasure of alternatives. This quandary is evident in a claim made by a supporter of the Ganges name: "Making Indian, Singaporean, Hong Kong English and even instruction sheet 'Engrish' coequal with the language of educated native speakers is a recipe for disaster. Chide all you want but educated native English speakers should have the final say. Then if I attempt to contribute to Hindi or Nepali Wikipedia, the shoe is on the other foot" (LADave, April 19, 2014). This suggestion was one among many that presented a slippery-slope scenario wherein the grant of one such request would open the floodgates to other name change proposals based on similar arguments. Claims that the matter should be decided by "native English speakers" appeared in different forms throughout the debate and was sought to be resolved by either side once again by showing that the numbers were on their side. Even as it globalizes, hybridizes, and mutates, the global lingua franca of English simultaneously engenders impassioned defenses of an authentic or standard version that needs to be preserved from contamination. Pleas for preserving a standard version of English on Wikipedia so a general readership can read it unknowingly conflate that readership with an Anglo-American demographic, thus pointing to the tension between fixity and mutability within any globalizing language.

From the vantage point of the defenders of the Ganges name, the fact that 304 (Wikipedia, n.d., "List of Wikipedias") language versions of Wikipedia exist, thus making it already balkanized theoretically, provides all the more reasons for further resisting the hybridization of the English version. Fears of the creolization and hybridization of colonial languages, especially when contrasted with an imagined past of "fixity, of certainty, centeredness, homogeneity" (Young 1995, 3), are a recurring trope within discourses of colonialism. These constructions of an immutable and pure origin conceal what is "rather often the opposite, a sense of fluidity and a painful sense of, or need for, otherness" (3). Young (1995) develops this fascinating dialectic of fear and desire by drawing their analogous operation in the seemingly distinct realms of language and sexuality in a passage worth reproducing: "The historical links between language and sex were, however, fundamental. Both produced what were regarded as 'hybrid' forms (creole, pidgin and miscegenated children), which were seen to embody threatening forms of perversion and degeneration and became the basis for endless metaphoric extension in the racial discourse of social commentary " (5). The fears of opening the floodgates for the degradation and defiling of the standard version of English, repeatedly expressed in this Wikipedia debate, are not too different from these notions of purity and the suppressed (but real) fear of the Other. In addition to showing numerical proof of the English-speaking population, each side also used Wikipedia's traffic from different regions of the world to argue that readership should be factored in to determine the version of English used. The Ganga side of the debate cited Alexa (the website that conducts global web traffic analysis; Alexa, n.d., "Wikipedia. org Competitive Analysis") to show that up to 7.5 percent of traffic to the English Wikipedia came from India, which they claimed was more than from England (4.5 percent), the home of English. Wikipedia's own statistics for September 2018 show the two countries neck and neck, but with the United Kingdom (748 million) ahead and driving the fourth highest traffic to all Wikipedia editions (after the United States, Germany, and Japan), immediately followed by India (734 million), which sends the fifth highest traffic (Wikimedia 2018b).

When narrowed to only the English Wikipedia, however, these rankings change (as Germany and Japan fall out) to make the United Kingdom second (sending 5 percent of the world total) and India third (sending 4.9 percent of the world total). However, the argument based on comparative traffic that shows India to be an equal stakeholder in English was promptly disputed by the supporters of Ganges, who countered that while Ganges is used both in India (albeit sometimes) and outside, those outside India would never have heard the name Ganga. As support they presented evidence of the usage of *Ganges* by the *Times of India*, in hotel names across India (including in Varanasi on the banks of the river), and by the government of India. Expectedly, the Ganga side sought to similarly show the innumerable usages of *Ganga* by prominent Western news networks (CNN, BBC), scholarly works, and textbooks to dispute claims that *Ganga* was unfamiliar outside India.

The fact that both sides could marshal supporting facts in favor of their version of English showed the inadequacy of Wikipedia's rules in resolving the stalemate about whose version should prevail. Elaborating on the role played by Wikipedia's rules, Jemielniak (2014) claims that despite their intentions of "establishing well sourced information" they "also encourage disagreements" (78). He distinguishes between disputes that can be settled by clearly "establishing the facts" and that are much easier to solve and those where supporting facts exist on either side (as in the case of the Ganga/Ganges debate), which he calls "nonfactual conflict" (78). The quandary of supporting evidence on either side of this debate was acknowledged (albeit grudgingly) by users on both sides—so much so that a user made a plea for the name change based on kindness and goodwill instead of contentious arguments: "Please let's remember that there are *innumerable* articles where Indian users of Wikipedia find article names that do not correspond to Indian English usage. Indians don't say railroad car, they say bogie. . . . Indians don't say warehouse, they say godown. . . . Please let's give them *this article*, on their national and holy river, in their own language. Thank you" (JN466, November 29, 2010). Even though the request was promptly rejected, the making of such a request (from a user who admitted to being based in Germany) is atypical within the archives of the decade-long debate on the name change. Such a plea reflects an acknowledgment that repetitive arguments based on facts and rational propositions were repeatedly leading to an impasse, as both sides were able to marshal those facts equally well. Hence a consideration based on equity and fairness instead of being based on "facts" would perhaps have more traction. Other scholars who have studied Wikipedia conflicts (Rogers 2013; Jemielniak 2014; Tkacz 2015) cite the determination and tenacity of participants as key distinguishing factors between opposing sides in the debates. Typically, the more adamant and unrelenting side, the one that can wait for the other side to be "bored to death" (Jemielniak 2014, 79), prevails. However, when both sides show equal resolve and are willing to entrench themselves for the long haul (as has happened in the case of the Ganga/Ganges debate), voting that Wikipedia rules (Wikimedia, n.d., "Polls are Evil") has called "evil" seems the only way out. Consequently, the Ganga/Ganges debate has gone through at least four different votes (archived within its talk pages), each of them unable to garner enough numbers to change the name to Ganga. The final outcome of this debate, therefore, is not based on evidence, facts, citations, or arguments but, as claimed by Sue Gardner above, on the demographic of Wikipedia's editors. That a collaborative encyclopedia with global ambitions would determine its content based on voting means that its content is more likely to reflect epistemologies and worldviews of those with a higher numerical representation.

The Politics of Postcolonial Names

Given that Ganges is a name given to the river by the British, the debate saw its inevitable and frequent association with colonial rule in India. As with colonial rule in other parts of the world, contestations about naming and renaming of places are infused with politically charged debates laden with emotive themes of colonialism, cultural/national/ethnic identity, and linguistic/cultural imperialism. While the renaming of places to their local precolonial versions has been a frequent source of controversy in India, this is just as potent an issue at other postcolonial locations around the world (Berg and Vuolteenaho 2009; Nash 2009). Naming was a crucial manifestation of power through which a place was enfolded within the history and culture of the colonizing nation. The close association between place names and linguistic identity has ensured that pronounced struggles to rename places have continued in postcolonial sites such as Hawaii (Herman 2009), New Zealand (Berg and Kearns 2009), Ireland (Nash 1993, 2009), and India, where key metropolitan cities such as Bangalore, Bombay, Madras, and Calcutta have been renamed (to Bengaluru, Mumbai, Chennai, and Kolkata respectively). In many of these cases, including India, the politics of these name changes have been driven as much by a desire to erase colonial markers as by attempts to assert regional ethnic and linguistic identities against the homogenizing narratives of the nation-state.

The Ganga/Ganges debate saw repeated assertions from the supporters of Ganga that *Ganges* was a colonial imposition and hence had distasteful associations for Indians. A telling quote from a user claiming to be British and "one of the old colonial oppressors" asked, "I think we really should leave the days of colonialism behind us, don't you?" before imploring the Wikipedia community to stop "enforcing a WASP perspective on the world" (Guy, November 22, 2010). The unpleasant colonial connection was acknowledged by Sue Gardner (then the director of the Wikimedia Foundation) when she stated that the name Ganges "bears the stench of colonization for many Indians" (Valby 2011).

As with other arguments above, charges of colonial connection and cultural insensitivity also met with stiff resistance from the opposing side, who dismissed them citing convenience and the belief that *Ganges* is more recognizable and easier to pronounce for a majority of Wikipedia's readers. In making this plea—which is commonly repeated against requests for name change globally—one user from the Ganges side argued that the name "Ganga" "sounds funny, being as it is a common word for marijuana" (kwami, October 22, 2010). Repeated references to Ganga's similarity to *ganja*, colloquial for marijuana, and the resulting confusion it may cause among Western readers unable to differentiate between their pronunciations sought to present arguments of convenience and utility against charges of cultural insensitivity made by the Ganga supporters. One supporter of Ganga responded: "Ganga is pronounced gun-ga (Gun as in a gun = firearm and ga as in radio ga ga), it is not pronounced gan ja, of course ganja is cannabis, but you wont find that in a dictionary, it is an Indian word. Gan as in GANdhi and ja as in JAcket" (Yogesh Khandke, October 22, 2010).

Resistances to name changes because of the inconvenience caused to certain speakers recurs across other conflicts (e.g., New Zealand and Hawaii) over name changes at postcolonial sites. Berg and Kearns (2009) found strikingly similar objections to proposals to change place names from their existing ones given by European settlers to the original names in the Maori language spoken by the native Maori people of New Zealand. They cite one submission as lamenting "to change such well known names as Long Beach and Murdering Beach to long, hard to pronounce and hard to spell Maori names is quite unacceptable and unnecessary" (Submission ED, 10/11/90, cited in Berg and Kearns 2009, 36). Complaints about the difficulty of pronouncing new names represent a "devaluation of the Maori language" (Berg and Kearns 2009, 36), given the assumption that since the Maori population already speaks English, it is easier for them to pronounce anglicized names than it is for the non-Maori population to pronounce Maori names, since they do not know the language. The Maori name in this case becomes a metonym for other aspects of Maori culture so that "everything Maori is always already tainted by inferiority" (36). Resemblances between settler and native population conflicts in New Zealand and the Ganga/Ganges dispute on Wikipedia are hard to miss; the latter debate too saw the argument that it was a smaller burden on fewer people if those in India learned and understood *Ganges* rather than having the global English-speaking population learn what *Ganga* means.

More importantly, Ganges supporters argued that India's familiarity with the English language (a fact supporters of Ganga also deployed in their favor) was in fact proof that if they could speak the language, they could also use the anglicized name. Laments about *Ganges* being a foreign imposition on an Indian cultural symbol by Ganga supporters were responded to by suggesting that English too was an imposition; as one user advised, "So stop speaking English. Problem solved" (Choyooł'įįhí:Seb az86556 27, November 2010 [UTC]). Yet another user said, "PS: As far as your foreign name-post is concerned: You do realize that you are using the foreign language of your former colonial power?" (Flamarande, November 27, 2010) The Ganga side had presented India as having the second largest English-speaking population to stake a claim on English, and that was precisely the argument being turned around on them. Repeated provocations to solve the problem by forsaking the English language presented language usage as a choice that global citizens could exercise at their will.

These exhortations ignore the varied historical, cultural, and economic reasons that weigh in to influence and determine the linguistic landscape in the postcolonial globalizing world. Choosing between the colonial and the native language is a part of the "the ongoing struggle over identity that is at the heart of the postcolonial condition" (Herman 2009, 102) at all postcolonial locations around the world. Enduring aftereffects of cultural and linguistic impositions make these postcolonial sites multilingual and fractured spaces wherein historical violence and coercion must be juxtaposed with explicit and implicit incentives to learn the colonial language. These incentives have continued in different ways in postcolonial times given the economic and cultural capital accruing from learning the hegemonic colonial language.

Documenting the processes by which the Hawaiian language was pushed to the brink of extinction, Herman (2009) shows the coercive push toward assimilation that functioned implicitly to connote that a speaker of the Hawaiian language was a "backward, ignorant person" (122). The widespread adoption of English was in fact led by "Hawaiians, eager to prove their worth as equal citizens with the haole (and under social pressure to do so), abandoned the language that made them stand out as different" (122). In the case of India, scholars (Viswanathan 1997) have convincingly shown that the imposition of the English language arose from the colonial desire to strike a balance between winning the loyalty of the colonized subjects and diffusing the moral and intellectual ideals of Europe. Similar to Hawaii, the success in presenting the English language as desirable shows that "cultural domination works by consent and often precedes conquest by force" (Viswanathan 1997, 113). Presumptions that people in the postcolonial spaces speak the colonial language "willingly" ignore the preexisting and coercive ideological and cultural structures that shape linguistic choices.

Movements against colonial cultural impositions have invariably leveraged nationalism as the bulwark against external power. Postcolonial nationalism is borne out of an irreconcilable struggle between precolonial community affiliations and capital that was a frequent handmaiden of colonial rule (Chatterjee 1993). Resistances to cultural domination made in the name of equity and justice also contained within them the dialectically opposed values of jingoistic nationalism and imaginations of homogenous national identity and were called out as such by the colonial powers being challenged. This contradiction has repeated itself in contestations over name change around the world, including the Ganga/Ganges debate. Supporters of Ganga were frequently called out as being "jingoistic," "nationalistic" and "right-wing" during the debate. As a supporter of Ganges said to another user frequently called out for his overt nationalism, "If you're not jingoist then I'm the emperor of China" (Flamarande, November 30, 2010). Yet another user argued that the name change to Ganga "will appease the nationalists but reduce readability and increase confusion among the users of Wikipedia" (Gizza, April 21, 2014). Wikipedia's rules about neutrality, which simultaneously caution against pushing a personal point of view, were cited as cautionary notes against letting the debate be hijacked by individual and nationalistic agendas.

The dialectic of nationalism wherein it assumes a homogenous national identity while simultaneously being the vantage point of anticolonial resistance (discussed more fully in the chapter on sovereignty) is a reminder against simplistic approaches (of acceptance or rejection) toward nationalistic discourses. Those calling for a revival of the Hawaiian language, for instance, have historically been accused of being "advocates of Hawaiian sovereignty" (Smyser 1991, A14, quoted in Herman 2009, 126), and allowing the revival of the language was "one step towards allowing them to reclaim the Islands themselves" (Herman 2009, 126). At a different postcolonial location, attempts to reinstate Maori names of places in New Zealand were similarly labeled as threats to a homogenous national identity by those seeking "Maori sovereignty and self-determination" (Berg and Kearns 2009, 44). Notably, the call to de-emphasize nationalistic fervor came from both sides of the Ganga/Ganges debate. A Ganga supporter cautioned against allowing "the various move discussions [to] get hijacked by nationalist editors because the common name argument to switch to Ganga is quite a reasonable one" (regentspark, September 28, 2011). But the supporters of Ganga also continued to call out the other side for labeling them nationalists: "The biggest problem I see with Wikipedia is this strong cartel of god-knows-what-ists that go overboard in labeling anyone who argues for primacy of local notions (in an Indian context) as right-wing whatever" (Fgpilot, October 25, 2011).

The recurring thematic of nationalism and neutrality as contradictory ideals is central to understanding a key dimension of the debate as it played out on Wikipedia. To be sure, Sahana Udupa (2016) has persuasively shown the reversal of these positions wherein the weaponization of historical facts to advance nationalistic versions of the past have similarly sought to appropriate the discourse of neutrality to "remedy the imbalance" (10) against "biased" versions of history. These online epistemic battles over history are a key facet of the polarized political discourse in India, where crowdsourced historical facts and knowledge are curated into digital archives (Udupa 2016) ready to be deployed at strategic moments in online debates.

Undoubtedly, some supporters of the Ganga name were inspired by a sense of nationalism, and yet it is just as true that those opposing them (and resisting the name change) were blind to the ways in which the abstract universal category of neutrality can function as a guise for hegemonic points of view (Gadamer 2004; Grasswick 2011). The unmarked neutral proclaims its Other as biased (as Wikipedia's rule on POV implies) but remains blind to the ways in which seemingly invisible infrastructures of media, culture, and knowledge such as language, technologies, and deliberative rules and conventions are just as rooted within particular cultural and locational frames. The move toward toponymic modernization, premised on the virtues of convenience, universal legibility, and access, conceals the obverse of the same movement which is "the erasure of the inherited heteroglossia of local names and even definite 'toponymic silencing' . . . of indigenous cultures" (Berg and Vuolteenaho 2009b, 4). The Ganga/Ganges debate reveals how the conflicting aspirations of national, regional, and linguistic identity and the desire for an elusive neutrality became a key pivot around which the debate was carried out.

To Vote or Not to Vote

In striking a balance between enabling collaboration across time and space, preventing vandalism while also not impeding the volunteer spirit, Wikipedia's governance rules have undeniably succeeded in drawing contributors and editors and expanding the online encyclopedia's content and reader base. The decline in recent editor population, widely ascribed to steps taken to stop mischief and vandalism, has nevertheless left a committed core of editors who continue to run and maintain Wikipedia. This committed group is also well versed in the expanding body of rules and policies on Wikipedia that have gradually been added to improve the quality of its content. As its procedural infrastructure expands, however, "you can always find one that agrees with you" (JN466, November 28, 2010), and often following a rule means "you often have to break another" (JN466, November 28, 2010).

As the decade-long Ganga/Ganges debate reveals, conflicting rules can be deployed by either side in a debate to stall and postpone resolution. Despite a significant number of willing editors presenting relevant verifiable facts, existing rules seemed incapable of resolving the intractable dispute. The fact that the discussion repeatedly went to vote, despite Wikipedia's clearly stated position against voting (it is suggested as the last resort under Wikipedia, n.d., "Polling Is Not a Substitute"), only emphasizes the inadequacy of the existing rules in resolving the issue. The frequent resort to polling as well as the discussions leading up to the votes reveal several invisible dynamics of Wikipedia's working, discussed below, that remain concealed within its seemingly well-meaning rules and policies.

While not all threads of discussions in the debate led to a vote, each time they did, Ganges supporters outnumbered those supporting Ganga by significant margins. A vote held in November 2010, for instance, was the most participated in; out of a total of thirty-seven votes cast, twenty-three voted for keeping the name Ganges and thirteen voted for changing it to Ganga. At least two other votes in September 2011 and as recently as February 2015 led to similar results, even though the number of voting participants was reduced. Wikipedia's recommendation for seeking consensus as the ideal route to solving disputes is premised on four arguments against voting: voting could obscure a solution that could exist between "discrete options" (Wikimedia, n.d., "Polls Are Evil"), it could promote factionalism, it could lead contributors into mistakenly believing that the majority will have their way, and if practiced frequently voting could gradually be used to arbitrate on content, thus undermining other rules about verifiability, notability, and so on. The discouragement of voting is strong enough that Wikipedia (n.d., "Polling Is Not a Substitute") encourages editors to use other terms such as *polling* and *iVote* (read a not-vote) to "serve as reminders that while we do vote on things, votes without reasonable accompanying rationales receive little consideration unless you also explain why you are voting the way you are." These cautionary notes against voting are frequently used by the losing side (who in the Ganga/Ganges case were also the initiators of the poll) to challenge a singular dependence on numbers for making a decision. But given that years of discussions had failed to reach consensus and persuade the opposing side, critiques of voting carried little traction with the winning side.

Despite Wikipedia's caution about the use of voting except as an absolute last resort, it has been unavoidable as a mechanism to get out of the most intractable edit wars. Its use has also led to just as dissatisfying an outcome as in the case of the conflict over the naming of the Wikipedia page for the Polish city of Gdansk/Danzig. Just as in the Ganga/Ganges debate, the lack of a consensus in the Gdansk/Danzig debate too was finally solved through "the brute force of widely discouraged vote" (Jemielniak 2014, 78), thus showing the limits of existing rules in resolving the naming dispute. In analyzing the trajectory of other similar conflicts on Wikipedia, Jemielniak (2014) argues that as long as each side is following the rules (thus obviating a situation of elimination) and is equally committed, intractable edit wars invariably lead to a stalemate. Once a dispute reaches this state, it becomes a test of the persistence and commitment of the other side in order to see who blinks first. Jemielniak (2014) explains what follows: "Thus, disputes on Wikipedia often do not end because one side persuades the other and is able to reach the holy grail of a consensus, to live happily ever after, but because the other side is bored to death and finds continued participation in the discussion a waste of time. In Wikipedia discussions, it is more important to be persistent than right (78–79)."

The willingness to commit time, labor, and affective investment therefore emerges as a key attribute in determining the winning position and in shaping the dominant worldview in Wikipedia disputes. Persistence is particularly incentivized in a scenario of conflicting rules where one rule could be cited against another to defend one's argument and avoid closure. These conflicts get a further boost because of the overarching rule in Wikipedia (n.d., "Ignore All Rules") that asks users to "ignore all rules," specifying that "if a rule prevents you from improving or maintaining Wikipedia, ignore it." Instituted in its early days to ensure that volunteers are not discouraged by overwhelming styling and formatting guidelines (Havenstein 2007), the rule has evolved to mean a healthy skepticism toward the policies, especially if they come in the way of "improving or maintaining Wikipedia" (n.d., "Ignore All Rules"). Despite its well-meaning intentions, however, when juxtaposed with rules that can contradict each other, the invitation to ignore rules allows the exercise of editorial authority to be tinged with arbitrariness. In this open-ended situation, incentives weigh toward unyielding tenacity, favorable interpretation of rules, pitting contradictory rules against each other, and pedigree, experience, and status within the community (elements that Wikipedia seeks to de-emphasize as factors within deliberations), as happened in the Ganga/Ganges debate.

Given that most editors with experience happened to be on the Ganges side of the debate, assertions of pedigree and experience, often indirect and subtle but present nevertheless, were more frequent from that side. When expressed, it was invariably meant to show better knowledge of rules and chide the other side for their unfamiliarity with them. A case in point is a comment wherein a user states (kwami, October 23, 2010), "Yogesh, read WP:RS. That is how we work here" before going on to elaborate on some examples that he claims "we use here." Yet another editor cites his long-running contributions to the article to express frustration at old arguments being repeated anew by pleading, "Those of us who have worked on the article, have brought it to its current level of completion, whether popular or not, are aware that it is called 'Ganga' in India" (Fowler&fowler, April 19, 2014).

These subtle and implicit allusions to seniority and a sense of territoriality point to how even well-meaning egalitarian structures can gradually develop their own status markers. In a similar conclusion about how the benefits of longevity and learning the modes of argumentation used on the site can benefit the argument being made, Tkacz's analysis shows how disputes over content on Wikipedia are instances of "frame wars" where opposing sides are using different and often irreconcilable frames to make their arguments. "The more a contributor masters the frame, the more likely it is that person's contributions will be valorized within it and, in turn, that the quality of that person's contributions will increase access to positions of authority and leadership" (Tkacz 2015, 86), he claims.

This mastery comes from factors such as the longevity of one's role at Wikipedia, the number of overall edits made, and informal and formal recognition (e.g., Barnstars) from peers that make the Wikipedia community one with "established stratification and very real power play" (Jemielniak 2014, 31). Even though the debate is not eventually decided on the basis of status or pedigree of the user/editor, contributing users' invocation of those elements function to create an "us versus them" discourse wherein new users with lesser experience and inadequately skilled or knowledgeable in the ways of Wikipedia will invariably be undermined and be silenced by older ones. Wikipedia's rules make it clear that deliberations about article content must be based on argumentative reason relying on facts, evidence, and the agreed-upon rules, but since those rules and policies are open to interpretation by editors, they create space for maneuvers, deals, and behind-the-scenes alliances that can be leveraged by those more familiar with the system. In defending his use of the term *cabal* in describing the editing community at Wikipedia, Jemielniak (2014) elaborates on editors and administrators seeking support from others through private and "secret" (51) email lists to create an exclusionary effect: "However, we naturally tend to ask for help from those whom we know well and can expect to share our point of view and often do so outside Wikipedia, and so the user, unaware of this background, obviously feels singled out and surrounded. Such a user may not verbalize it, but she or he is right to feel a subject of power play, even if just because she or he did not have the same means to defend her or his ground, contacts on Wikipedia, or an established position" (52).

These subtle, almost invisible ways in which back-channel power plays shape Wikipedia's content and the implications of the process in a world where half the population is yet to come on board the internet allow us to pose broader questions about the state of collaborative knowledge production on the web and interrogate Wikipedia's claims of being "the sum of all human knowledge." While acknowledging that entirely horizontal entities

Table 3.3 Correspondence between location and vote in the Ganga/Ganges debate

Position	Location	Number
Against Ganga	India	0
	West	13
	Unknown	10
Supportive of Ganga	India	6
	West	2
	Unknown	5
Neutral	Unknown	1
Total Votes		37

SOURCE: Created by the Wikipedia user zuggernaut (November 2010) and archived at https://en.wikipedia.org/wiki/Talk:Ganges/Archive_1. The author adds, "I've assumed the definition of West as those who live in North America, EU and Australia. Of the two people from the West who voted in favor of Ganga, one is an Indian living in the UK."

invariably develop power structures, these revelations nevertheless show us how the goal of a globally representative encyclopedia that embraces the differences, multiplicities, and pluralities in the world remains an elusive one. Even though voting has resolved the Ganga/Ganges debate, it has led to a temporary and unstable equilibrium at best that will continue to give way to an eruption every time a new user stumbles on the talk page and decides to renew the campaign for name change. Results of the voting process show that the existing name "Ganges," arrived at through a vote, therefore is more a reflection of the demographic distribution of Wikipedia's editors and administrators than of the merit of one side's argument over another. Table 3.3, created from the first vote count (by the user zuggernaut, November 2010), captures this point and shows a striking congruence between the users' locations and the vote they had cast.

A contributor's location can be deduced only if they have openly stated it in their description or if they are an unregistered user and have their ISP publicly visible. While the table gives us a partial picture (since many users' locations can remain unknown), it reveals a notable correlation. It shows us that out of a total of thirty-seven votes cast, twenty-three voted for keeping the name Ganges and thirteen voted for changing it to Ganga (one vote was neutral). In making the point that the debate was about cultural affiliation, ideology, and politics rather than evidence and arguments, zuggernaut (November 2010) found that ten out of the twenty-three pro-Ganges voters were based in the West while six out of the thirteen pro-Ganga voters were located in India. If we look only at the voters whose locations are known (for purposes of analysis), we can see that all voters located in India supported the change to Ganga and not a single one of them supported continuing with the name Ganges. On the other hand, of the fifteen voters with a Western location, only two voted for Ganga and thirteen for Ganges.

The alignment of 100 percent of voters from India voting with one position and of 86 percent voters from the West voting for the opposing position not only showed that the supporters of Ganges are located almost entirely in the West (as no resident of India supported the Ganges name) but also that the supporters of changing the name to Ganga are overwhelmingly based in India. This resonance between editors' locations and their votes on the issue confirms key arguments about the ways in which the prevailing dominant opinion on Wikipedia is shaped by editors' demographics rather than an open and fair exchange, as would occur in a free marketplace of ideas. More importantly, it corroborates claims about the enmeshing of the process of knowledge production with culture, politics, and ideology (Grasswick 2011; Gadamer 2004). This enmeshing is visible as much in the positions editors take as in the conventions, policies, and rules that regulate knowledge production online. When these procedural and cultural architectures combine with the imbalance of demographic distribution on collaborative digital platforms, they create an insurmountable barrier to free, uncoercive, and inclusive deliberation. The analysis above establishes how this skews the content on digital platforms such as Wikipedia.

Conclusions

In closely studying how Wikipedia's architecture of conventions (rules, policies, guidelines, and procedures) and the demographic distribution of its editors subvert its stated goal of creating a collaborative global encyclopedia, this chapter has sought to instantiate the cultural, political, and ideological valences of seemingly neutral infrastructures. It has shown that the historically salient relationship between knowledge and power extends into the digital domain since the ability to shape its conventions and protocols combined with the digital divide skews online knowledge production with distinct Euro-American leanings. Analyzing the Ganga/Ganges debate shows how key policies of Wikipedia, such as what counts as evidence, the definition of a neutral point of view, who makes up the general reader, and norms to be followed in naming article pages can function to reproduce and amplify the inequities within knowledge production in the off-line world and in so doing undermine the goals of democracy and egalitarianism that animated the ethos of the early web.

This analysis gains importance in the context of the historically contested terrain of knowledge that has been instrumental in the cultural and epistemic hegemony as well as physical domination of the colony by the metropole during colonialism. While this chapter has focused on Wikipedia and zeroed in on a particular edit war to make its case, the broader web is equally apt for an analysis of this nature. How does the broader ecology of online knowledge production (scholarly search engines, the self-referential citation practices within academic knowledge production, the inaccessibility of academic journals hidden behind paywalls, etc.) shape the global balance of power in the realm of knowledge creation and distribution? Has it enabled a more equitable distribution by creating spaces for alternative modalities of knowing or further entrenched and amplified the existing hierarchies of knowledge production in the world? Entities such as Google scholar, Google Books, and the digital domain of academic journals that regulate access behind password-protected paywalls are other similar sites of contestation.

In their role as mediators and channels, these digital gatekeepers of knowledge form key pillars of the infrastructures of knowledge (Bowker 2018) that exercise power through regulating the boundaries and distinctions between legitimate and nonlegitimate knowledge, between sayable and unsayable truths, thus creating the Foucauldian "fellowships of discourse" (Foucault 1972, 225). These boundaries function "to preserve or to reproduce discourse, but in order that it should circulate within a closed community, according to strict regulations, without those in possession being dispossessed by this very distribution" (225). The two-step move here operates first by creating boundaries and then restricting access within the walls through various mechanisms. While restrictions on access to published knowledge that was regulated through prohibitive costs of journals in the real off-line world continues through paywalls in the digital domain, the ways in which those hierarchies and orderings permeate into seemingly democratic spheres of knowledge such as Wikipedia are equally worthy of analysis. This is because the egalitarian, open, and democratic spaces on the web that sought to make the web (and in effect the world) more representative than the world they were replacing are the sites where these operations are more invisible.

The critique of online cultures of knowledge production gains urgency because Wikipedia's utopian ideal of creating a repository of global knowledge has a self-admitted deadline. The admission on its page (Wikipedia, n.d., "There Is a Deadline") that "practically every day, distinct forms of knowledge are lost forever and no copies are available" is cited in its own documents to emphasize the urgency for expanding their editor and reader base to global populations beyond the West. This chapter's attempt at showing the exclusionary effect of its procedures and norms of deliberation are an important corrective to that vision. Forms of knowledge that remain off-line, that escape digitization, and that comprise the excesses irreducible to criteria such as empirical verifiability, neutrality, and having prior published proofs deserve just as legitimate a seat at the table of global digital repositories of knowledge on the web as do those that fit the existing criteria (Srinivasan 2013).

This chapter's critique of Wikipedia holds an implicit invitation for creating systems and structures that enable and invite local and culturally situated knowledge, oral histories, experiential, narrative nonlinear, and nontextual (Bowker 2018) forms of understanding, knowing, and meaning making so that we come closer to the unrealized potential of a truly representative global web. If the end goal of the early visionaries of the web was a plural and globally representative web, it requires that the next half of the web's population be given the same choices to shape their internet experience as the first half did. By enfolding users within their digital enclosures and seeking to shape their digital experience, the big internet oligopolies undercut the inspiring vision that the web started out with. Specifically, in the realms of information and knowledge, a plurality of voices, perspectives, and epistemic systems is far more desirable and amenable to achieving the ends of global democracy and self-governance.

Notes

1. It is important to note here that in some cases merely the number of articles is misleading because of wide usage of software (bots) to create Wikipedia articles. In particular the high rankings of the Swedish, Waray Waray (Philippines), and Cebuano (Philippines) editions of Wikipedia can be credited to such a bot created by the Swedish physicist Sverker Johansson (Tomlinson 2014; Guldbrandsson 2013).

2. Each week, the list can be found on Wikipedia (n.d., "Wikipedia: Top 25 Report").

3. The wording of this section has changed slightly since this page was accessed in July 2020, but the meaning remains the same.

4. The sentence mentioning the Ganges/Ganga page as an exception has since been removed, but it was present during a majority of the duration of the debate, including when the page (Wikipedia, n.d., "Article Titles") was previously accessed for this chapter, on July 30, 2015.

5. Among Rushdie's more famous works that bring forth this linguistic play are his *Midnight's Children* and *The Satanic Verses*, whose intermingling of English with local Hindi has led to significant scholarly and critical attention. Ezekiel (1924–2004) famously took liberties with grammatical rules to capture the unique blend of Indian languages and English spoken in India. The repeated use of the present continuous tense in poems such as "The Patriot" and "Goodbye Party for Miss Pushpa" are instances of blending at work.

4

SELFHOOD

IN ADDITION TO THE APPROPRIATION OF THE DIGITAL commons and privileging of particular epistemologies, which the two preceding chapters have focused on, the ongoing global spread and uptake of a wide range of digital platforms and websites has ensured their emergence as key gateways to the web for billions of users while also shaping and modulating their behavior and interaction. The dual function whereby these digital media platforms mediate but also channel the online experience of netizens in particular directions is being studied by scholars of all backgrounds and from divergent perspectives (Boyd 2014; Marwick 2013; Turkle 2017). This chapter seeks to analyze how the global dominance of key social media platforms is reshaping global culture by elevating particular notions of selfhood as aspirational ideals. As the global digital divide narrows and a larger number of new users get online, social media platforms such as Facebook, Twitter, Instagram, and Snapchat as well as search engines such as Google and peer-sharing sites such as YouTube become primary entry points to users' online experiences.

By focusing on the global role of social media platforms where online sociality is increasingly learned and enacted today, this chapter shows how the infrastructures of control delineated in this book regulate users' digital experiences—and in doing, so simultaneously privilege specific cultural and societal norms. I show this by delineating a global scenario where local players, despite their presence in the field of digital sociality in many countries and regions, typically cede ground to the dominant Western ones (Jin 2015; Smyrnaios 2018) that continue to grow and add users at exponential rates globally. Interrogating the consequences of the dominant players' global sweep is important given that their uptake across national and cultural boundaries occurs along with particular norms, values, and ideologies embedded within the cultural architecture of these social media platforms. To dismiss the issue of cultural change is to accept the fallacious notion that media technologies are neutral, acultural tools that users fashion to their own ends. Arguments opposing such claims have established incontrovertibly that, far from being empty channels, media technologies including digital platforms "are neither neutral nor value-free constructs" (van Dijck, Poell, and De Waal 2018, 3) that, as with other technologies (Winner 1980), allow them to shape and modulate the behavior of users through their affordances of allowances and limits (Hutchby 2001; Peters 2017). To accept that technologies have a directionality and culture (Heidegger 1977; Ihde 1979) but to somehow exclude social media platforms from such interrogation would be an untenable omission.

Accordingly, the question pursued by this chapter aligns with similar interrogations by scholars who have asked, "Do social media also shape our world, or our everyday lives?" (Schroeder 2018, 82). I pursue seriously the implications of their conclusion that among the changes engendered by social media, "there are some patterns that are quite similar across the globe" (83). Specifically, if media technologies have cultural and political orientations inherent within them, what are the ways in which those notions are transcribed within and on users? In addition, how is users' agency circumscribed within the contours defined by the said technologies? This last question is part of a broader historical enquiry that has focused on the ways that power operates through the circulation of media and cultural texts globally. Earlier iterations of this exploration looked at prior media forms and technologies (Schiller 1992; T. Miller et al. 2005; Dorfman and Mattelart 1975; Kraidy 2007), posing this question to critique global inequities. They showed how the asymmetries within circulation and consumption of media and culture were advancing particular ideologies, values, and ways of being. Their conclusions connected cultural inequity directly to economic disparities, suggesting that the largely unidirectional flow of cultural texts reordered aspirations to the benefit of Western corporate capitalism (Dorfman and Mattelart 1975).

While those prior theories of cultural dominance were justifiably challenged and corrected over time (most stridently through theories that made a case for hybridity), posing the above questions anew in the context of the latest media technology—the internet—holds much value. Continuing interrogations of the digital domain (Ebo 2001; Kraidy 2001; Gittinger 2014) have sought to examine varied dimensions of the global and geopolitical aspects of the web, and yet they have been few and far between. Such critical enquiries (about the dynamics of global cultural power on the web) have often ceded ground to emancipatory narratives such as the "dominant and invariably celebratory account of horizontal social media 'revolutions'" (Aouragh and Chakravartty 2016, 560). This erasure perhaps could be ascribed to the unquestionably diffused, decentralized, and liberatory dimensions of the web, as evidenced by its ability to create unprecedented solidarities and alliances to subvert structures of power (Tufekci 2017). While acknowledging the emancipatory potential of the web, this analysis nevertheless seeks to focus on the novel mechanism of control that it simultaneously represents.

In seeking to understand *how* infrastructural control operates on the global web, this chapter's analysis seeks to unpack the ways in which seemingly freely available choices can nudge user behavior in particular directions through persuasive mechanisms such as "choice architecture" (Thaler and Sunstein 2008), captivation metrics (Seaver 2019), and behavior design (Leslie 2016) that deploys the seductive power of "variable reward" (Eyal 2014). Just as a combination of arrangements, placement, and design as well as trigger, action, and reward can regulate human action in real life, their digital versions can similarly shape and channel user behavior to particular ends while discouraging and penalizing unwanted online behavior. Not surprisingly, the so-called desirable behaviors on the web are precisely those that help the digital platforms' ability to monetize user interactivity. By rewarding behaviors such as self-revelation and interactivity and discouraging attributes such as reticence and asociality, the design of digital platforms, as manifested in their affordances, default settings, and algorithmic regulation, exercise a nuanced, surreptitious, but effective form of power over their users. Just like the "sanctions and seductions" of an earlier era (Rose 1999) helped moderate social life by presenting normative ideas as aspirational templates to be emulated, the cultural architecture of social media platforms realizes "an idealized self and an idealized or desired lifestyle" (Schroeder 2018, 98) that is gradually visible within global iterations of online sociality analyzed within this chapter.

This normative idea of selfhood gradually diffusing globally through the uptake of dominant platforms has key and distinctly visible attributes being reified through a dialectical effect of prize and penalty. Those features, increasingly visible within online social cultures today, include a radically individual self, a readily self-disclosing being, and a subject that performs the traits of self-entrepreneurship and responsibilization. Inculcating and fostering these norms aligns well with the larger goals of digital platforms as their success is premised on the outcomes and consequences of the widespread adoption of this idealized subjectivity. Notably, scholars have also shown these dominant values to have specific cultural and historical origins borne within particular contexts and ideological frameworks that formed their habitus. Genealogies of human subjectivity (Taylor 1989; Rose 1999; Elias 2000) that have sought to excavate the processes and means by which particular notions of selfhood were idealized show that the emphasis on the self-revealing entrepreneurial individual is a relatively recent phenomenon and uniquely tethered to the growth of liberal capitalism from within the social, political, and cultural churnings of European modernity.

That this ideal subject emerges from the sociocultural contingencies of Western Europe gives it indisputably cultural roots, as emphasized by scholars (Rose 1999; Taylor 1989) who connect the birth of that selfhood with other specific ideological formations of the moment. In challenging the universality of this ideal subject, Rose roots it within key ongoing movements of the time such as Protestantism, Romanticism, capitalism, and the broader doctrine of Christianity, thus locating its rise within specific axes of time and space. He claims this conclusion was supported by "anthropologists in the twentieth century, who suggested in many societies that they investigated the notion of the person as a unique individual was unknown" (Rose 1999, 221). Rose does not elaborate on the specifics of the societies that were studied by said anthropologists, and while such claims elide over innumerable analyses on the nature of self in other non-Western societies such as Japan, India, and other cultural sites and traditions (Dasti and Bryant 2014; M. Miller 2018; Allen 2018), it is also true that the *nature* of the idealized self, originating in each cultural milieu was different. In presenting a genealogy of the subject being globalized through the dominant social media platforms, therefore, the goal here is to draw on these scholars (Rose 1999; Rose 2000; Taylor 1989; Elias 2000) to challenge claims of universality made about normative attributes of the globalizing online social self. I hope to show that the simultaneous global spread of digital media platforms and appearance of key cultural formations globally are far from a coincidence and in fact signal an evident causal relationship.

The chapter concretizes its argument by analyzing three cultural formations—the global selfie, lifestreaming, and influencer cultures—within which, it claims, the emerging normative subject of the globalizing social web finds expression. The selfie culture's focus on the unique attributes of the self, the lifestreaming culture's emphasis on seemingly unfiltered self-expression, and the influencer culture's privileging of an entrepreneurial self-branding subject represents the apogee of those traits expressed globally, no doubt within culturally distinct ways and yet with palpable overarching global commonalities. By showing the global burgeoning of these traits, the goal is to understand the relationship between the gradual reshaping of global culture and the spread of digital sociality. As with any process of globalization, the emerging norms of selfhood are undoubtedly a negotiation between the values and ideals foregrounded through the social web and the distinct cultural norms and codes within particular locations. The negotiations and the multiplicities they produce between the global and the local, as well as between code and culture, are best understood through the focus on local cultural practices emerging through interactions with and visible on the social web across the world. This focus on the cultural manifestations of media technologies takes seriously and advances arguments made by scholars (Hillis, Petit, and Jarrett 2013; Turner 2010) that ideological visions encompassing the habitus around the birth of technologies inhere within their design and percolate through their cultural architecture. It only extends the well-argued point that technologies (including digital platforms) "have values inscribed in their architectures" (van Dijck, Poell, and de Waal 2018, 3), and while their eventual effect on the ground is a process of sociocultural negotiation, the inherent qualities within them (Winner 1980) assert a cultural force with enduring social and ideological consequences.

From Cultural Industries to Platform Dominance

As opposed to the dominant media systems of the past that were primarily unidirectional, the web's radically differentiated and networked architecture allows for multidirectional and distributed flows of content, thus turning viewers and audiences into potential creators and disseminators of seemingly democratized culture. Its disarming ability to empower seems to obviate the need for the kind of critical analysis of its global dimensions that earlier media technologies with their unidirectional, top-down architectures were subjected to. Those critiques (Schiller 1992; T. Miller et al. 2005; Thussu 2018) showed how the global dominance of Western media and film industries exacerbated inequities in the global cultural flows of texts, images, values, and ideals, thus imposing upon and reordering the priorities of weaker, developing nations. Theories of global cultural dominance were key to those analyses as they sought to call out the continued influence of former imperial powers of the world (Thussu 2005), focusing on the manifest, measurable aspects of their global cultural dominance. However, as those critiques justifiably showed, the totalitarian, monopolar force imagined by theories of cultural dominance neglected to focus on the creative ways in which users and audiences reappropriated and resisted global culture (Appiah 2006; Canclini 2006; Pieterse 2006). While posing important correctives to claims of cultural dominance, theories of cultural hybridity had their own blind spots as they failed to acknowledge that, even as hybrid cultures speak back to the dominant ones, encounters between dominant cultures and receiving sites occurs on asymmetrical terms and are rarely bidirectional. Moreover, the appropriation of the discourse of hybridity to further the very goals of cultural and economic domination (Kraidy 2007) that critical scholars warned against shows the continuing role of power inequities within global cultural circulation.

The radical break in the technological architecture of media heralded by the web invites us to reconsider those prior arguments and explore the nature of cultural power on the globalizing web. To be sure, this exploration has occupied media scholars since the earliest days of digital culture (Schiller 1992; Ebo 2001; Kraidy 2001; Bhuiyan 2008; Fuchs 2010). In extending those important prior critiques, this study on the globalization of aspirational notions of the self, while recognizing the web's disarming ruse of democratized cultural production and organic ground-up expression, also points to how the web's technological affordances are increasingly moving away from the plural utopian dream that inspired critical media scholars of yore. My claim that digital cultures spawned by the web simultaneously herald a novel modality of surveillance, discipline, and control (Cheney-Lippold, 2018) that is unprecedented in human history is driven by a similar utopian dream. The goal here is to show that its immanent and hence elusive power operates by permeating the quotidian aspects of our lives, through the very devices and platforms that allow us to express, produce, and connect but that simultaneously function to locate, track, and shape our subjectivities.

The role of platform affordances in bringing about social, cultural, and behavioral changes (Cirucci 2015; Boyd 2014) is already acknowledged by scholars of digital culture, and this chapter (in keeping with this book's argument) extends those prior insights to focus on the relatively underexplored *global* scale of platform dominance (Jin 2015; van Dijck, Poell, and de Waal 2018) in nudging normative subjectivities into being. In foregrounding the global effects of the soft infrastructures that make up the pathways and sinews of digital culture, this chapter extends analyses of their social and cultural effects (Marwick 2013; Carr 2011; Turkle 2017; Boyd 2014) to show their role in a global cultural reordering similar to the cultural hegemony of the media and cultural empires of the past. As the next half of the global population gets online, new users enter into a dialectical relationship with the digital world wherein their ability to connect, share, and express is simultaneously circumscribed by conditions, conventions, affordances, and algorithmic regulation that, akin to global cultural industries of the past, normalize particular behaviors, values, and ideologies. The radically different nature of this cultural power is marked by a reciprocity between the technology and the body populace, thus instantiating a dispersed, agile, and scattered modality that the Deleuzian notion of control anticipated (Deleuze 1992; Rose 2000; Guins 2009; Cheney-Lippold, 2018). In its shaping, modulating, and hence controlling through pervasive immersion within quotidian social life, it is an evolution from the prior centralized top-down mode that operated through cultural hubs and centers—or what Foucault described as confined spaces and institutions that we inhabit.

The social iterations of these dialectical effects of online culture are primarily mediated through digital platforms such as Facebook, Twitter, Snapchat, and Instagram as well as search engines such as Google that increasingly mediate global users' experiences of the web. In certain cases, as discussed in the chapter on frontier, these platforms are conflated with the entirety of the internet (Silver and Smith 2019; Milani 2015), thus pointing to their success in articulating themselves as the singular gateways to the web. As has been shown convincingly by others (Jin 2015), a global survey of dominant platforms reveals a disproportionate preeminence of those originating within prior technological centers, where they benefit from the dense ecosystem of entrepreneurs, financiers, and technical skill sets as well as the deep institutional and cultural memory of the successes and failures associated with the early days of the web. That a majority of the globally dominant platforms in distinct areas such as social networks, search, video sharing, streaming, e-commerce, email, maps, and peer collaboration can be traced directly or indirectly to these technology hubs underscores that media industries have an affinity toward particular centralized locations where they benefit from preexisting networks of knowledge and skill sets (Curtin 2004). The global dominance of these Silicon Valley–affiliated platforms, no doubt aided by the network effect and the winner-takes-all (Coyle 2018) nature of the platform ecosystem, is also notable given that in large swaths of the global digital landscape (barring China and Russia) their popularity and usage override local platforms that benefit little from cultural proximity toward the specific location.

The Global Dominance of Western Platforms

Despite the infamous opacity and secrecy around platform membership numbers as well as the continuously changing user base and nature of the digital ecosystem, various publicly available parameters at particular moments reflect the disproportionate global sway of particular websites, platforms, and social networking sites. An analysis of the most popular websites globally as well as the list of most popular websites within each country (as extracted from Alexa.com in December 2017) reveals the disproportionate popularity of global versus local platforms and websites within a country. If the site of their hosting is an indicator of their cultural and linguistic orientation, then it is worth noting that twenty of the fifty most popular websites in the world (in 2017) provided a location within the United States as their official/business address. Moreover, twelve out of the remaining thirty were the country-specific versions of Google, thus taking the number of US-hosted websites to thirty-two out of the top fifty global sites. In terms of linguistic distribution, about half (twenty-four) out of the top fifty global websites (listed by Alexa) were in the English language, with Chinese-language websites being the second most popular at eleven (out of the top fifty). If one delves deeper into the rankings of the top ten websites within different countries, the claim about a preponderance of Western sites gets further boost. Analyzing the top ten websites in a random sample of 19 countries (choosing every tenth country starting from the first—i.e., Afghanistan) out of a total of 186 countries listed on Alexa (December 2017), one finds only 3 countries that had fewer than five US-based sites among their top ten most popular sites.

Besides, there is not a single country (in the random sample of nineteen) wherein Google was not among the top ten sites; it often sat closer to the top position in most. Other US-based sites that figured repeatedly among the top ten in the sampled countries included Yahoo, Wikipedia, YouTube, Amazon, and Facebook, all of which are the leading platforms in their respective areas. That countries ranging from Azerbaijan to Bhutan and Gabon to Swaziland have their digital sphere dominated by US websites is an indicator both of the digital divide manifested in their underdeveloped internet ecosystem and of the technological and financial advantages of Silicon Valley–based American media and technology corporations.

This picture emerging from the analysis of the most popular websites gets further support when juxtaposed with the dominant social media platforms globally. A list of the twenty most popular social media platforms in the world in 2017 (Clement 2017) determined by their global usage numbers (sourced through the business intelligence portal Statista) included eleven US-based social network sites, six Chinese, one Japanese (Viber), one Korean/Japanese (LINE), and one (Telegram) whose home location was concealed. A clearer picture of dominance emerges when looking at the top four on the list (Facebook, YouTube, WhatsApp, and Facebook Messenger), whose combined user count in 2017 (approximately 6.1 billion) equaled almost the same as that of the remaining sixteen on the list (approximately 6 billion). In terms of user distribution, all eleven US-based social networking sites accounted for almost 8.4 billion users while the Chinese social networking sites totaled about 3.2 billion; the two Japanese and Korean social network sites accounted for 474 million users. These ratios remained largely analogous two years later, in July 2019 (Clement 2019b). The same US-based platforms held the top four positions in 2019 too, and the total count of US platforms went up to twelve (Statista's public version ranked the top eighteen in 2019 instead of the top twenty in 2017) due to the entrance of Reddit and the gaming platform Discord. The combined user count of US-based platforms exceeded ten billion active users in 2019. The additions of Chinese platforms TikTok (500 million users) and Douban (320 million users) to the list in 2019 were accompanied by the exit of Baidu and YY, taking the combined user base of Chinese platforms to 3.7 billion users.

Additionally, the global reach of the dominant US-based platforms is underscored by the fact that a majority of their users are now based in countries outside the United States, thus making them global digital empires in the true sense due to their memberships transgressing national (and cultural) boundaries. In the case of Facebook, for instance, only about 240 million of its approximately 2.32 billion global users in 2019 (Facebook Investor Relation 2019) lived within the United States, and the largest number of Facebook users (almost 300 million) now reside in India. The case is the same for Twitter: approximately 62 million of its users were based in the US in 2020 (the percentage hovering between 21% and 22 % of all Americans; see Perrin and Anderson 2019; Clement 2020), which constituted only about 22 percent of its global user base of 320 million in 2019 (Jamie 2019), thus making about 78 percent of Twitter users non-Americans. The case is similar for Instagram, where in 2019 only 110 million (Clement 2019a) of its approximately 1 billion global users (Clement 2019c) came from within the United States. The pattern emerging from these statistical distributions of the user bases of social networking sites and the analyses of the most popular websites in each country show the preponderance of global platforms and websites over the local ones (with the exception of China). That the dominant social networking platforms globally are primarily US-based digital media empires brings a notable inflection point to the ways in which the corporate logic of monetizing interactivity and user information through encouraging particular forms of interaction continues to shape global online sociality.

This asymmetrical dominance of US-based social media platforms invites an analysis of their global effects. How does their continued global expansion and their gradual enfolding of internet users across countries, cultures, and languages shape global culture? An attempt to answer this could pursue evidence of "any common or global patterns" of "globalizing social media sociability" (Schroeder 2016, 5637). Even a cursory perusal of the global social media culture as evidenced by phenomena such as the global rise of selfie culture, the growth of live-streaming practices such as vlogging, and a pervasive online influencer culture shows irrefutable support for Schroeder's tentative question. Even as we acknowledge the grounds for naturally occurring cultural differences, they coexist alongside broad, overarching commonalities within patterns of online sociality on global digital platforms, thus pointing to their roles in reshaping global culture. Schroeder (2018, 98) sees these threads of "homogeneity" amid "diversity" within the globalization of an aspirational idealized self and in notions of tethered togetherness that the subsequent sections of this chapter extend by delineating the specific parameters of that emerging self and the social ecology it inhabits.

This analysis is premised on the claim that the simultaneous rise of two parallel global phenomena—the global uptake of social media platforms on the one hand (as described above) and the rise of normative notions of idealized selfhood on the other—are not entirely disconnected processes but represent a causal relationship. Simultaneously co-occurring phenomena may not always be causally related, and yet dismissing investigations of causality due to that caution risks missing palpable relationships that may hold deep insights about trajectories of global digital culture. Showing the global influence of digital social platforms helps correct claims about digitized social media as a terrain of unhindered and organic self-expression. By emphasizing the surreptitiously coercive effect of the rules, procedures, default settings, and affordances of social media, we begin to understand how they shape, nudge, and regulate user sociality by normalizing certain aspirational notions of selfhood. Before analyzing the effects of social media affordances, it is important to briefly trace the roots of this normalizing selfhood to the uniquely contingent sociocultural churn occurring within the simultaneous processes of modernity, the Enlightenment, and colonialism that sought to spread "civilization" globally, as the section below will show.

Genealogy of the Globalizing Aspirational Selfhood

That we all sense a shift in our being because of our immersion within the all-engulfing tentacles of digital culture is a widely accepted truism and a subject of daily lament in a world saturated with networked devices and social media platforms. Their affordances and designs entice us with increasingly successful addictive traps that compete for our time and mind space and require us to constantly feed snippets of our lives into the digital vortex. The pervasive effect of the nudges, triggers, and seductions of the digital ecosystem can be gauged by the fact that having a digital presence is increasingly not a choice but a necessity given the undesirable social and professional consequences of resisting it. Marwick (2013) cites the CEO of a reputation management firm who claims that for a potential employee, "not using social media marked unsophistication and backwardness" (214).

The social pressure to have an online presence, when combined with the power of globalizing digital platforms, whose cultural and technological architectures are designed to make our interactions monetizable (van Dijck, Poell, and De Waal 2018), provides strong clues about the ever-expanding nature of the "idealized self" (Schroeder 2018, 98) that is increasingly emerging across platforms, albeit with variations along linguistic, national, and cultural axes (Schroeder 2016). This section explores the unique conditions of origin of these notions of selfhood and delineates how the distinctive contours of this idealized personhood were normalized over time. These normative notions of personhood, which were globalized historically and that culminate on the social web today, can be traced to unique historical and sociocultural processes that shaped and carved ideal citizenship and subjectivity during specific moments of Western modernity. Shining a light on that history allows us to challenge claims that this increasingly ubiquitous notion of selfhood on the social web is inherently "universal" or somehow new and radically discontinuous from prior iterations of subjectivity.

This section proceeds in two broad steps that first delineate the processes (the how) by which this ideal subject was brought into being through a plethora of institutional and discursive mechanisms that reified a system of gradual but definite modulation of human behavior. A genealogy of this subjectivity shows that the rise of Western modernity was accompanied by a profusion of new sciences that progressively made the human subject an object of study, analysis, and control (Rose 1999, 2000; Elias 2000; Deleuze 1992). The public manifestation of these sciences in the form of confessional accounts (written diaries and confessions spoken to a pastor), therapeutic discourses, manuals of self-help, and prescriptive regimes of normative social behavior set in motion widespread social and cultural ideas about conceiving the human subject at both the societal and the individual levels. After elaborating on these inculcating processes (the how), the analysis proceeds to the next step (the what) that concretizes the particularities of that selfhood citizens were supposed to aspire to. As shown below, those particularities were rooted within uniquely contingent sociocultural processes occurring within the specific axes of time and space that intersected "within the modern West" (Taylor 1989, 11) and converged to create the contours of the "western concept of the person" (Rose 1999, 221) whose digital iteration is increasingly global today.

How the Normative Subject Was Produced

Desirable social norms of behavior and personal etiquette extended the lessons emerging from laboratories and clinics into the social world. They did so by creating a discursive regime of truth around norms and behaviors through the assimilation of ideas from the so-called upper levels of society to the lower ones. Just as the structure of rewards and sanctions that shape the social self on digital platforms today (as will be elaborated on in subsequent sections), these prior regimes sought to modulate human behaviors by creating systems "in which behavior that tended in the desired direction was 'rewarded' while that which was undesirable was either ignored or responded with 'negative reinforcement'" (Rose 1999, 239). These programs sought to diffuse the lessons learned from newly emerging "programmes, strategies and techniques for the conduct of conduct" (Rose 2000, 322) such that the entire social milieu became an extension of the field of experiments so that "institutionally desired behavior is made translatable into a universal reward of tokens, points, or money, which can be exchanged for those things that the subject considers desirable" (Rose 1999, 240). Illustrating how these structural pathways worked in the economic realm, Rose explains that "these enwrap each individual life decision and action—about labour, purchases, debts, credits, lifestyle, sexual contacts and the like—in a web of incitements, rewards, current sanctions and forebodings of future sanctions which serve to enjoin each citizen to maintain particular types of control over their conduct" (Rose 2000, 326).

Adding to this modulating regime was one of praise and shame to mold the "drive economy" (Elias 2000, 414) and suppress (Freud 2004) and channel the untamed human instincts toward desirable and socially acceptable categories of behaviors. Norbert Elias (2000) painstakingly elucidates how binaries that categorized human behavior along the lines of civilized versus uncivilized or along the polarity of acceptability and shame created a structure of incentives that gradually percolated into society through "the progressive imposition of constraints upon the human instincts" (Rose 1999, 224). Elias (2000) explains how this gradual process worked as "constraints through others from a variety of angles were convened into self-restraints, how the more animalic human activities were progressively thrust behind the scenes of people's communal social life and invested with feelings of shame, how the regulation of the whole instinctual and affective life by steady self-control became more and more stable, more even and more all-embracing" (365).

The similarities between these dialectical mechanisms of inducements and restraints or praise and shame that sought to bring an idealized subject into being and the nudges, triggers, and constraints on behavior that are realizing an aspirational notion of the self on digital platforms today are impossible to miss. Watching different cultural iterations of this process being performed online and popularized globally has elevated them as scripts for digital life to be emulated and aspired to. Similar scripts were rampant in the discourses that presented elaborate descriptions of ideal behavior detailed within popular and official cultural, textual, and literary artifacts of the day. They included a "tradition of books on manners" (Elias 2000, 63) that joined other textual artifacts such as pamphlets and "a series of poems designed as mnemonics to inculcate table manners" (53). In the ensuing years, the literary novel, with its thick description of particular archetypes of selfhoods (Taylor 1989), performed a similar discursive role of providing templates for how life was to be lived. Elias makes note of how German literature emphasized "with mockery and scorn, a very serious need for a 'softening of manners'" (Elias 2000, 65). The modern novel's rise, therefore, was an inseparable dimension of the broader discursive regime that, along with systems of social and economic rewards, introduced an "order sui generis" (Elias 2000, 366) that progressively altered aspirational norms of the ideal human subject. Disciplinary domains through which subjects navigated—such as schools, hospitals, the church, factories, and prisons—were key sites where these dual regimes of social and cultural prescriptions and popular discourses engrained normative behavior.

Contours of the Emerging Ideal Subject

Definitions of ideal citizenship and selfhoods have existed across time and cultures (Allen 2018), and yet the earliest, most enduring, most continuously documented, and most socially enforced versions of it come to us from colonial-era Europe, whose simultaneous rise as a political and economic power helped entrench and globalize ideas about what it meant to be an ideal human. While discourses about cultivating refinement and standards for taste (Hume 1965; Arnold 1993) were a part of broader processes for creating social stratification, there were some fundamental changes underway in the nature of subjectivity itself. The multifaceted contours of this subjectivity had three foundational characteristics that formed inevitable precursors to the dominant notion of self whose culturally variant iterations we find within digital culture today.

The first characteristic is a concept of the self as a unique individualized subject with an interiority irreducible to any another. The second related characteristic is its self-expressive dimension that relies on self-disclosure of one's unique innerness to constitute itself. Both of these lead us to the third, which is that of an entrepreneurial self who takes responsibility for the shape and direction of one's destiny. Notably, each of these finds strong resonances in dominant narratives of online selfhood today that require an active "management" (Schroeder 2016; Marwick 2013) of one's digital identity through selective and desirable disclosures about one's life. Even though these threads of personhood are distinct, all are also intertwined in a causal relationship, thus making them symbiotic on each other. One's radical individuality is realized only in its self-expression, thus making the latter an imperative for and constituent of the former. And continuous and public self-revelation automatically opens up those accounts to public scrutiny, thus creating the imperative to manage them to project a desirable public image, a process akin to hawking one's unique identity within the digital marketplace. These features, whose accentuated versions we witness in contemporary digital culture, heralded a departure from communitarian ideas of identity, thus making the individualized self "responsible for their own destinies" (Rose 2000, 324).

The first characteristic of this ideal person in this emerging era of individualism was to manifest in a unique and discrete self that was supposed to embody "a bounded sphere of thought, will, and emotion; the site of consciousness and judgement; the author of its acts and the bearer of a personal responsibility; an individual with a unique biography assembled over the course of a life" (Rose 1999, 221). The rise of individualism (and its interrelated ideas of the expressive and entrepreneurial self) are key by-products of Western modernity, and Charles Taylor (1989) connects it to the birth of "inwardness" that was marked by "partly unexplored and dark interiors" (111) that were hardly a universal phenomenon but were "a function of a historically limited mode of interpretation, one which has become dominant in the modern West" (111). Taylor locates this self with a marked interiority as a culmination of a trajectory that can be traced to St. Augustine's turn to inward self-reflexivity as opposed to an external source of inspiration.

Secondly, the individualized subject was manifested only in the act of articulating and proclaiming their unique inner-ness across various interpersonal and mediated networks. Various modes of such disclosures arose during this era (e.g., the confession, artistic expression, journal writing, therapy sessions), all of which shared a presumption of a unique innerness that must be tapped in to and coaxed out. Among the most rigorous investigation of this relationship between self-disclosure and personhood comes to us from Charles Taylor's *Sources of the Self* (1989), which establishes the "expressivist turn" as a key milestone in the formation of the modern Western subject who "can only find an identity in self-narration" (289). This turn premises itself on the belief that one's inner voice is an authentic expression uncontaminated by the vagaries of culture and modern life, and one can only fully hear that voice in the process of its external enunciation. Self-expression helps the "inchoate, and partly formed" self to take "final shape" (374) that cannot be fully apprehended separately from and prior to its articulation.

The world of art wherein mimesis (or copying reality) gradually gives way to expression provided a realm where, Taylor argues, one could dive into one's inner depths to bring forth a slice of it. Alongside the cultures of self-expression, a proliferation of the "technologies of the self" (Rose 1999, 224) from institutional apparatuses and therapeutic discourses founded on the idea of studying, analyzing, and making meaning of human experiences thrived in a culture of self-expression. And in an ironic inversion that bears a striking resemblance to today's era of digital surveillance, what started out with the assurance of individual liberty and freedom (as radical individuality was presented to be) soon morphed into a regime of subjectivation and control. Rose powerfully explains this reversal: "In compelling, persuading and inciting subjects to disclose themselves, finer and more intimate regions of personal and interpersonal life come under surveillance and are opened up for expert judgement, and normative evaluation, for classification and correction. In the name of the recognition of the subjectivity of the client or patient, a more profound subjection is produced" (Rose 1999, 244). Freedom morphs into control.

The commonalities between this mutation of an empowering process into one of discipline and surveillance, delineated above, and the coercive invitation to participate, contribute, and self-disclose, presented as a mark of our freedom and individuality, on the social web are difficult to gloss over. The inversion of "freedom as a disciplinary mechanism" (Guins 2009, 6), a hallmark of the Deleuzian notion of control, finds its epitome in the digital ecosystem today, thus serving the very regimes of power and commodification it promised to liberate us from.

Lastly, the two features of the individualized self and self-expression find a natural culmination in the third facet of this idealized personhood—a sovereign subject taking charge of their destiny so "each of us is to be our own rock" (Rose 2000, 328). This individual self, with progressively weakening ties to communal structures of premodernity, had to embody an entrepreneurial spirit of the kind whose strong echoes we see in the influencer culture and the branding of the self on the social web today. Assuming control of one's life trajectory relegated fates such as failure or success, destitution or prosperity, entirely to the hands of the individual rather than in any external structures. Scholars have connected this entrepreneurial self as inextricably tied to the secularization of society and the concomitant rise of capitalism, whose emphasis on choice, responsibility, personal initiative, and rational decision-making percolated into social life more generally.

Self-reliance through making prudent choices within a world of options epitomized freedom—an abiding credo of liberalism and capitalism. Rose (1999, 1996) locates the birth of this emphasis on individual choices primarily within the realm of economic actions, but the role of choices in calibrating and emphasizing the uniqueness of our selfhood and as an "emblem of our identity" (Rose 1999, 231) is easy to see. The move to differentiate oneself from others through cultural taste and to assert one's individuality through consuming and associating with particular cultural objects (e.g., movies, music, literature) hold a similar instantiation of the relationship between choice and individuality that we see in the digital realm today. Moreover, the ways in which this delegation of responsibility to the individual, who embodies "personal responsibility, self-reliance" and "self-governing" (Guins 2009, 7), and the gradual abdication of it by the state can generate debilitating social inequalities are an extreme manifestation of this very equation of freedom with consumer choice in what Rose (2000, 325) calls "advanced liberal societies" witnessing a late form of capitalism.

These three facets of the idealized self-emerging from within the churns of Western modernity were meant to symbolize freedom from the chains of tradition and a validation of one's ego-satiating uniqueness, but that freedom could be realized only by paying the wages through the risk of taking responsibility for oneself and recusing the state, society, or community from that charge. In this emerging schema, even as the self is invited to show its freedom through expressing its innerness, it must also be ready to endure the public gaze and the scrutiny that comes along with evaluation, correction, and norming to mitigate deviant social tendencies. The transposition of discourses of freedom and liberty into regimes of discipline, surveillance, and power—a relatively untold story of liberalism—helps us understand the historical mandate through which control functions under the ruse of empowerment. This sobering dialectic pervades the technological and cultural architecture of the digital ecosystem today, where technologies that seek to empower simultaneously enfold us into logics of commodification, monetization, and control.

How Digital Infrastructures of Control Shape Global Selfhood

Having delineated the historic genealogy of the aspirational selfhood, and the system of social rewards and strictures that nudge it into being, prepares us well to consider how the technical architecture of the social web shares a similar recursive logic of feedback loops in order to emphasize desirable aspects of a normative self. Arguments about the cultural and political effects of technologies (Winner 1980) and media technologies in particular (Peters 2017; Hutchby 2001) must simultaneously eschew the two extremist positions that debates about the effects of media must nevertheless navigate. At one extremity lie those who ascribe no social effect whatsoever to technologies, locating its meaning and power entirely in the interpretive domain of users and scholars, and on the other end are those arguing for a crude version of technological determinism that presents a dystopian techno-centric future devoid of human agency. The former position of radical constructivism, while underscoring a useful reminder about the contextual and contingent meanings of technology, nevertheless risks pushing the production of that meaning so far in the symbolic and discursive domain that it entirely ignores the material specificities of the medium. In a world increasingly saturated with technology, where "much of our infrastructure is digital and thus seemingly personal and flexible" (Peters 2017, 21), eliding questions that interrogate the effects of digital technologies on human life is tantamount to "giving up on critique" itself (21). It is therefore a worthy reminder that "our interpretations and uses of technological artefacts, while important, contingent, and variable, are constrained in analyzable ways by the ranges of affordances that particular artefacts possess" (Hutchby 2001, 31). Moreover, materiality need not always be thought of in physical terms as, for Hutchby, elements such as design, cultural architecture, and user interfaces that we have called "soft" infrastructures can similarly shape navigation and influence user experience with just as determining an effect as the material dimensions of technology.

As opposed to the visibly coercive effects of insurmountable physical structures, soft infrastructures (Punathambekar and Mohan 2019; Aouragh and Chakravartty 2016) exercise power over us through the design, organization, and arrangement of choices and pathways in our quotidian lives. More importantly, in the digital domain, we witness the synergistic convergence of the power of seemingly soft elements such as design, algorithmic regulation, and infrastructural nudges with knowledge from the subfield of behavioral psychology about shaping and modulating human action. Insights from these two streams cohere in a powerful new discipline called "behavior design" (Leslie 2016), which is singularly focused on deploying the wealth of prior research to understand how placement, layout, and design as well as a combination of triggers, incentives, and variable reward (Eyal 2014) can mold human action online.

The Modulating Power of the Nudge

The immense enduring power of seemingly neutral arrangement of elements in free space, presented as equally available choices, accrues from how nuances such as sequence, ordering, shape, sound, color, and lighting can leverage the inherent irrationalities of human beings (Thaler and Sunstein 2008) to prod them into behaving in particular ways. At issue here is the tussle between the seemingly rational human impulse that evaluates all options equally to decide which is best for one's self-interest against the more irrational tendencies (e.g., pleasure seeking, immediate gratification) that are persuaded by formal elements such as placement, order, layout, and design as well as the triggers of past learning. The tendency to assume rational decision-making as the only mode exercised by human beings severely undermines a fuller understanding of the motivations that propel human action while also ignoring research that "has raised serious questions about the rationality of many judgments and decisions that people make" (Thaler and Sunstein 2008, 7).

While his Nobel Prize has shone light on Thaler's emphasis on the importance of irrationality in human decision-making—ideas that have long been prevalent in disciplines such as communication and media studies—the deeper import of Thaler's lifelong challenge to the mainstream economics discipline points to the ways in which irrationality can be leveraged to "nudge" human decision-making through a noncoercive, benevolent mechanism that he calls "libertarian paternalism" (Thaler and Sunstein 2008, 14). In elaborating on his notion that there is "no such thing as a neutral design" (3), Thaler and Sunstein (2008), have posited how seemingly irrational factors such as layout, sequence, and order of objects positioned in real or virtual spaces, which they call "choice architecture" (81), can significantly influence human decision-making while still maintaining the illusion of free choice since they do not foreclose any option. Deceptive factors that influence decision-making—such as "status quo bias" (83), the "planning fallacy" (7), the "path of least resistance" (83), and the strikingly different responses to opting in versus opting out of "default options" (85)—are often leveraged by private and public institutions (and, as we will see below, digital media platforms) to "nudge" human behavior in particular directions, thus underscoring the power of design, visual placement, and ordering of choices in shaping the decision-making process.

There is hardly a better instantiation of this power of designed nudges in channeling decision-making while maintaining (the illusion of) free choice than Natasha Dow Schüll's masterful exposition of the role played by design in the gambling industry of Vegas in *Addiction by Design* (2012). The industry whose profits increase proportionate to the time players devote to the gambling machines has applied the entire gamut of available knowledge about the power of design (or what Thaler and Sunstein would call "choice architecture") and sensory cues (from behaviorism) to create arguably the largest *infrastructural nudge* in the casinos of Las Vegas. Detailed minutiae that include the angles at which alleys turn (avoid ninety-degree turns), the height of ceilings, the patterns on the carpet, the tempo of the music, the ambient odor, the shape of the slot machines, the sounds both background and emanating from slot machines, the lighting intensity, and "casino atmospherics" are all designed to "turn attention toward machines, and keep it focused there" (Schull 2012, 99). The goal, claims Schull, is to simulate "structured chaos" with the singular purpose of extracting maximum "revenue per available customer" (63). The contribution of Schull's riveting analysis would have been confined to helping us understand gambling addiction and would be a sidenote in a study, such as this one, focused on the digital realm were it not for the striking parallels between the role played by designed triggers in fostering gambling addiction on the one hand and their manipulative deployment to bait and keep users glued to social media platforms on the other—a similarity pointed out by several former employees of these platforms (Bosker 2016).

To be sure, soft infrastructures such as design achieve the trade-off between freedom and coercion by meeting users halfway through leveraging preexisting tendencies, desires, and wants within subjects both in the arena of gambling and similarly on the social web. Just as the power exercised by the casinos in Las Vegas (and elsewhere) must align "what players want" (Schull 2012, 170) with their own end goals, social media affordances can be effective only through a system of rewards and incentives such as peer recognition, a sense of value, rewarding self-esteem, and (an illusion of) networked sociality. Players come to casinos with (varying degrees of) pre-existing desires to play, but then the "sensorially attentive design" turns those incipient and often nascent desires to drive players to "the point at which player funds run out" (171). This form of immanent, immersive, and modulating power operates from within the environment akin to Deleuze's well-defined conception of control. As distinct from the "the rigid molds of disciplinary enclosures (like the prison)" (Cheney-Lippold 2018, 147), the dispersed and scattered modality of control circulates and flows within the sinews of "a continuous network" (Deleuze 1992, 6) that subjects inhabit. Deleuze explains it through the metaphor of a highway on which "people can drive infinitely and 'freely' without being at all confined yet while still being perfectly controlled" (Deleuze 1998, 18). An array of seemingly equal options can simulate the conditions of free will such that "choice is enabled through the control of options" (Guins 2009, 7). The menus of options presented to us on various social media platforms exemplify how a carefully preprogrammed and yet algorithmically modulating (Cheney-Lippold 2018) array of choices can accrue immense power to its designer—a phenomenon that former Google employee and design ethicist Tristan Harris describes succinctly: "If You Control the Menu, You Control the Choices" (Harris 2016).

The coercive power of choices operates through a diagrammed movement of subjects in an immersive environment laden within an assortment of controlled alternatives and selections (e.g., consider the controlled set of choices for privacy settings on Facebook), thus ensuring that "rule is imposed through active choice" (Guins 2009, 7). Even as the multiplicity of options simulates freedom, the omissions from the list of options often go uninterrogated and unquestioned. In understanding how this logic of manipulative arrangement can shape user behavior in the digital ecosystem, it is important to remember its parallels with the earlier iterations of rewards and derision, sanction and seductions, as well as shame and praise for modulating human behavior that scholars such as Rose (1990, 1996) and Elias (2000) have elaborately detailed for us.

The Proddings of Social Media Affordances

Such ecosystems of multitudinous choices, each leading us toward already determined pathways and thus masking the nature of control with the ruse of enabling freedom, are fully entrenched on digital platforms today, whose affordances constitute the all-enveloping "infrastructure of online cultural life" (Seaver 2019, 11). These platforms, frequently presented as sites of unencumbered and organic expression, are teeming with nudges directing users toward specific ends that go a long way in creating the "globalizing social media sociability" that Schroeder (2018, 5637) argues is a consequence of the global spread of digital platforms. Platforms as diverse as those focused on peer video production and sharing such as YouTube; those focused on social networking such as Facebook, Instagram, and Snapchat; and microblogging platforms such as Twitter are rife with programmed choices that seek to channel user behavior through circumscribed and yet seemingly autonomous action. Closely analyzing these features and choices, broadly summarized under the term *affordances* (Bucher and Helmond 2017; Hutchby 2001), which are a combination of allowances and constraints on user behavior, can help underscore how digital media platforms normalize aspirational notions of selfhood that the web globalizes.

From the arrangement of buttons to the design and options available in menus and drop-down lists, the default settings, the temporal movement of content on a page (e.g., the extent one can scroll to or "pull to refresh" on smartphones), the nature of notifications, and a fine-tuned system of triggers followed by variable rewards and penalties, the "choice architecture" within social media is the digital equivalent of the designed nudges of the gambling havens of Las Vegas with their enticing slot machines that exploit human vulnerabilities to drive users to "the point of extinction" (Schüll 2012, 171). Just as addiction to gambling is premised on a reciprocal cycle of betting and reward that infinitely extends playing time by spreading out and making the prize unpredictable and variable, the affordances of social media platforms entice us to reap the spoils (likes, comments, appreciation) resulting from our wagers of posting content and sharing details about our lives. The euphoric intensity after a successful bid in a slot machine is not too different in its ephemeral superficiality and addictive power from the rush created by likes, retweets, or validatory comments from friends and strangers on social networking sites. The mystification at work in both cases is the inversion of user desires and wants to serve the goals of the entities masked behind the gambling enterprises or digital platforms. Just as the design that glues gamblers to slot machines in a state of suspended and self-destructive stupor, with the singular motive of transferring money from the players to the companies, the architecture of social networking sites constitute "infrastructures" that "are already traps" (Seaver 2019, 12) to lure users to surrender their time, attention, and self-revealing information and data to be captured and monetized. These damning comparisons between the incentive structures of gambling and those constituting the digital ecology of platforms and applications have been made frequently by key insiders working for digital platforms and involved in designing their architecture (Harris 2016; Silverman 2017), whose powerful effects are analyzed sequentially below.

The nudges to disclose our inner selves on digital platforms are a combination of multiple prompts that create a diagrammed apparatus comprising textual and symbolic cues, default settings, carefully designed options, and drop-down menu items as well as algorithmic modulation (analyzed below in this sequence) to create a carefully planned architecture of control. The process of nudging user behavior toward desirable end goals begins with personalized *textual* proddings such as Twitter's invitational "what's happening?" in the empty tweet box to Facebook's endearing question "what's on your mind, Sangeet?"; both simulate a personalized friend-like curiosity into users' lives to prompt a response. These nagging cues seek to tease open the folds of our inhibitions by reassuring us through validating words that anything and everything on our minds is worth sharing with the larger world. These textual prompts continue with invitations to tag, comment, or reply to other comments and tweets through effortless clicks and algorithmically induced suggestions. Such personalized cues proliferate across digital platforms, such as on Netflix (Jenner 2018), where they are used to provide personalized recommendations. Individualized nudges such as "'Because you watched . . .', 'Recommendations for [insert first name/ screen name of viewer]' or 'Because you added [a specific text] to your list'" (Jenner 2018, 129) are similar attempts by Netflix to ingratiate itself to users by showing an ability to know them and achieve the desired end goal (e.g., binge-watching).

Textual signals coexist with the *symbolic* ones represented by buttons that are often semiotically redefined to articulate new meanings within the confines of social media platforms. Buttons that invite us to like, retweet, and share content or follow and friend someone are digital, nonverbal equivalents of verbal cues in the off-line world, each of them open to interpretive rearticulations. Their polysemic nature is underscored by examples such as explicit statements and clarifications from users that foreground users' intended meanings of the semiotic acts (e.g., the clarification that "retweets ≠ endorsements" often placed by users in Twitter bios). Changes in the type and function of buttons over time are also a testament to the evolving character of social interaction on the web and highlight the continuous mode of trial and error by platforms to gauge user responses and shape them more effectively. For instance, the significantly undermined importance of the Facebook poke button (from a prominent position on the top right corner of a friend's page to obscurity under "see more" on the bottom left) exemplifies the semiotic richness of these buttons, which (in the case of the poke button) led to frequent speculations (Willett 2015; Wickman 2014) about its intended meaning. Similarly, the replacement of the star with a heart-shaped button to favorite a tweet on Twitter led to much heartburn among avid users of that button (Bucher and Helmond 2017).

The Power of the Default Setting

Buttons and textual cues also play a crucial role in entrenching the role of *default settings*, whose power lies in their ability to leverage the inbuilt human affinities toward inertia, habituation, and the status quo. The ecology of digital platforms is rife with the manipulative deployment of default settings to maximize desirable user choices (i.e., beneficial for the platforms) and minimize the undesirable ones. A clear ubiquitous use of default settings is in presenting a (preselected) default option that a user can opt out of (if they decide to) instead of presenting all choices and then asking the user to choose one. Behavioral biases toward the status quo and inertia ensure that a majority of users are far more likely to continue with the default option, which is the path of least effort—a fact that social networking sites such as Facebook, Twitter, and Instagram use expediently to achieve desirable goals such as liberal privacy settings for user profiles. It is perhaps his knowledge about the power of default settings that Mark Zuckerberg unwittingly gives away in his now famous words "we are building a Web where the default is social" (Schonfeld 2010). By invoking the notion of the default, Zuckerberg is tacitly alluding to this insight from behaviorism about how the power of inertia significantly increases the likelihood of users continuing with default options, thus making seemingly equal choices not really equal.

Such use of default settings to encourage a certain version of online sociality that is often posited in opposition to its obverse (i.e., antisocial) allows sites such as Facebook to push a normative notion of the public/private divide that seeks to foster more interaction (the more people post, the more validating feedback, thus creating an upward spiral) but only so as to meet their broader goals of monetizing interactive user data. These online affordances that normalize particular cultural and ideological values instantiate a distinct form of cultural power by gradually altering the ideological underpinnings that shape and regulate human conceptions about selfhood and normative behavior online that are bound to seep into life off-line. Dana Boyd elaborates on this ripple ideological effect of social media affordances that diffuse into the off-line world by showing how the setting of "public-by-default, private-through-effort mentality" (Boyd 2014, 62) gradually coaxes users to invert how they think about privacy even in the off-line world. "Rather than asking themselves if the information to be shared is significant enough to be broadly publicized, they question whether it is intimate enough to require special protection" (62), thus showing how the social web reshapes off-line culture more broadly.

The power of default settings is also used to meet the end goals of *stickiness* of apps and platforms to help them in the increasingly desperate scramble for the finite resources of user attention and time. Just as the profits in the slot machines of Vegas increase proportionate to the time users spend on them, the more content social media platforms can capture, the more they can monetize, thus making user time an immeasurably valuable good online. An instance of the use of default settings here is the phenomenon of autoplay when watching videos on sites such as YouTube, Facebook, or Netflix, which ensures the next video begins to upload at the very moment the prior one ends, thus relying on user inertia to keep viewers in a zone of suspended animation. Just as on other streaming platforms, on Netflix too the autoplay feature "creates an almost seamless flow from one episode to the next" (Mareike 2018, 115), thus making viewers unknowing captives to the screen. The feature has continued despite intense user dislike (Murgu 2015) precisely because of the behavioral knowledge that "automaticity makes it difficult for viewers to Escape" (Perks 2014, xxvi). No doubt users can select to opt out of autoplay on each of these platforms, and yet even the seemingly minimal effort and initiative needed to make that change requires moving against one's inertia, thus making the autoplay feature the preferred "choice" for a majority of users. Such presentations of choices as default options ensure that "a large number of people . . . end up with that option, whether or not it is good for them" (Thaler and Sunstein 2008, 83)—a fact used as much by digital platforms as by subscription services that automatically renew unless users take action to cancel a free trial.

Default settings are also deployed to pursue stickiness by seducing users back into their digital enclosures through automated notifications, alerts, and personalized recommendations. These features that deploy knowledge from one's online behavior and profile to create what Perks (2014, xxiii) has called "entrance flow" are invariably a part of the default settings—unless they are turned off—and further help colonize user attention and time. Harris explains how these notifications deploy the semiotic power of the trigger, such as a bright-red color that makes it far "more likely than some other hues to make people click" (Bosker 2016). More worryingly, Harris claims, these default settings of instant notifications and read receipts (that alert a sender when a message has been read) "[activate] our hardwired sense of social reciprocity" (Bosker 2016), nudging us to respond immediately as the designers and social media companies "stand back watching as a billion people run around like chickens with their heads cut off, responding to each other and feeling indebted to each other" (Bosker 2016). While design ethicists such as Harris or critical scholars such as Thaler and Sunstein (2008) implore that the knowledge of human vulnerabilities such as the bias toward inertia and status quo and the radically different outcomes of opt-in versus opt-out options be harnessed for channeling people toward the right decisions, social media platforms deploy it expediently to create environments of entrapment (Seaver 2019) for the pure pursuit of user attention and time so they can maximize profit but also bring about behavioral change in their wake.

How Sequences of Choices in Menus Coax Decisions

In addition to textual/symbolic cues and default settings, the *manipulative arrangement* of drop-down menus and lists (e.g., search results) and the exclusion and inclusion of choices therein is the third way in which social media affordances channel and shape user behavior. The sequential arrangement of choices, in a drop-down menu or the order of Google search results, is no accident but in fact presents an argument about the relative importance of those alternatives. For instance, the positioning of the log out option on a platform, website, or email account, which is invariably located toward the bottom if not at the absolute end, is a clear illustration of nudging users away from a particular action. On Facebook the log out option is the last one in a drop-down menu when clicking on your account icon at the top right, thus betraying the platform's obvious intention to enforce stickiness and discourage users from logging out of their services. On Twitter, recent changes on the platform's interface have hidden the logout option under the "more" button, making logging out a three click process. The first click is on the "more" button, the second is on the logout option, and then the third click is to confirm that you indeed wish to log out (just in case the prior two clicks were mistakes). Besides, on platforms such as Google and Facebook, logging out no longer signs you out entirely from the account, which requires further clicks on one's username (in the case of Gmail) or profile picture (in the case of Facebook) to fully log a user out, requiring a total of three clicks for Facebook and five for Google.

The multiple steps needed to sign out of most social platforms, when contrasted with what is invariably a single click to post, comment, like, share, or tweet our thoughts or watch and consume content, shows the deployment of behavioral design to make desirable actions easy and undesirable ones arduous. Such nudges to remain logged in through the design of a platform's interface relies on key insights from research on behaviorism that "to initiate action, doing must be easier than thinking" (Eyal 2014, 59). This credo animates the architectural landscape across the social web. The power to nudge particular actions through ordering and arrangement is also visible in Google search results, which leverage the tendency of a significant majority to click on the top few results to create an implicit hierarchy of diminishing attention that drives traffic to the top results and create proportionately decreasing clicks on the lower results. Nudging and prodding users toward desirable actions such as self-disclosure, interactivity, and lifestreaming (each through a single click) while decreasing or delaying undesirable actions such as logging out, restricting privacy settings, and changing default options (by requiring multiple clicks and arduous navigational decisions for them) instantiates how the order and sequence of choices on social media are deployed to foster particular habits and hence subjectivities. The value of these habits and notions of selfhood increase proportionally to the amount of content produced by adopting and following them.

Given how they help feed data-hungry social media platforms, the specific contours of the self-revealing subject are hardly accidental but encouraged precisely because they directly add economic value to these platforms' bottom lines. After all, "the more information that Facebook can compel users to input, the more money each user is worth" (Cirucci 2015). Key to eliciting more information from users is the deployment of the liberatory discourse of openness and transparency to normalize this continuously self-revealing selfhood, as in the words of Franklin Foer (2017): "Though Facebook will occasionally talk about the transparency of governments and corporations, what it really wants to advance is the transparency of individuals—or what it has called, at various moments, 'radical transparency' or 'ultimate transparency'" (Foer 2017, 3). Deploying the ruse of emancipatory discourses of freedom, openness, self-expression, and transparency, all abiding liberal credos, for furthering the dual goals of control and the pecuniary interests of social media platforms makes them key enablers of the Deleuzian societies of control that consist of "constant and never ending modulation" juxtaposed alongside the "flows and transactions between the forces and capacities of the human subject and the practices in which he or she participates" (Rose 2000, 325). The networked affordances of social media are teeming with choices that have enabled a culture of expression, and yet those avenues of freedom provided by the platforms also function as bait to ensnare users into a new regime of power that the digital platforms are globalizing today.

Algorithmic Modulation of Online Behaviors

In addition to the design and affordances of digital platforms, the continuously modulating *algorithmic regulation* to control and shape the dynamic and constantly varying elements of our experience on the social web go beyond the already powerful ways in which textual/symbolic cues, default settings, and arrangements of choices (analyzed above) normalize particular conceptions of selfhood. While affordances are the fixed pathways that a channel user experiences, continuously changing elements such as content recommendations (on streaming platforms such as YouTube, in our Facebook newsfeed, or on our Twitter time lines) and decisions about the extent and nature of visibility (of profiles, posts, actions, etc.) as a reward being made in real time attain their power by continuously moderating themselves according to a slew of factors they take as inputs. A pertinent analogy of such modulation is the continuously rerouting software on our GPS systems that seeks to correct each wrong turn by treating our location as the starting point for the journey to the destination. Unlike the default settings, choices, and user cues that are embedded within digital platforms, the dynamic and continuously self-correcting algorithmic features can endlessly personalize the "user's informational choice context" to create a "hyper

nudge" (Yeung 2017, 119) that encourages particular choices and online behaviors. In analyzing user behavior on Instagram, Cotter (2019) shows how
the perception that increased engagement and follower counts are rewarded
by the "powerful and mysterious" (904) algorithm while inactivity, stagna-
tion, and banning others are penalized nudges users to increase the former
type and decrease the latter type of behaviors online. Such a dynamic and
modulating choice architecture combines insights from behaviorism (about
rewards and sanctions) and the role of design in influencing choice with
a personalized data set gleaned from a deep dive into our online profile
and history. When every aspect of interface design is a nudge, they become
"landscape traps," turning into "environments where prey is already effectively caught" (Seaver 2019, 12). This potent trifecta (of choice architecture/
design, behaviorism, and modulating personalized algorithms) creates an
inescapable and immersive milieu that is perhaps an unprecedented infrastructure of priming and prompting users toward desired behavior.

A pertinent instance of how such a dynamic algorithmic architecture
can continuously intermix sanctions and seductions through nudges is
how they grant visibility and salience to desirable content and users (Cotter 2018), thus upholding them as worthy of emulation at the expense of
others that may be suppressed or rendered invisible. In analyzing the role
played by Facebook's algorithm EdgeRank, Bucher (2012) argues that the
algorithm normalizes and encourages self-disclosure by making users fear
"the very real possibility of becoming obsolete inscribed through the 'threat
of invisibility,'" thus inculcating "a desire to participate" (Bucher 2012,
1175). They do so through promoting content with high engagement (e.g., a
large number of comments and likes), thus "making it appear as if everybody is participating and communicating" (1175). This simulation gives the
phenomenon an effect of realness (akin to how Google's PageRank gives
top results an effect of "truthiness" as described by Hillis, Petit, and Jarrett [2013, 182]), instantiating a process wherein an algorithmically created
simulacra of truth perpetuates itself by triggering a scramble to replicate
the desirable norm.

Their active role in the distribution of rewards and penalty, by peddling
ample amounts of attention and visibility to users and content that fit their
larger goals (more disclosure, self-revealing content) and withholding visibility by making obscure those users and content that do not, makes movement
along these infrastructural pathways (like Deleuzian highways) seemingly
free expressions of user agency. The algorithmic power to tantalize users

through the lure of reward is akin to the promise of "a little dopamine hit every once in a while, because someone liked or commented on a photo or a post or whatever" (Price 2017) and entices a Pavlovian response from users who post, share, and self-disclose ever more private aspects of their lives. As subjects plunge into ever deepening folds of their innards to come up with content in the hope of rewards of greater visibility and approval (through interactive feedback such as likes and comments), they reproduce the logic of wagering ever larger bets in the hope of bigger prizes in a slot machine.

Even as we acknowledge the all-encompassing power of these digital infrastructures, including its dispersed and continuously recalibrating modality, it is important to underscore that their end goals and desirable outcomes have cultural and ideological underpinnings that are rooted within the particularities of the dominant cultures they emerge from. The embedding of these values, ideals, and norms within the architectures of code advance a "particular philosophical frame on the world" (Kitchin and Dodge 2011, 247) and hence is hardly acultural or apolitical. As Nieborg and Poell (2018) have proposed, the protocols, standards, and conventions that undergird the affordances, designs, and algorithmic modulation of "US-owned and operated GAFAM platforms effectively [entail] a globalization of US cultural standards concerning what is and what is not permitted" (4285). Recognizing their ideological and hence political orientations allows us to apprehend how the global spread and uptake of these soft infrastructures facilitate cultural and behavioral change, thus manifesting a form of global cultural reshaping whose progressive effects are increasingly visible in specific cultural practices within global digital cultures today. These cultural practices are key to constructing, privileging, and fortifying the globally prevalent "idealized self" (Schroeder 2018, 98) that finds expression within specific cultural formations of online sociality, as discussed below.

Performing the Global Digital Self

Understanding these mechanisms through which online sociality is brought into being positions us well to interrogate the specific instances of the idealized subject being affirmed and realized online. Given the global arc of this book's argument, it is pertinent to analyze the visible consequences of the persuasive nudges of social media affordances and algorithmic regulation in specific cultural practices around the world. Such an exploration is the direct corollary of the question that asks, "What types of selves are people encouraged to create and promote while using popular technologies like Facebook, Twitter, and YouTube?" (Marwick 2013, 5) It is the goal of this section to show that the modalities of power on digital media platforms, as illustrated in the preceding section, emphasize and accentuate specific features, such as individuation, self-expressivity, and self-entrepreneurism, that are continuations and digital iterations of idealized selfhoods emerging from the unique historical churnings of European modernity. This study locates those dimensions of subjectivity within three distinct cultural formations increasingly visible across linguistic, cultural, and national boundaries. These cultural practices, visible globally and analyzed below, are first the global rise of the selfie culture, second the related global culture of lifestreaming and vlogging, and third the increasing prevalence of the global influencer culture. Each of these have notable correlations with attributes of radical individualism, expressive self-disclosure (as a mode of constituting a public self-identity), and an entrepreneurial notion of self that this study has respectively located as key elements of the idealized subject emerging within Western modernity.

To claim that networked digital sociality encourages particular broad behavioral categories is not to discount the role of individuals and cultures in shaping social media platforms in specific ways that are locally rooted. In continuing the interactional perspective that eschews the polarities of absolute social constructivism on the one hand and inescapable media determinism on the other, the analysis here underscores the valuable contributions made by wide-ranging scholarship that has emphasized the cultural, national, and regional differences (Cunningham and Craig 2019, 2021; Goggin and McLelland 2009) within online digital cultures of creation and expression. Such pluralities are particularly evident when combined with the unique sociocultural histories within which the web has evolved across the world (Goggin and McLelland 2017) as well as in the globally expanding "creator culture" (Cunningham and Craig 2021). Nuanced variations also emerge in reasons for social media usage in different countries that have been established through ethnographic studies on social media adoption around the world (D. Miller et al. 2016), thus challenging claims of overarching global commonalities or patterns in their uptake. Differences in behaviors such as the percentages of clicked photos that users post online, the likelihood of playing online games, conceptions of privacy, and the usage of anonymous accounts as well as in online spending habits show behavioral patterns that align along national digital cultures. Underlying those differences and in a dialectical interplay with them, however, are central commonalities that are palpable within key sites of the expanding digital infrastructures.

To be sure, studies emphasizing these variations while providing granular accounts of local digital cultures can simultaneously create their own generalizations, such as about commonalities in behaviors among large numbers of users composed of national groups (e.g., Brazil, Italy, Indian, or Chinese) online. Depending on their level of focus (or chosen zone of magnification), all studies of the social invariably seek to strike their own balance between broad overarching tendencies on the one hand and nuances and variations within them on the other that can progressively differentiate and fragment down to the individual level. In acknowledging the quandary arising from one's level of focus, this project takes seriously the caution to not elide consequential regional differences, even as it points to emerging global tendencies toward particular types of behaviors within digital culture. Seemingly diverging trajectories of differences and similarities are in a continuous dialectical interaction within social milieus, and even studies focused on differences, such as Daniel Miller et al. (2016), cannot entirely avoid making claims about common proclivities, such as "in taking selfies individuals actively craft the impressions they hope to give, making such images a significant form of self- expression" (158). Even as it acknowledges the contribution of such studies that focus on the "content rather than the platform that is most significant when it comes to why social media matters" (1), my project adds to such scholarship to claim that the design, arrangement, affordances, conventions, and protocols (that compose the medium) of media technologies are *also* profoundly consequential.

It is indeed true that "genres of content, such as schoolchildren's banter, happily migrate to entirely different platforms" (D. Miller et al. 2016, xi), but my analysis proceeds with the caution emerging from traditions of scholarship on media technologies that the process of migration to another medium invariably inflects the meaning of the content, even if ever so slightly. This vantage point gives a constitutive role to media technologies (such as digital platforms) rather than positioning them as mere conduits (McLuhan 2011; Innis 2008; Peters 2017). Not only is a letter fundamentally different (in its meaning) from an email, but so is a tweet distinct from a Facebook comment (despite having the same content), and both are different from a Snapchat or a LinkedIn update, just as a video carries a different meaning than an Instagram post. Today, as increasingly large amounts of our infrastructure are digital, ignoring the role of the medium in shaping behaviors, influencing dominant norms and ideologies, and asserting power is akin to "giving up on critique, that is, reflection on conditions of possibility" (Peters 2017, 21). This emphasis on the medium (alongside the content), is only presented as a complement to other perspectives and lenses with the understanding that no single vantage point determines the social outcome in the last instance, which is always an unfolding interactional process.

While media technologies that preceded the digital moment all had their own social effects and altered our notions of time, space, the body, death, and art (Kittler 1999; Innis 2008)—ideas that are germane to the human condition—the digital moment's emphasis on the individual accentuates its effects related to human subjectivity and notions of selfhood. Key to this amplifying effect is the online profile. An imperative in today's world, it sits on the confluence of the three strands of individual distinctiveness, self-disclosure, and self-branding. Our online profile is a careful curation of data about the self that utilizes the affordances of the social web to project a desirable public identity. Cultural choices such as film, music, books, affiliation with organizations, advocacy of causes, lifestreaming activities from vacations, working out, and eating form the eclectic range from which choices are made to project a digital social identity. And if the profile stands in as the symbolic representation of the self in the digital domain, it is also situated in and constructed through a relational tangle with other profiles with which it shares relationships of immediate reciprocity, feedback, and validation loops. These interactive relationships, through device- and platform-based sociality, reorient our conception of selfhood by making it a dialectically produced, always evolving, and anxiety-laden process.

If the presence of the Other is key to our own self-conception, the expanded, distributed, and networked notion of the Other on the social web is key to the anxiety-inducing experience of digital sociality, wherein "people are constantly monitoring themselves against the expectations of others" (Marwick 2013, 220). It is safe to claim that online relational dynamics, when combined with the effect of the teeming number of images about normative ways of being that proliferate in the digital domain, add to and fortify the power of affordances, behavioral knowledge, and algorithmic power in advancing particular norms of online selfhood. This mechanism functions through the suasive force of the "power of the image" (Rose 1999, 243) in providing scripts of life that, similar to the discursive regimes about behavioral norms elaborated by Elias (2000), become idealized templates for millions to emulate online. In words written two decades ago to describe the power of images in constructing a normative self in Western modernity, but prescient enough that they could just as well have been written about the cultural power of images today in creating a normative self online, Nicholas Rose elaborates, "According to this meta-world of images and values, more luminous and real than any other world we know, the self is to be reshaped, remodeled so that it can succeed in emitting the signs of a skilled performance. And of this continuous performance of our lives, we each are, ourselves, to be the sternest and most constant critic" (Rose 1999, 243).

The new entrants on the social web and digital platforms need only emulate those aspirational profiles that have attained a certain status of popularity and repute (often attaining the tag of social media influencers) to learn the gamut of ideal practices that create a desirable digital identity. As it does with everything, the social web amplifies this ability to observe and emulate at a computational scale wherein the taking of a selfie, the outpouring of one's life online, or the strategic positioning of oneself as a brand (which define the three traits in focus here) seem logical attributes of following the well-worn commonsensical paths online. It is no surprise, therefore, that evidence of the three digital cultural practices presented here as the defining features of the ideal online subject emerge within media reports, popular culture, and critical commentary emerging from across the world. There surely are variations within how these practices find expression in distinct cultural milieus, and yet the broad parameters of their imbrication within the digital ecology have left few parts of the digitally connected parts of our planet untouched. The combined power of social media affordances, algorithmic rewards, and the persuasive power of images creates a gestalt effect realizing these three prominent cultural practices, analyzed sequentially below.

The Global Selfie Culture

The sweeping scale of digital culture is often best represented by key quantifiable parameters that give us a sense of its expanse, and the selfie culture today (which is global in every sense of the word) is one such parameter. When NASA decided to celebrate Earth Day in 2014 by creating a "global selfie" (Northon 2014), it did so through a collage of 36,422 selfies from 113 different countries in all five continents to draw attention to the precarity of our planet and the imminent threats to its sustainable future. The choice of selfies, "from Antarctica to Yemen, Greenland to Guatemala, Micronesia to the Maldives, Pakistan, Poland, Peru" (Cole 2014) to create a global mosaic underscored a recognition of the global scale of the cultural phenomenon of selfies. In the year 2015, Google alone reported a staggering 24 billion selfies uploaded by 200 million people on the Google Photos application (Gray 2016), and other estimates include a million selfies a day (Walden 2016), with future projections signaling exponential growth. The global expanse of the practice is evident in the ubiquity of the selfie but also in media coverage of the phenomenon in addition to books and academic studies analyzing its medical, legal, social, and psychological dimensions. A collection of scholarly essays on selfies was introduced by the editors with the question "What Does the Selfie Say? Investigating a *Global* Phenomenon" (Senft and Baym 2015, my italics), thus signaling that the diverse national iterations of the selfie phenomenon explored by scholars in the collection spanned national and cultural boundaries. Aided by the saturation of social life with camera-fitted and networked smartphones and endorsed by global and local celebrities taking and posting their own selfies, the global selfie culture instantiates, in each act of its clicking and sharing, the ideology of individuation that animates the liberal subject of modernity.

The percolation of the term *selfie* (and the culture it signifies) within popular discourse is a key marker of the spreading global phenomenon. In 2013 the *Oxford English Dictionary* deemed it the word of the year, defining it as "a photographic self-portrait; esp. one taken with a smartphone or webcam and shared via social media." There is also a Wikipedia page devoted to the term. In addition to those key exemplars of an idea's cultural salience, as of 2020 there were at least two movies (one English and one in Russian), a television show, and several songs in various languages bearing the word *selfie* as a title. Cultural and consumer products that use variations of the term abound globally, including songs and movies such as *Selfie Raja* (2016) in Telugu (see Chowdhary 2016) and *Oru Vadakkan Selfie* (2015; translated as "A northerner selfie") in Malayalam; accessory products (e.g., the selfie stick); and fictional and academic books. As the culture has globalized, so have the risks associated with it, including the spiraling number of selfie-related deaths each year, which have earned a derivative moniker of *killfie* (Lamba et al. 2016). An indication of the prevalence of the practice in non-Western locations can be gauged by the fact that the country with the largest number of selfie-related deaths is India (Coffey 2017), which accounted for 60 percent of all global selfie-related deaths that occurred within the two-year period from March 2014 to September 2016 (Lamba et al. 2016). The phenomenon has also led to the coinage of the term *selfitis* to denote a condition of taking and posting an excessive number of selfies (Balakrishnan and Griffiths 2018; Knapton 2017) as well as official government advisories about safe selfie-taking practices (Thiagarajan 2017) and legal demarcations such as no-selfie zones to prevent accidents.

This global resonance of the selfie culture can be explained, at least partly, by two technological differences that make it distinct from prior photographic practices. The first is that the combination of a camera-enabled smartphone with an outstretched arm obviates one's dependence on a second person for taking one's photograph. This assemblage of the camera and the stretched arm creates sufficient distance between the lens and the object (the self) to be photographed, thus framing one's entire corporeal presence and especially the face within the composition of the image. The second technological distinction from earlier photography lies in the networked camera that makes the instantaneous distribution of the image on social media the "the very raison d'être of a selfie" (Tifentale 2014, 11). The act, therefore, is simultaneously personal and intimate but also public and social, encapsulating a binary that is symptomatic of the individuated subject whose unique interiority is inculcated for and in the process of public narration and expression. As elaborated on in exploring the genealogy of the normative subject of modernity above, the public, expressive side is an inseparable dimension of the individuated subject and in fact *constitutes* it. It is, after all, in the expressions and confessions "that are true to an inner reality, through the self-examination that precedes and accompanies speech" that "one is subjectified by another" (Rose 1999, 244). The selfie is expressive of one's unique personhood, and its online social dissemination is key to constituting the digital self that encases and projects that unique singularity.

The selfie emphasizes the unique me-ness of the subject of the image by making him or her the central focus of the camera's gaze, thus telling its viewers, "See me showing you me" (Frosh 2015, 1610). Its centrality of the individual is underscored by other linguistic iterations of the term such as *ego portrait* in Quebecois French (Walden 2016) as well as studies that claim that habitual selfie takers have a much higher "self-favoring bias" than others (Boult 2016). The emphasis on one's uniqueness—a key hallmark of the individuality of the globalizing selfhood—is borne out by the increasingly perilous global practice of taking extreme selfies clicked in situations of high risk, often leading to death or injury. The daring, courageous, and maverick self sought to be portrayed in extreme selfies is constituted within the cycle of clicking, sharing, and feedback that makes up the selfie loop. That the me-ness of the selfie is enacted through a visual rather than a textual portrait is explained by the designed centrality of the photograph within the affordances of social media platforms (Marwick 2013). Social networking sites such as Facebook, Instagram, and Snapchat as well as popular photo sharing and storing applications such as Flickr, Google Photos, iPhoto, and Imgur emphasize visuality as the key to online sociality and in many cases entirely obviate the need for textual descriptions by substituting them with the hashtag #selfie. On Facebook, a culture of anti-anonymity and an interactional immersion in each other's digital lives is premised on crafting a visual culture wherein photographs are far more likely to be rewarded with likes, comments, and interactions (Cirucci 2015).

The global adoption of social media platforms is key to the rise of the selfie culture, as it is only through pictures that users get to know other users and validate the authenticity of their profiles on digital platforms because "the myth of photographic truth lends photography a credibility that text lacks" (Marwick 2013, 143). In presenting the global selfie culture as a symptom of the radical individuality of the globalizing selfhood, the goal is to exemplify the aspects of individualism that are key to the ideal subject, brought into being through the sanctions and seductions of social media platforms. It would not be a stretch to surmise from our analysis that the ideologies of selfhood made pervasive on the web must percolate into off-line life, thus fashioning social life more generally in the real world—a fact just as true for the characteristic of self-revelation (expressed in the lifestreaming culture) that this study identifies as a second key dimension of this ideal subject.

The Global Lifestreaming Culture

If the global selfie culture's emphasis on "me-ness" validates key attributes of individualism, then the practice of continuous self-revelation through pouring out our innermost thoughts and banal details of our quotidian lives online symbolizes the second related dimension of this normative digital subject. Broadly labeled as lifestreaming, which is the "the ongoing sharing of personal information to a networked audience" (Marwick 2013, 208), it is a pervasive aspect of digital culture today, as seen in the expressive practices of social media updates, blogging, and vlogging, among others. It is a consequence of an always-on digital culture wherein the traces we leave behind cumulatively create "a digital portrait of one's actions and thoughts" (208) pointing toward one's unique "inner domain" (Rose 1996, 23). Just as the selfie culture has a global span and presence, the phenomenon of lifestreaming comprising continuous self-expression is a global consequence of the web's affordances that foster the creation and sustenance of a public online identity carved over time through innumerable digital traces. These streams of online self-expressions are only the digital avatar of prior practices of confession, therapeutic self-excavation, and the overall emphasis on articulating one's unique innerness that was an essential component of the idealized subjectivity emerging along with Europe's modernity.

Lifestreaming, which emphasizes the public articulations of one's innerness, is the obverse side of individuality since it helps both constitute and express it. This relationship between self-expression and a distinct self that is "the site of consciousness and judgement" (Rose 1999, 221) was apparent within the medico-legal as well as the sociocultural discourses during middle-century Europe. Elaborating on the role played by the "confessional diary," one site of such self-expression, Rose shows how it functioned as a mirror of "one's sinfulness" that "both calibrated one's lapses and bore witness to the survival of one's faith; the self was to become both sinner and judge (Rose 1999, 224). The simultaneously public and personal act of diary writing, or journaling, emerges as a key precursor to how "expressive individuation has become one of the cornerstones of modern culture" (Taylor 1989, 376). Revealing our inner core by parsing away the repressive sociocultural layers enfolded within the psyche was a means to psychic freedom and "the apotheosis of the celebration of the individual in capitalist ideology" (Rose 1999, 219). The proliferation of various therapeutic mechanisms that placed the subject under a pervasive gaze represented an ironic inversion of technologies of freedom metamorphosing into structures of discipline and control.

Even though the expressive individuality encapsulated within practices of lifestreaming has manifested itself through different channels that have evolved along with the web, its definitive earliest iteration was the blogging culture in the first decade of this millennium that witnessed common users taking to the internet to deliberate on a multiplicity of issues ranging from the personal to the political, the public to the private. Even as the expectation that online financial transactions leading to sustainable, profit-making internet businesses would form the initial bedrock of digital culture was belied with the dot-com bust at the turn of the millennium, it was the organic blogging culture that steadily grew from under the shadows of the big digital media entities that "closed the gap between Internet and society" (Lovink 2008, 4). Situated at the intersection of the public and the private and often displaying a conversational and confessional tone, the increasingly widespread culture of blogging soon earned the moniker of "public diaries" (7), capturing its simultaneous public and private dimensions.

In the broad range they encompassed, blogs also shared the entrepreneurial spirit foregrounding the individual voice of the writers who, in carefully crafting their commentaries on the issues of their choice, were also cultivating public identities by positioning themselves within a global conversation. Their episodic rhythms and personal tones and the particularities of style, choice, and positionality on a topic represented perhaps the first digital iteration of the idea "that each human being has some original and unrepeatable 'measure'" and that "we are all called to live up to our originality" (Taylor 1989, 376). In building the groundwork for an expressive, participatory ethos on the web, the early blogging culture, which was soon global, was a vital precursor to and charted the path for a much deeper and extensive mode of online expression and interactivity as represented in the subsequent social media explosion during what has been called Web 2.0.

That explosion has further deepened the global culture of lifestreaming and finds expression in global social media practices such as microblogging sites (e.g., Twitter), through video blogging on platforms such as YouTube (henceforth termed vlogs, a neologism of video weblogs), and live video blogging through platforms such as Facebook Live and Twitter-owned Periscope. The move from text-based to video blogging (Biel and Gatica-Perez 2010), while a reflection of the changing technological underpinnings of the digital sphere, significantly transforms the nature of lifestreaming wherein a conversational monologue facing the camera and addressed to an imagined audience is able to muster a multitude of affective, gestural, tonal, and nonverbal cues that written text is incapable of transmitting. The global proliferation of vlogs (as illustrated through a simple search on video-sharing platforms such as YouTube) is a "direct multimodal extension of traditional text-based blogging, where spoken words (i.e. what is said) are enriched by the complex nonverbal behavior displayed in front of the camera" (Biel and Gatica-Perez 2010) and have expanded and democratized the global conversation by giving a voice to anyone with access to a computer or a phone.

The burgeoning culture of video blogs finds expression on peer-sharing platforms such as YouTube and Twitch (as well as on social network platforms such as Facebook), which are teeming with conversational videos of faces talking into cameras from living rooms, thus replicating a genre that "opens up a world of strangers to strangers, where biographical sharing creates an intimate, highly personalizing 'publicly private and privately public' sphere" (Lange 2007, quoted in Gibson 2016). While there is an established subculture of monetizing the vlogging genre by influencers (discussed below), the personal and intimate aspects of these vlogs thrive outside market-driven logics (Luers 2007) and instantiate the expressive individuality that animates the cultural practice of lifestreaming. Vlogs that are often numbered in order to show their chronological sequence (just like a dated diary) are both an account for the audiences who may stumble upon them and a biographical record for the future self of the vloggers, thus functioning as a log of one's life journey. Milestones on that journey include personal growth, academic and professional achievements, and as tragedies and life events such as birth and death. For instance, the growing role played by personal vlogs as a medium of seeking cathartic solace during bereavement and mourning from strangers in the digital community has made "grieving publicly and seeking support among strangers . . . a normative social act" (Gibson 2016, 638), thus making platforms such as YouTube "not secondary or supplementary" but " a primary social space" (637) for seeking comfort and consolation. The fact that there is virtually no aspect of our lives that remains outside the purview of these vlogs underscores how broadcasting ourselves through the process of lifestreaming is a key element of normative subjectivity within the digital sphere.

The global geographical span of the vlogging culture, while increasingly self-evident within the digital and popular discourse, can be established using freely available geo search tools that allow one to conduct searches for geotagged videos uploaded on platforms such as YouTube to determine their geographical locations. The open-source YouTube geo search tool (GitHub, n.d.) hosted on the software depository GitHub provides a search interface through which one can search YouTube videos by keywords and locations in addition to being able to define a preferred radius from the chosen location (0 to 1000 kilometers) as well as the video upload time (ranging from "anytime" to "the past year," with intervals in between). It can be turned into a useful research tool for assessing the geographical distribution of YouTube's content on a particular topic with the important caveat that only a certain percentage of videos uploaded on YouTube are geotagged (YouTube-GitHub, n.d.). But since that is an equally randomized filter, one can safely assume it does not introduce a significant bias in the search results. Additionally, the tool returns a maximum of fifty videos per search, which is sufficient for a project such as this where the goal is to ascertain the breadth of the global spread of the vlogging culture and not so much the depth of its concentration in particular locations.

A snapshot of the search results for videos with the term *vlog* in their titles reveals (see table 4.1) that their global spread corresponds with availability and access to the internet. While no major city in the world is untouched by the vlogging culture, what supports the larger point about the truly global footprint of the genre is the uploading of vlogs from regions and cities such as Tierra del Fuego in Argentina (five videos), Luanda in Angola (nine videos), Fairbanks in Alaska (fifty videos), Ashgabat in Turkmenistan (seven videos), and Ulaanbaatar in Mongolia (twenty-three videos). There are vlogs uploaded from small island nations (e.g., Vanuatu, Samoa, and American Samoa in the Pacific Ocean and the Faroe Islands in the North Atlantic Ocean) as well as the remotest parts of the world such as Antarctica (five videos), Godthaab in Greenland (twenty-six videos), and Irkutsk in Siberia (thirty-nine videos). By searching geotagged videos in smaller and relatively lesser-known places, the goal here is to establish the ambit of the global vlogging culture, which, while expectedly thriving in the well-known urban centers, has visibly emerged in seemingly distant and unlikely sites. When layered over with the reach of live-blogging applications such as Facebook Live and Periscope as well as with image and multimedia messaging platforms such as Snapchat, the global sweep of the emerging culture of lifestreaming as a key component of the individuated subject is well established. No doubt there are nuanced cultural, linguistic, and regional differences in what people talk about and how, but those differences are in a dialectical interplay with and layered over the common genre of looking into a camera and broadcasting one's life. And just as the centrality of the individual culminates in the global selfie culture and self-disclosing innerness is represented in the culture of lifestreaming, the normative notions of personhood also have entrepreneurial and performative dimensions, as symbolized by the global culture of influencers analyzed below.

Table 4.1 Delineating the global spread of vlogging culture by region

Continent/region	Asia			
	Country	City	No. of Videos	Radius/km
	India	Patna	21	100
		Indore	13	10
		Srinagar	8	10
		Ranchi	8	10
		Vishakhapatnam	5	10
	Nepal	Dharan	2	10
	Japan	Tokyo	50	10
	Mongolia	Ulaanbaatar	23	10
	Turkmenistan	Ashgabat	7	10
	Kazakhstan	Almaty	50	10
	Azerbaijan	Baku	50	10
	China	Beijing	50	10
	Kyrgyzstan	Bishkek	24	10
	Philippines	Manila	50	10
	Russia	Tyumen	44	10
		Yakutsk	39	
		Vorkuta	23	10
		Irkutsk	39	10

Continent/region	Middle East and North Africa			
	Country	City	No. of Videos	Radius/km
	Saudi Arabia	Riyadh	50	10
	Iraq	Karbala	1	10
		Baghdad	0	10
	Iran	Tehran	35	10
		Tabriz	17	10

Continent/region	Africa			
	Country	City	No. of Videos	Radius/km
	Tanzania	Dar es Salaam	7	10
	Zimbabwe	Harare	4	10
	Uganda	Kampala	16	10
	Kenya	Nairobi	50	10
	Botswana	Gaborone	1	10
	South Africa	Bloemfontein	11	10
	Namibia	Windhoek	8	10
	Angola	Luanda	9	10
	Sudan	Khartoum	1	10

Table 4.1 (*continued*)

Continent/region	Latin America			
	Country	City	No. of Videos	Radius/km
	Argentina	Tierra del Fuego	5	10 Km
	Chile	Punta Arenas	4	10 Km
		Puerto Montt	11	10 Km
	Brazil	Manaus	50	10 Km
	Suriname	Paramaribo	4	10 Km
	Venezuela	Barquisimeto	5	10 Km
	North America			
	Country	City	No. of Videos	Radius/km
	USA	Fairbanks, Alaska	50	10
	Canada	Whitehorse	1	10
	Europe			
	Country	City	No. of Videos	Radius/km
	Greenland	Godthaab	26	10
	Iceland	Reykjavik	50	
	Estonia	Tallinn	50	10
	Antarctica			
	N/A	N/A	5	10
	Islands			
	Country	City	No. of Videos	Radius/km
	Vanuatu	Port Vila	3	10
	Fiji	Suva	1	10
	USA	American Samoa	1	
		Kapalua, Hawaii	9	10
		Captain Cook, Hawaii	1	10
	Denmark	Faroe Islands	4	

Note: The number of videos with *vlog* in the title uploaded within a given radius of the named cities. N/A = not applicable; No. = number.

The Global Influencer Culture

The logic propelling both the global selfie and the lifestreaming cultures converges in and allows for the emergence of the rapidly growing global cultural phenomenon of social media influencers who encapsulate the entrepreneurial dimension of the normative subject of social media. Across social media platforms and linguistic, cultural, and national boundaries we see the rise of individual profiles that have gradually begun to command a bevy of followers, fans, and audiences by circumventing the mainstream media institutions. Constructed through the careful and strategic cultivation of their online persona, replete with an abundance of textual and visual lifestreaming updates, bolstered through an interactive presence and a uniquely tailored individual online profile (the combination of which was impossible to create within the prior legacy media ecologies), these star profiles emerge as hubs of attention and engagement within the cacophony of conversations on the social web. Categorized as influencers, who are the "shapers of public opinion who persuade their audience through the conscientious calibration of personae on social media" (Abidin and Ots, 2016, 155) and "deliver curated content to audiences," they often (though not always) use their social capital to "earn income by collaborating with major brands" (Hund 2017, 1). Social media influencers and their related category of micro celebrity-hood (Senft 2008) represent an accentuation and culmination of the prior two features of fetishizing the self (that the selfie culture represents) as well as its construction through an expressive, self-revealing subjectivity (that the lifestreaming culture represents). The culture of influencers and microcelebrities strategically deploys these two prior facets of the selfhood to sculpt one's online self as a brand by invoking and deploying the same strategic steps that solidify and entrench brand identities in the corporate world.

Endorsements of the global emergence of the influencer culture from important quarters within the popular media, especially those focused on business and corporate news, underscore its global cultural salience. In launching *Forbes* magazine's first ever Top Influencers global list in April 2017, Christina Vuleta, the vice president of Forbes Women's Digital Network, affirmed that "it's time to recognize the influencer economy as a legitimate entrepreneurial pursuit," thus giving the media empire's backing for this increasingly visible global trend. As the global list maker of record, with annual lists (*Forbes*, n.d., "Forbes Lists") in areas as diverse as the world's top billionaires, top-earning dead celebrities, best value colleges, the highest paid athletes, and the world's most powerful people and women, *Forbes's* decision to launch its inaugural list of top global influencers underscores their role in cultural, political, and social life globally. Going beyond its list of the top global influencers, *Forbes* now also breaks down its lists by separately ranking the top influencers

(*Forbes*, n.d., "Top Influencers of 2017") in distinct areas such as parenting, fashion, entertainment, fitness, food, technology and business, and (not surprisingly) kids.

The importance of the influencer culture is also affirmed in research reports such as the *Influencer Marketing Report* released by Business Insider Intelligence (Business Insider Store 2019),which predicts the global advertising spend on influencer marketing to touch $15 billion. The growth and entrenchment of this cultural phenomenon can be seen as a continuation (in the digital realm) of analogous cognate ideas such as "early adopters" (Rogers 1983), who are opinion leaders and whom others look to for knowledge about the latest innovations in different aspects of social life. The digital avatar ensures that while earlier opinion leaders relied on word of mouth and traditional media channels, social media influencers disseminate their ideas and thoughts through their personally owned social media profiles, thus having complete control over the frequency, length/amount, and nature of content. The personalization of the process of strategic messaging to present a carefully constructed narrative and garner audience attention is similar to the attempts to construct brand identities, which is the purview of corporations and public relations agencies (Ewen 1996). The appropriation of those strategies by entrepreneurs to create brands represents the culmination of the entrepreneurial subjectivity whose early traces we see within the idealized subject of modernity.

Indeed, the analogies between these temporally apart but culturally similar notions of the ideal person are strikingly similar. Just as their personification of a culture of self-entrepreneurism represented by influencers today, the valorized subjects in seventeenth- and eighteenth-century Europe were "entrepreneurs of themselves, shaping their own lives through the choices they make among the forms of life available to them" (Rose 2000, 230). Similarly, by forswearing reliance on mainstream media institutions and by cultivating direct channels of access, these influencers take charge and become "responsible for their own destinies" (324), thus instantiating the characteristic of responsibilization that defines the ideal neoliberal subject existing and navigating outside the institutions of the welfare state. They represent the apogee of "humans as selves with autonomy, choice, and self-responsibility, equipped with a psychology aspiring to self-fulfillment, actually or potentially *running their lives as a kind of enterprise* of themselves" (Rose 1996, 33, my italics). The culmination of the logic of radical individualism and self-disclosure within the influencer culture ensures that in the digital ecology, we are all managers and shapers of our brands and must make prudent choices to construct their public identities. Crucially, the cultural idea of individual responsibility and entrepreneurship of the self arises directly from the economic logic of enterprise that animates capitalism. It aligns seamlessly with the free-market notion of autonomous individuals functioning as discrete economic units pursuing their rational self-interests through well-calculated economic decisions. On the social web, ascriptions of choice signal a unique taste and play an important role in curating the discrete selfhood that is a necessity for self-branding.

These cultural, political, and social choices are also vital to the performance of authenticity that helps anchor the individuated self deep inside the core of their being, thus providing a criteria for distinguishing contrived and inauthentic identities from "real" ones. Successful influencers therefore must pass the test of reflecting their true inner selves, which requires walking a "very tenuous definitional frame" given that authenticity is at best "a social judgment that is always made in distinction to something else" (Marwick 2013, 120). Consistency of one's views and online posts over time, despite being an entirely subjective attribute of authenticity, is a key strategy through which realness is projected online. Successful self-branding efforts, therefore, often use the judicious curation of information that performs a longitudinally consistent online identity.

The global influencer culture visible today in the form of opinion leaders and hubs of attention and interactivity within different areas of online culture represents the culmination of the three dimensions of normative subjectivity this chapter has presented as the defining parameters of an ideal personhood being globalized by the cultural architectures of the social web. It also encapsulates within it the prior cultures of selfies and lifestreaming that form the foundation on which the influencer culture thrives by democratizing celebrity hood, as it theoretically opens up the hallways of fame and prominent visibility to all. In a world where everyone is potentially fameworthy and capable of being an influencer, the globalizing digital ecology functions to articulate new meanings for categories such as fame, celebrity, influence, and community. Infrastructural nudges that valorize this trifecta of the self arguably take up space by interacting with and often displacing other cultural notions that held sway in different milieus. The attempt here to both show the globalization of this distinctly cultural phenomenon and emphasize its distinct historical and geographical roots seeks to underscore that its democratizing aspects must be dialectically juxtaposed with the novel manifestation of power it represents.

Conclusions

To show the specific norms of selfhood globalizing through mechanisms such as the affordances, default settings, algorithmic regulation, and the power of the image is to also understand the complex nature of global power today. Far from the top-down, unidimensional imposition that some prior theories of cultural dominance imagined, cultural power today operates through negotiated and circumscribed pathways that represent the dialectic of expression and restraint (Guins 2009; Deleuze 1992). To acknowledge the simultaneously enabling and constraining potential of digital technology is to advance a nuanced understanding of its modalities of control that both sees truth in the visions of the global web as an organic, ground-up expression of the demos (Jenkins 2008; Benkler 2007) and represents an unprecedented force for reshaping global culture. While the effects of digital culture in shaping behavioral norms are widely being studied, this project extends but also departs from their trajectories to show how ongoing changes cannot be divorced from *global* relationships of power.

Continuously being resisted and hence never complete, always processual, visible more in dominant trends rather than in complete, total, and final imposition, the social web's ideal subject undoubtedly competes with parallel visions and narratives of selfhood that it must coexist with. Showing its contingent origins is to also challenge claims of universality that invariably align with the emancipatory readings of the global web's uptake. After all, the position that the internet is what we make of it and that it allows users to be who they are rather than imposing cultural and behavioral change as a precondition of participation obviates and sidesteps the need for analysis of the specific modalities of power on the web. By taking an interactional position instead, this study presents cultural change as the result of a negotiation between the inherent cultural, social, and political values embedded within the cultural architectures of the web and what users bring to the medium. This dialectical position channels the debate about technological determinism (Hutchby 2001; Peters 2017) that eschews both the extreme positions of radical constructivism and absolute determinism to point to a more interactional understanding of how media technologies reshape culture in their wake. Similarly, tracing the genealogy of the social web's self within particular historical conjunctures is not to proffer an unbroken cause and effect link between the processes that gave rise to the modern Western self and the current digital practices of selfies, lifestreaming, and self-branding. Instead, pointing to prior traces of these features of subjectivity and their renewed expression in the digital realm that globalize them, far more than ever before, allows us to historicize the present.

5

SOVEREIGNTY

T HE EXTENT TO WHICH THE DIGITAL DOMAIN WOULD emerge as a site of geopolitical contestations in the post-COVID-19 era could hardly have been predicted. Instances such as the US push towards a "clean network" (targeting Huawei and other Chinese tech companies), India's banning of a slew of Chinese apps (including TikTok), and the increasingly assertive attempts by nation-states to align the digital domain with their political goals and agendas are only precursors to how intense such conflicts will be in the future. Increasingly, the ways in which the expanding digital culture conflicts with the authority of the nation-state, the most prominent repository of power in modernity, are vital to understanding the cultural and political sway of the global digital infrastructures that compose the web. A nation-state's ability to regulate information and enforce its laws within its geographically demarcated boundary has been historically solidified through mutually beneficial arrangements among countries in the post-Westphalian global order. These agreements constrained states into reciprocally binding commitments that respected mutual territorial integrity (except, of course, in cases of wars and conflicts) and withstood (in varying degrees) challenges such as the headwinds of globalization, which directly impinged on the preeminent authority of the nation-state (Sassen 1998, 2007; Held 2004; Rosenau 1999). The global rise of the internet, whose decentralized architecture presents new centrifugal pressures over the centralizing and centripetal tendencies of the nation-state, gave rise to intense debates in the early years of the web (Wriston 1997; Perritt 1998) about the latter's ability to weather the challenges posed by networked digital technologies. Almost two decades of global adoption of the internet presents us with an apt moment for evaluating how the early anxieties about the relationship between the web and sovereignty of nation-states have panned out. What are the ways in which nation-states find themselves challenged because of the technological architectures of the emerging global digital culture? How do digitized networked media further entrench the power of states by aiding in their ability to enforce laws and monitor and discipline "deviant" behavior?

In answering these questions about the relationship between nation-states and the internet, this chapter evaluates one of the most prominent sites of conflict: where the influence of the digital ecosystem's "soft infra-structures" has been felt and resisted. The anxieties expressed about the en-durance of sovereignty in the face of challenges posed by the web and digital media technologies, just as they were being adopted globally at the turn of the millennium, arose from new media's ability to bypass state control to create a "global conversation" that was bound to put "pressure on sovereign governments" (Wriston 1997, 175) by spreading the "virus of freedom" (172). In distinguishing the internet from prior media technologies such as the tele-graph, telephone, radio, and television, scholars pointed to how the internet was "not susceptible to the same physical and regulatory controls" (Perritt 1998, 427). Almost two decades later, some of those concerns seem to have been unfounded in the light of the continuing resilience of the nation-state (Kohl and Fox 2017), despite the rapid global adoption of the web. However, there is also significant evidence to show that in key areas such as secu-rity, legal jurisdiction, and the flow of cultural and informational content, nation-states find themselves challenged by the technological novelty of the medium in unprecedented ways. Situated at the midpoint of the web's glob-al adoption (with just over 50 percent of the global population connected today), recent scholarship on the web's effects on national sovereignty has the luxury of being concrete instead of conjectural, as one can evaluate the specific areas of challenge and pushback (Kohl and Fox 2017; Kumar 2010) in the ongoing tussle between the nation-state and the internet.

In navigating through the debate, this chapter advances the idea of differential sovereignty by pointing to radical disparities and variations in power wielded by nations in their ability to engage with and respond to its challenges. It argues that while the challenge posed to national sovereignty by the cultural and political dimensions of what this book calls infrastruc-tures of control has been met and responded to in increasingly ingenious ways, states' abilities to assert sovereign authority in key areas are also sig-nificantly compromised in comparison with the predigital era. More cru-cially, this chapter shows that the degree and extent to which nation-states are able to assert their influence in the digital domain are determined by the prior alignment of the web's cultural and political architecture with those of particular nation-states. That ability is also directly proportional to the power wielded by nations in the off-line world. The ideologies inherent within the dominant parts of the web's soft infrastructures (e.g., conventions, standards, and protocols) and the geographical distribution of its material infrastructures (e.g., offices, servers, data centers, cables, and financial gateways) make the digital ecosystem more susceptible to pressures from some nations as opposed to others. This claim of differential power locates digital media networks within the economic, political, and technological force field of global geopolitics, thus making them sites of and subject to the same maneuverings and tussles that define other aspects of relationships among nations.

The fact that the spread of networked media technologies impacts nations differently has already been acknowledged by prior scholars (e.g., Perritt 1998, 431) who argued for the variable effects of the internet by claiming that the centralized "non-liberal governments" were at far greater threat from the globalizing information technologies than the liberal states where power was already decentralized. Subsequent events, such as the tide of color revolutions in the new millennium that sought to topple illiberal regimes by effectively deploying the subversive affordances of the web, have borne out claims of variable effects of the digital information technologies. In extending that argument to the broader gamut of the ongoing global tug-of-war between the digital ecosystem and national sovereignty, this chapter pushes back against claims that present the global comity of nations as a homogenous group facing similar challenges and that can similarly counteract the influence of the web. While the tussle between older and newer forms of power, represented respectively by the nation-state and networked digital media technologies, has continued across different areas of social, political, and legal domains, the outcome of those conflicts is not predetermined and often is contingent on the specific actors involved in the case.

This claim about variable power presumes that the post-Westphalian world system, first globalized through colonialism and then through the emerging postwar, postcolonial global order, has created a hierarchical structure of states with varying degrees of capacities, access to resources, and ability to assert sovereign authority within their boundaries as well as externally. Among the globalized order of nation-states, the postcolonial nations, newly emerging from the ravages of colonialism (Premnath 2003; Braziel

2006; Chatterjee 1993), form a distinct category defined by their common challenges of underdeveloped institutions, lack of resources, and nascent civil societies thus providing a weaker foundation to these newly emerging countries. Their desire to resist both the poles during the Cold War through the Non Aligned Movement (NAM) and the ensuing call for a New World Information and Communication Order (NWICO) to gain true information sovereignty (Macbride and Roach 1989; Kleinwachter 1989) is a key precursor that signaled early attempts to both preserve their precarious sovereignty and assert themselves in global affairs through collective power. The subsequent rise of postcolonial nation-states and newly emerging formations such as BRICS (Thussu 2015) point to a resurgence that should nevertheless not blind us to the continuing disparities in technological infrastructure as well as corporate, political, and military power that countries can exercise on the global stage. These dissimilarities affect their ability to resist the challenges posed by networked digital media that can arguably chip away at the specific functions that define national sovereignty.

Exploring the conflicts between national sovereignty and key dimensions of digital culture, as this chapter does, also necessitates taking a position on the role of the nation-state in our world. A relatively recent emergence in world history, the present form of the nation-state has acted as the representative of its citizens within global affairs and claimed rights to be the legitimate repository of sovereign authority within its territory. This perspective on the state, acknowledging its role as a protector of its citizens, has touted it as a bulwark against the forces of imperialism, capitalist expansion, and cultural domination (Hall 1997; Kennedy 2001) within the area under its suzerainty. However, this picture of global geopolitics shaped by nation-states would be grossly incomplete in not emphasizing the other violent, homogenizing impulses of nation-states whose emergence has also been premised on brutal marginalization and dehumanization of significant populations that we continue to witness today (Baishya 2012). In this version, the nation-state has been the primary cause of conflict (external and internal) that has used its monopoly on the exercise of violence to suppress dissent, plurality, and human rights and liberty. Both these perspectives on the nation-state are embedded and amply visible within its short but checkered history, which has also been marked by recurring predictions of its impending demise (Appadurai 1996; Hardt and Negri 2000). By acknowledging its dual tendencies, this exploration of the confrontations caused by nation-states facing challenges from digital networks seeks to eschew easy judgments about the value of the nation-state in the present world. Its goal instead is to focus in on the moments and sites of struggle between states and the internet to extend the larger argument about differential sovereignty in the digital realm.

The Evolution of Sovereignty

The origin and evolution of the concept of sovereignty and its various iterations are germane to understanding how the global adoption of networked digital media technologies are challenging the power of nation-states. It helps us underscore why an exploration of the kind attempted in this chapter is both timely and rooted in important historical questions about the nature and status of sovereignty in our world. Historicizing the concept reveals moreover that while this challenge to nation-states is radically distinct from prior ones, it is hardly the first time their absolute sovereignty has been contested and undermined. In fact, the history of the global order from the emergence of the concept of national sovereignty until now has been one of external and internal contestations that have repeatedly sought to undermine the *"supreme legitimate authority within a territory"* (Philpot 1995, 357, italics in original) or a "political community" (Hinsley 1986, 1) that is the nation-state. The difference of the new challenge lies in the combined effect of three distinct features that make it uniquely insurmountable.

The first is that it is posed not by other nations but by nonstate actors, the second that its effects are felt in variable ways depending on the nation-state being challenged, and the third that this challenge is uniquely technological and being posed by a medium whose slippery and unregulatable nature amplifies its disruptive effect. Taken together, these features have created an unprecedented dent in the historical ability of states to assert their writ in key aspects of social life within their defined geographical boundaries. Historically, the notion of sovereignty has been an aspirational ideal with varying levels of concreteness as well as cultural variability determined by the historical moment and the specific nation in question. Treating the idea as some unchanging, homogenous concept that can be equally applied therefore leads to grossly inaccurate generalizations that invariably end up presenting the experience of particular nation-states as representative of the entire global comity of nations and in the process eliding over significant differences in internal and external powers to withstand challenges to their warrant.

As is the case with many abstract concepts, the idea of sovereignty is easier understood than defined. Etymologically, it has roots in the Latin word *superanus*, meaning "above," and the adjectives *superus* and *superbus*, denoting "elevated above others" (Kreijen 2004, 27). Notably, as opposed to raw power that relies on asymmetrical force alone, sovereignty denotes legitimate authority that is rooted in "law, consent, tradition or divine command" (Philpott 1995, 55) and has the general endorsement of those it holds power over. This distinction allows for different iterations of sovereign power over time (Couture and Toupin 2019) with the nation-state being only its latest manifestation. Carl Schmitt defines the sovereign as "he who decides on the exception" (Schmitt 1985, 5) and locates the origins of sovereignty in divinity by arguing that "all significant concepts of the modern theory of the state are secularized theological concepts" (36). Each iteration of worldly sovereignty ranging from monarchy to the nation-state is, for Schmitt, derived from this notion of absolute undivided power residing in the idea of the "engineer of the great machine" (48). For him the sovereign's decision of "exception," which suspends jurisprudence and exists outside the rule of law, is analogous to the miracle in theology that similarly exists outside worldly rationalistic explanations.

The devolution of sovereign power from divinity, onto monarchy, and then to the nation-state represents its morphing nature not only from a decisionistic, personified, and unitary form to a split and fragmented entity (due to checks and balances in a democracy) but also of its changing grounds of legitimacy from a transcendental theistic basis to a popular democratic one. The sovereign nation-state of modernity distinguishes itself from the earlier iterations by being governed by a constitution and gaining its legitimacy from being a representative of the people so that "the general will of Rousseau became identical with the will of the sovereign" (Schmitt 1985, 48). In its present avatar, the nation-state is a necessary condition for the notion of sovereignty, and in fact once the nation-state comes into being, "the concept of sovereignty is sooner or later unavoidable" (Hinsley 1986, 17). This gradual move from transcendental overarching unified power to an immanent and fragmented one that resides in the people (at least theoretically) had an important milestone in the Westphalian peace accord of 1648, which formalized "the sovereign state as the legitimate political unit" (Philpott 1995, 364) and is widely regarded as a singularly important event in its emergence and gradual global adoption.

The importance of the Westphalian treaties in legitimizing the nation-state as the repository of sovereign power is widely acknowledged (Krasner 1999; Kreijen 2004; Philpott 1995; Hinsley 1986) even though the degree and extent of its role has been a subject of significant debate (Osiander 2001; Croxton 1999). The treaties signed in Westphalia at the end of the Thirty Years' War (1618–48) had key exclusions that negated their universal applicability (e.g., they were limited only to European Christendom while excluding non-European regions such as the Ottoman Empire), but they nevertheless started a process of the preeminence of the nation-state in global affairs that has continued an uneven but progressively forward journey since. The challenges now posed to nation-states from digital entities allow us a new vantage point from which to evaluate the endurance of Westphalian sovereignty and its founding premises of "territoriality and the exclusion of external actors from domestic authority structures" (Krasner 1999, 20) within the bounds of a country. As frequent world events show—from the Google Earth controversy (2005) and cyberattacks inside countries starting from the infamous ones in Estonia (2007) to the Iranian uprisings (2009), the ongoing WikiLeaks exposés, and the seemingly successful Russian attempts to subvert the US elections (2016)—digital media technologies have repeatedly helped undermine the sovereignty of nation-states by intervening within and shaping events in ways and to a degree no prior media technology has been able to. By doing so they have disrupted nation-states' claims to be the "sole arbiters of legitimate behavior" (Krasner 1999, 20) within their defined territory.

Even though the challenge of new and digital media technologies is unique, this is by no means the first contestation to national sovereignty given that the evolution of the global order since the treaties of Westphalia has been marked by an unstable disequilibrium, with tussles and conflicts that have routinely violated the policy of nonintervention in a sovereign state. Even setting aside the exceptional instances of war, armed conflict, and other uses of military power, the rules and norms ensuring sovereignty of nation-states have been followed only when it has been in the interest of particular actors and ignored when not, thus creating a system of "organized hypocrisy" (Krasner 1999, 24). Scholars have broadly classified these compromises under the four categories of conventions, contracts, coercion, and imposition, which include actions ranging from conditional monetary aid to economic and political sanctions, interventions to protect human rights, gunboat diplomacy, and postwar treaties that limited sovereign powers of defeated nations.

What is common among all of these mechanisms, however, is that they presume a global order of nation-states where one group or individual country is acting against another. Our present global moment is distinct from the preceding ones due to the increasing preeminence of nonstate actors (including but not limited to the global digital oligopolies) asserting themselves against state actors. Not only do they fail to meet the key conditions of statehood—defined by some as a permanent population, defined territory, government, and the authority to enter into interstate relations (Kreijen 2004)—but their centrifugal, fragmented, and dispersed nature epitomizes the very obverse of the unifying and centralizing tendencies of the nation-state. It is within this broad classification of nonstate actors that we can locate the emerging digital media entities whose constraints on the nation-state we discuss next.

Digital Media's Challenge to National Sovereignty

If academic debates point toward the pressing issues of a time, then debates about the future of the nation-state as internet and digital communication technologies grew and expanded at the turn of the previous century suggest that it consumed scholars from disciplines as diverse as communication and media studies, legal studies, political science, international relations, and sociology (to name a few). Evaluating the apprehensions and prognostications expressed in those debates two decades later, and with the benefit of hindsight, is a valuable exercise not only to gauge the early understandings of the nature and effects of the nascent web but also to analyze claims about the resilience of the nation-state in the particular domains and areas pointed out in those debates. Expectedly, positions in those debates ranged from alarmist claims about a stateless future in disarray (Rosenau 1999; Wriston 1997) to the other extreme of a nation-state structure further strengthened by emerging media technologies (Goldsmith 1997; Trachtman 1998; Perritt 1998). Subsequent global events have proved both those positions to have been partly correct, and yet the reasons proffered within them are useful to our current analysis of the effect of the web and digital culture on national sovereignties.

Even in their disagreement, both these paradigms of alarm and reassurance about the future of the nation-state acknowledge the technological novelty of the emerging media apparatus while disagreeing on the uses and end goals it could be put to. Claims about the withering power of nation-states located the emerging digital media networks as part of larger unfolding processes such as globalization (Appadurai 1996; Sassen 1998, 2007; Held 2004; Rosenau 1999; Hardt and Negri 2000) and the resulting proliferation of nonstate entities that challenged the traditional domain of nation-states. The centrifugal forces of subnational hierarchies such as transnationally connected "global cities" (Sassen 1998, xx) "in which multiple global circuits intersect" (Sassen 2007, 20), networks of NGOs, and social movements as well as the restraining effect of supranational hierarchies (that exist above the nation-state structure) such as global covenants, organizations, and global financial and trade markets (Sassen 2007; Krasner 1999) had already begun the process of undermining the traditional structures of hierarchy of the state-centric global order from above and below. The arrival and rapid growth of the internet leading to the emergence of digital media oligopolies therefore only marks the culmination of a process of the continuous and gradual withering of the nation-state in the face of strengthening nonstate actors during the last decades of the previous century.

A Different Type of Nonstate Actor

The global digital network presents itself as yet another nonstate actor but one whose radical novelty arises from its technological architecture, which presents a structural break from prior media technologies. Its fundamental differences are rooted in the reasons that led to its invention, which included the pressing need to create a "survivable" network that would last "long enough in a nuclear strike" (Peters 2016, 95). The drive to invent "a nuclear-proof method of communicating" (Ryann 2010, 13) at the height of the Cold War proved true the adage that wars or threats of them have historically played a vital role in the development of media and communication technologies (Mumford 1934). While an exhaustive description of the technological foundations of the internet is outside the scope of this chapter, it is important to gesture toward the central attribute that differentiates it from the prior media technologies and makes its regulation through routine mechanisms by the nation-state a "Sisyphean task" (Morris and Waisbord 2001, viii). That difference lies in the nonlinearity of its process of data transmission, also called "packet-switching" (Banks 2008; Peters 2016; Ryann 2010), which is a mechanism through which a piece of data can be broken down into multiple tiny parts that can each independently travel along potentially different but the shortest possible routes to the destination node (or computer) and be reassembled there to re-create the whole. The software governing this process, called TCP/IP (transfer control protocol/internet protocol), has been called the "essence" of the internet (Ryann 2010, 39) that encapsulates the design of a "distributed network" (Deibert 2002; Peters 2016) wherein data can reroute itself around the damaged parts of a network in real time. Not only was this modality of data transmission distinct from the existing protocols adopted by the communication industries (e.g., telecom networks such as AT&T), but its centrifugal, decentralized, and dispersed ethos is diametrically opposed to the centripetal tendencies of the hierarchical, unifying, and top-down structure of the nation-state. This stark difference (from prior media technologies) in its organizational design has earned it the rubric of "anti-Westphalian" by scholars (Mueller 2017) and forms the bedrock of the structural and technological challenge that the digitally networked World Wide Web poses to the classical sovereign.

The web's seemingly unregulatable design weakens states' abilities to enforce their power in key areas of social and political life, including the control and regulation of the flow of information within and across their borders. Their ability to regulate the flow of information has been a primary concern of nation-states (Morris and Waisbord 2001) that have invariably scrutinized trade and flows of media, cultural, and information products just as closely (if not far more so) than other categories of products. This is explainable given the centrality of cultural texts in the construction of national identity that are foundational to a nation-state and the resulting strategic importance of telecommunication and media networks through which those texts flow. Nation-states ranging across geographical regions, with varying political and cultural orientations and encompassing radical disparities in resources, wealth, and technological progress, all have specific regulations about media ownership (Valcke 2009; Harcourt and Picard 2009; Kumar 2014) that govern the flow of cultural, media, and informational goods across their borders.

Given its importance, this domain has witnessed a constant struggle wherein the degree and extent of a nation-state's success in shaping informational and cultural flows to align with its national and cultural identity has been determined by its technological and institutional strengths. It was precisely this asymmetry in the global trade of information and cultural products that led to the demand for a New World Information and Communication Order (NWICO) that called for the "decolonization of information" (MacBride and Roach 1989, 4) and a restoration of balance within the global milieu. The fact that this call arose primarily from nations recently liberated from the clutches of colonialism with comparatively underdeveloped cultural and media industries underscores the claim of variable power in the face of challenges from global information industries that this chapter seeks to advance. As the specific case studies of conflict discussed below will show, given the technological nature of the digital media infrastructure, the differential power is far more pronounced in states' abilities to regulate it than it was in the case of prior media technologies.

The Technological Nature of the Challenge

The continuing tussle between media technologies and the nation-state represents only "the latest assault on state sovereignty" (Morris and Waisbord 2001, 8), but its technological challenge makes it the most persistent counterforce yet subverting the national regimes of media, culture, and information. To be sure, this counterforce has not been ignored, and nation-states have scrambled to mitigate its disruptive effects (to their authority) despite the seeming technological impossibility of doing so. In a reprise of the NWICO debate, this need to contain the effects of the all-pervasive web within their borders has been felt far more urgently by the developing, non-Western, often postcolonial states, a phenomenon explained perhaps by the Euro-American dominance of the web in terms of content, its technological and logistical underpinnings (e.g., domain name registration), its cultural architecture (see the chapter on selfhood), and the physical location of its dominant hubs. These concerns have been raised in key stakeholder meetings such as the annual World Summit on Information Societies (WSIS) that have provided a forum for conversations about broader stakeholder participation in the process of internet governance, including discussions about and the gradual devolution of American control over ICANN (Internet Corporation for Assigned Names and Numbers), the body responsible for domain name registration for websites (Mueller 2017; DeNardis 2014).

The areas of conflict over the emerging medium's challenge go far beyond governance issues, and so the pushback too has included a complex mix of technological and nontechnological measures to create cyberborders including strategies such as filtering and geo-blocking of sites (Deibert et al. 2008, 2011), deletion and removal of content from sites, and legal and financial means to penalize offending actors. Determining the precise location of entities (sites, users, servers) is a prerequisite for creating digital enclaves on the web, and that is now easy and commonplace with a host of geo-identification technologies that can identify locations with substantial accuracy, thus helping block sites and preventing content originating from particular locations from being accessed by users in other regions (Svantesson 2017). The availability of these and other technologies has ensured that the general ability of states to regulate the internet has been gradually strengthening, with scholars tracing the tightening controls from a phase of open commons (1960–2000) to one of increasingly denied access (2000–2005) to the diversification of controlling mechanisms in the access-controlled phase (2005–10) and finally to the current phase (2010 and beyond) of public contestations over access (Deibert et al. 2011). States now routinely delegate the task of restricting access to parts or the whole of the web within their countries to second- and third-tier intermediaries such as ISPs, cybercafe owners, and last-mile providers of the physical network that control access lower down the chain (Wei 2017), financial intermediaries that support them, and search engines and browsers that function as gatekeepers to the online content.

Today, extreme steps such as the complete shutdown of the internet or the blockage of entire platforms, far from revealing the strength of a state, in fact reveal its inability to assert its leverage to negotiate with actors to remove content; they also show the lack of technological ability to micro target those specific web pages or content they find problematic. In an age of expanding discourses of rights and freedoms, total shutdowns also mean that states have to withstand intense global and national scrutiny, thus making it an undesirable option but often the only one available. These total blockages are especially self-defeating because even as cyberborders become easy to create, so are they becoming easier to bypass and circumvent with the growing sophistication of geo-evasion technologies (e.g., virtual private networks, evading identification through the Tor browser, and the ability to mirror sites on different parts of the web through new technologies [IPFS, n.d.]), allowing users to dodge surveillance mechanisms in a constantly unfolding tactical cat-and-mouse game wherein each side is continuously trying to prevail. Scholars contend that this "world historical" struggle (Mueller 2017) where "a new world order is at stake" (van Dijck, Poell, and De Waal 2018, 165) will continue into the unforeseeable future as states attempt to align the web to their national, cultural, and legal values and ideologies. Strategies of national securitization, territorialization of information flows, and the control of critical internet resources will increasingly be deployed to mold the web according to national preferences.

National and Regional Attempts at Alignment

Evidence of these attempts are visible in the legal arena as well through laws such as the Right to Forget law (Fazlioglu 2013) and the General Data Protection Regulation (GDPR) in the EU, court orders to block access to particular websites within countries, and the routine requests for removal of information from search engine results (Google Transparency Report, n.d.). While acknowledging these widespread attempts at alignment by sovereign states, it is equally important to note two crucial qualifications connected to the larger argument of this chapter and by extension of this book. First, the specificities of the technological infrastructure ensure that these attempts are never entirely successful, with substantial scope for leakages, circumventions, and alternative pathways of access (Svantesson 2017). In showing how state maneuvers toward alignment are "both irresistible for states to attempt, and impossible for states fully to achieve" (104), Mueller (2017) ascribes this partial failure to the "inherent clash between alignment and the economic efficiencies and capabilities of digital technology" (104). These failures and partial successes, however, have not stopped states from trying. The second point worth noting is that substantial differences exist between nation-states' abilities to even attempt the kind of controls described above. These differences in states' abilities to align the digital domain with their national priorities are evident in the recent enmeshing of the digital sphere within geopolitical conflicts. Even as a border skirmish between India and China led to India banning over two hundred Chinese applications in 2020 (Pham 2020), it is also true that four of the top five smartphone brands in India (as per their market share) continue to be Chinese companies (*Gadgets Now* 2020). US attempts at similar alignment, on the other hand, have not only successfully purged Chinese companies and apps from within its borders but also resulted in a gradually successful global campaign (Duckett 2020) to convince many other countries to take similar steps by signing on to its "Clean Network" program. These differences show how global disparities in diplomatic and political clout as well as access to financial and technological resources determine a state's ability to align the internet to their designs within and outside their borders. The unique case of China (discussed below) and other similar case studies of tussles between countries and the digital network explored in the subsequent sections aptly establish this differential power.

The case of the Great Firewall of China (GFW) presents a classic instantiation of the tussle between the dispersive, centrifugal ethos of the internet and the centralizing, hierarchical tendencies of the nation-state, and one that any discussion about the nature of sovereignty in the age of digital networks must engage with. Undoubtedly, the Chinese state has created one of the most sophisticated technological mechanisms to regulate access to the web, which functions like a "semipermeable membrane" (Goldsmith and Wu 2006, 92), thus creating an enclosure with a highly controlled and administered pathway to the rest of the internet. The technologies and strategies adopted to regulate internet access within China are a hybrid of hard and totalizing methods such as blocking entire websites and domains from being accessed in the country as well as soft methods that allow access but regulate content (Bamman, O'Connor, and Smith 2012), invariably with the help of a network of intermediaries. By making the granting of licenses to internet service providers contingent on their acceptance of the state's mandate on acceptable content (e.g., removal of content related to the nine basic prohibitions)[1] and by making the intermediaries liable if they fail to block or delete prohibited content, a regime for "mandatory self-regulation" (Wei 2017) has been instituted on the Chinese web. Over the years, these cyberborders have been successful in creating a thriving version of the Chinese web with a self-sufficient internal ecosystem and a culturally defined market where the "the content and the audience share common cultural traits" (Taneja and Wu 2014, 299). What is important to note, however, is that the mechanisms to create the GFW have combined top-down approaches with participatory ground-up mechanisms where users are actively involved in the process of regulating content (e.g., through community committees that adjudicate reviews, complaints, and disputes on China's microblogging platform Sina Weibo), thus necessitating a buy-in from the users for the rules to be effectively implemented.

These hybrid regulatory mechanisms that involve common users, when juxtaposed with the exponentially increasing usage of tools to scale past the GFW (most prominently the use of VPNs, which allow users to route their traffic to a blocked website through an external address [Yang and Liu, 2014]), present a substantial wrinkle in totalizing claims about the success of the Chinese state in regulating access to the internet within the country. To be sure, China has been more successful than perhaps any other state in aligning the web to its larger cultural, political, and social goals, and yet there is increasing evidence that the government has had to buy end-user approval for its policies through persuasive discourses (e.g., about security and nationalism) and, more importantly, through making increasing concessions to users (e.g., not strictly enforcing its rules, like the real-name policy on social platforms), thus allowing for a (limited) form of democratic governance of give and take rather than a top-down command and control logic. While a significant amount of censorship continues on the Chinese internet, the delegation of key regulatory activities to users, reliance on voluntary implementation of key online laws, and the necessity to gain legitimation for its prohibitions on the web means that the "regulatory legitimation has become an integral part of the regulatory process and this in turn has heightened the significance of individual rights and freedom, especially freedom of expression and the right to privacy. Although Chinese law recognizes these rights (albeit neither as fundamental constitutional markers to limit regulation nor within a liberal framework), it is only with the huge popularity of the internet and social media, that increasing public insistence on these rights has prompted the Chinese government to align their regulatory policies with the rights discourse" (Wei 2017, 80).

That a sovereign state with as strong an intent to regulate the internet as China has had to moderate its approach by building concessions, participation, cooperation, contestations, and negotiations into its regulatory regime points to the larger argument about how the technological features of the medium make it difficult to regulate through the traditional means. China's case, just as in the cases of other nations' tussles with the web elaborated below, underscores the novel challenge that the distributed network of the medium poses to the centralized organizational structure of the nation-state. These ongoing battles between the classical sovereign and the networked entity that seeks to replace it are marked by victories and defeats, but no nation remains untouched by its provocation. While the challenge is equally posed, the capacity to respond is variable and determined by the relative technological, financial, political, and institutional strength of each nation thus extending into the realm of digital media—a dictum widely held to be true within other aspects of international affairs. Just as differential power is visible in the ability of nations to shape global affairs in the realm of economics, politics, and the cultural domain, so is it true in meeting the challenge of networked digital media as well. In the past two decades this challenge and the ensuing conflicts have played out most prominently in three distinct domains: national security, legal jurisdiction, and cultural and informational content, which are analyzed sequentially below. Specific instances in each of these areas have shown nation-states struggling to respond adequately to the technological novelty of the medium and often resorting to the "all or nothing" approach of complete shutdown. As the analysis of each area shows, these conflicts illuminate stark global differences in meeting and responding to these challenges.

Security

Digital Networks and Challenges to National Security

The exclusion of external actors from influencing events inside the territorial boundaries of a nation-state is a key tenet of national sovereignty (Krasner 1999). In the digital era, however, conflicts between countries and digital companies and platforms have repeatedly shown how these networked media technologies can enable and even strengthen external interventions within countries. Understandably, these conflicts take on an alarmist dimension when regimes feel threatened or when other nation-states are perceived to have a hand in those interventions. There have been innumerable instances of these conflicts in the past two decades (coinciding with the global spread of the internet) that have engendered paranoid responses from states struggling to contain the effects of networked digital media, often leading to conspiracy theories about the hidden hand behind the actions of seemingly neutral and apolitical platforms. Specifically, the rise in resistance movements has targeted illiberal regimes where the affordances of digital media have helped citizens bypass state control to organize for collective action. The intensification of the color revolutions including Rose (Georgia, 2003), Orange (Ukraine, 2004), Tulip (Kyrgyzstan, 2005), Cedar (Lebanon, 2005), Blue (Kuwait, 2005), Saffron (Myanmar, 2007), and Green (Iran, 2009), as well as uprisings such as the Arab Spring and Hong Kong's Umbrella Revolution (2014) and more recent ones (2019) form only a partial list of popular insurrections wherein social media technologies have played a key role (Tufekci 2017; Castells 2013). All of these movements have expressed long-held resentments against oppressive regimes, but they also showcase the radical possibilities enabled by new technologies in circumventing state control.

The recent renewal of popular unrest against the Iranian government (December 2017–January 2018) is only the latest in a chain of protest movements wherein social media technologies have helped galvanize a campaign against a regime. But the latest goings-on in Iran cannot be fully understood without the background of the prior uprisings (against the results of Iranian presidential elections in summer 2009) that were labeled Iran's "Twitter revolution" and that led to the banning of Twitter and Facebook from the country. The recent uprisings there have focused on a wider range of issues (most prominently gender rights), but the prior one in 2009 was sparked primarily after large numbers of people disputed election results that declared the reelection of the incumbent president. While the hope of that moment seems misplaced in retrospect, a closer analysis of the role played by digital platforms in those uprisings complicates any simplistic reduction of neutral platforms being used by protestors to mobilize against the state. The now infamous revelation that the US State Department had emailed Twitter executives to postpone a planned maintenance shutdown so that the protests could continue unaffected provided grist for conspiracy mills on the Iranian side that "the Internet is an instrument of Western power and that its ultimate end is to foster regime change in Iran" (Morozov 2012, 10). The ensuing paranoia arising from the leaked State Department email and the resulting crackdown on activists that followed were justified as exercises necessary for resisting a Western conspiracy, a claim for which the leaked correspondence between Twitter and the State Department was brandished as evidence.

While the eventual outcome of the Green revolution was far from desirable, the incident showed the powerful role that platforms such as Twitter can play in enabling collective organizing and protest. The fact that Iran chose to completely shut down access to key sites and platforms underscored the fact that, unlike the US government's ability to influence Twitter's actions and policies, as revealed by the State Department's email, Iran had little leverage in shaping the platform's functioning. Undoubtedly this difference arises from the physical location of Twitter in the United States, which gave the latter far more leverage in aligning the platform's behavior with its own foreign policy goals. This alignment is important in light of the US government's stated position, as outlined in then secretary of state Hillary Clinton's (2010) speech that railed against "electronic barriers" on the internet and argued in favor of a "single internet," much to the chagrin of countries she named as indulging in "censorship" on the web (see also

Jin 2015). That official position and reactions to it upended arguments that position tussles, such as between Iran and Twitter, as between competing principles and ideologies (e.g., an illiberal Iranian regime vs a liberal US government) and locate it centrally within the power play of international geopolitics.

Differences in ability to shape the web have been on frequent public display in recent years as officials from globally dominant platforms have been repeatedly summoned by high officials and elected representatives of the US government. Testimonies by representatives of Facebook and Google before the US Senate Judiciary Committee and House Intelligence Committee about the controversy regarding Russian political advertisements on their platforms in the run-up to the 2016 US presidential elections (Shaban, Timberg, and Dwoskin 2017) are cases in point. The fallout from that controversy led to immediate changes within the platforms, as announced by Mark Zuckerberg (2017), who detailed nine specific remedial steps to prevent a similar episode in the future. Regular updates about the issue on their website and blog include a section titled "What is our action plan against foreign interference?" (Facebook Help Center, n.d.; see also Glaser 2017), thus signaling strong and proactive intent on their part. The controversy has also led to the introduction of a bipartisan bill called the Honest Ads Act (Congress.gov 2017) that would make it mandatory for all media outlets including online platforms to "make reasonable efforts to ensure that communications . . . made available by such station, provider, or platform are not purchased by a foreign national, directly or indirectly," thus ensuring that precisely those actions that the Iranian regime accused the United States of could not be repeated by another foreign country inside the United States.

In addition to pressures through the legislative and legal routes, there are various unofficial and informal pathways available for weighing in on digital corporations. Natasha Tusikov's (2017) account of the role played by private internet corporations and platforms in enforcing key policy and regulatory measures desired by states (specifically the United States and the European Union) emphasizes how nonbinding agreements arrived at through "closed-door meetings with little participation from consumer or civil-society groups" (Tusikov 2017, 4) enforce a state's writ in the digital domain. As a case in point, she narrates the series of pressures applied on WikiLeaks after its publication of the US diplomatic cables in 2010. WikiLeaks faced immediate retaliation from companies, such as Amazon,

PayPal, Mastercard, Visa, and EveryDNS (a domain registration company), that functioned as agents of the American state and helped enforce its authority by stopping the site from availing of their services. Even though the whistleblowing site survived this coordinated arm twisting, it was crippled significantly due to what Julian Assange described as an "economic death sentence" (Tusikov 2017, 38) as its payment gateways were choked. Notably, the private intermediaries acted not due to some official or formal diktat for them to do so but only from a public call issued by a US senator (Joseph Lieberman) and a letter written by the US State Department to WikiLeaks.

The difference between the Iranian response to perceived foreign interference within their country when contrasted with US responses such as in the case of WikiLeaks, the Honest Ads Act, and the steps taken by the platforms amid the US congressional hearings on Russian interference in the 2016 elections show the different purchase countries have on digital media entities. In this case, a host of factors, including but not limited to the physical location of their headquarters in the United States, shift the balance of power in favor of US sovereignty in the digital domain. As the Iranian protesters returned to the streets in 2017–18, the government in Tehran this time blamed the messaging service Telegram, which was (just like Twitter and Facebook in 2009) promptly blocked by the Iranian government (Frenke 2018; Etehad 2017). This was after the application (with forty to forty-six million users in Iran) refused to comply with government requests and the company's chief executive categorically stated that the company had "refused to shut down channels of peaceful Iranian protesters" (Frenke 2018). While in this case their challenge to the writ of nation-states has been in the form of their enabling role in organizing protests against illiberal regimes, not all perceived challenges to security by digital entities have been in the cause of supporting popular uprisings.

Google Earth's Challenge to Nation-States

Conflicts involving Google Earth, which has rankled world governments ever since its launch in June 2005, are among the most contentious and enduring controversies involving security issues of nation-states and digital platforms. These fears gained legitimacy with the increasing number of instances when the site was used to plot and launch attacks against governments (e.g., in the case of the Mumbai attacks of 2008 [Bedi 2008] and in the Iraqi city of Basra at the height of the Iraq conflict in 2007 [Harding 2007a, 2007b]).

Governments the world over were flummoxed at the ease with which this new media technology could combine satellite imagery with a networked web to bring an invasive gaze on the most classified and secretive sites inside their borders and then make it publicly available for anyone with an internet access.

The ensuing flurry, which involved state governments, military and security experts, media analysts, and conspiracy theorists represents a formative moment (and a relatively understudied one) in the tussle between the internet and sovereign states. One of the first publicly reported fears about Google Earth was expressed in Australia, where the Australian Nuclear Science and Technology Organization (ANSTO), which runs the country's only nuclear reactor at Lucas Heights in Sydney, called on Google to censor images of the nuclear site to prevent their misuse. Reporting on the issue, the Australian Broadcasting Corporation (Barlow 2005) quoted officials from ANSTO as well as several security experts as fearing that the images could be of "tactical and logistical" interest to groups seeking to do harm. A week after the Australian concern, on August 12, 2005, two Dutch parliamentarians, Frans Weekers and Aleid Wolfson, wrote to their government pointing out that terrorists could get help from images available on Google Earth (Sterling 2005). The letter asked the government of the Netherlands to find out how other governments such as the United States' were dealing with the problem.

These alarmist concerns continued the following month as the government of South Korea discussed with the US government its concerns about the availability of images of the presidential residence and military bases on Google Earth, especially since the country continued to be technically at war with North Korea (Associated Press 2005). The complaints soon gained momentum as a week after South Korea's concerns, similar reservations were expressed in Thailand, where the spokesperson for the armed forces stated that the government intended to address the issue after internal discussions (CIOL 2005). Besides Australia, the Netherlands, South Korea, and Thailand, objections to Google Earth continued to spring up from countries such as Ireland, Russia, and India. The *Irish Independent*, for instance, wrote about the numerous Irish government buildings visible through Google Earth (*Irish Independent* 2005). Similarly, the *Daily Record* quoted Lt. Gen. Leonid Sazhin of Russia's Federal Security Service as saying, "Terrorists don't need to reconnoiter their target. Now an American company is working for them" (Daily Record 2005). By the end of the year of Google

Earth's launch (2005), the global buzz created by these controversies was significant enough to result in lengthy articles on the issue in newspapers such as the *New York Times* (Hafner and Rai 2005) and the *Independent* (Shreeve 2005). These series of alarmist reactions show that the perceived threat was unprecedented. The reigning sovereign was apprehending the emergence of a counter force targeting its roots.

Among the most vociferous protests against Google Earth came from India, which initiated a year-and-a-half-long conflict with continuing lingering effects. A close analysis of the unfolding conflict is helpful both because it involved the highest office of the land, that of the president of India, and because it starkly reveals how nation-states were ill prepared to deal with this unprecedented technological challenge from a nonstate actor. The protracted conflict involved public and unimplementable threats from the Indian state and back-and-forth negotiations followed by frustration and finally a voluntary concession on Google's part in the midst of its vice president's visit to India. The issue was first raised through a media report on September 27, 2005 when the *Times of India* (henceforth *TOI*) reported the availability of high-resolution images of Indian security installations online. The story named the so called "sensitive sites" as the president's residence, the parliament house, the prime minister's residence, the Palam air force base in Delhi, and the Yelahanka air force base in Bangalore respectively (Assisi 2005). The story set off a chain of events and conspiracy theories voiced by no less than the president of India Abdul Kalam two weeks after the issue had been brought to light. He claimed that such high-resolution imagery was available only for security installations within a few developing countries (Farooq 2005), a statement that garnered global attention leading to many subsequent stories in the global press that cited the Indian president's concern to signal the importance of the issue (Deutsche Presse-Agentur 2005).

Within days of the Indian president's lament, Google's spokeswoman Debbie Frost responded to the brewing controversy by stating that "Google takes governmental concerns about Google Earth and Google Maps very seriously. Google welcomes dialogue with governments, and we will be happy to talk to Indian authorities about any concern they may have" (*Times of India* 2005). Frost also reiterated Google's position about the availability of the information on the website from other sources as well as reiterating its beneficial aspects in "fighting forest fires to emergency response, rescue, and relief in natural disasters, such as tsunamis and hurricanes" (Indo-Asian

News Service 2005). Despite these reassurances, however, nothing concrete happened even as press reports continued to stoke paranoia. Besides the issue of close-up images of security locations, the media also highlighted the "wrong" depiction of India's international boundaries. Indian law prohibits the sale within India of maps that depict Indian borders differently from the official version. Not surprisingly, Google Earth's version of India's map differed from the official version in crucial areas such as the disputed North Indian state of Kashmir (*Times of India* 2005). Given the many boundary disputes that the Indian state faces with neighboring countries (China and Pakistan), the depiction of boundaries differently from the official version was shown by media reports to be just as problematic as security threats.

Closely scrutinizing the Indian government's floundering response a decade later shows it to be a mix of panic, surprise, and technological cluelessness. As the events unfolded, solutions imagined and manufactured on the fly were being publicly pronounced. After the Indian president's publicly expressed apprehensions, the Ministry of Science and Technology in India "started taking steps" to address the issue (Mahapatra 2005), even as Google made an offer of dialogue to the government. Google's offer was met with suspicion, with the designated official, Secretary of Science and Technology V. S. Ramamurthy, saying, "We are not concerned with Google's reaction" and describing the task at hand: "The job entrusted to us is to evaluate in coordination with others the damage potential of these high-resolution pictures. . . . The challenge posed by these images is without precedent and it would take some time for the government agencies to evaluate and devise strategy, if at all required" (*Times of* India 2005). In light of these unfolding events, the Indian government finally protested to Google Earth through a letter sent to its CEO pointing out the "wrong" depiction of India's boundaries. The deputy Indian minister of external affairs also noted that the Indian embassy in the United States had been "instructed to take up the matter with Google Inc" (Siliconindia 2005). That the Indian state would engage diplomatic channels (with no leverage on Google) to apply pressure on a nonstate digital entity based in a different country is among the earliest instances of a phenomenon that has now become routine. This moment was pregnant with ushering in a new era for the struggle for sovereignty that is feverishly playing out today as nation-states around the world desperately seek any possible leverage against digital platforms.

In those early days, the morphing, modular, and agile nature of the digital threat drew nervous and often empty responses from governments that betrayed their cluelessness. Google's polite but firm refusal to accede to the Indian state's demands, for instance, prompted the Indian government to threaten it with altering the high-resolution images on its own and replacing them with low-resolution ones, a solution whose absurdity was only compounded by the fact that it was presented by a minister in the Indian parliament (on March 9, 2006) as well as reiterated to the press by India's army chief (on April 3, 2006). The unrealistic solution was immediately called out for its absurdity when the government could not explain how exactly they would do so, thus leading analysts to rightly speculate that any changes had to be made at the source servers by Google itself (Basu 2006). The inability of the government to implement its threats ensured that those images remained unchanged for a year and a half after first being identified until changes to them were voluntarily made in early 2007, to coincide with Google's vice president Vinton Cerf's visit to India. As such, it was more of an attempted gesture of goodwill than acquiescence to pressure from the Indian government. Even though the announcement brought an end to India's anxieties, such conflicts between Google Earth and other nation-states have continued in new areas including privacy of citizens, conflicting versions of national boundaries (analyzed in the subsequent section), and terrorist attacks where the site had been used to assess targets. An evaluation of Google Earth's global controversies by the Open Source Center, a branch of the US government, showed that governments worldwide had tried several strategies in the face of the threat from Google Earth such as (i) conducting negotiations with the company, (ii) banning its products, (iii) trying to develop similar products, or (iv) taking evasive measures (for the full report, see Open Source Center 2008). But notably their best hope of success remained if Google addressed the issue at its end on its own servers.

Such a conclusion, however, does not fully acknowledge the varying leverage that different countries have on Google. For instance, the United States was involved in a similar conflict with another site just a year before the Google Earth controversy. John Pike, the director of Globalsecurity. org, was asked to remove certain images from his website by the National Geospatial-Intelligence Agency, an arm of the US Defense Department. The *New York Times* stated, "Mr. Pike said he had complied, but added that the incident was a classic example of the futility of trying to control information" (Hafner and Rai 2005). Mr. Pike unknowingly echoed Google's position by saying, "To think that the same information couldn't be found elsewhere was not a very safe assumption" (Hafner and Rai 2005). Given that his website operated out of US territory, however, Mr. Pike had to abide by laws governing the distribution of images considered sensitive by the US government. The same laws regulate Google, and in fact the *New York Times* claimed that for a period images of US government buildings such as the White House and adjacent buildings appeared blurred on Google Earth because the source of those images was the US Geological Survey. The story elaborates, "the government had decided that showing details like rooftop helicopter landing pads was a security risk" (Hafner and Rai 2005).

While Mr. Pike's situation might have been an isolated one, it illustrates the disparities in the leverage states have in responding to a challenge from dominant global oligopolies. The imbalance also arises from the fact that in addition to policing end users like Globalsecurity.org, technologically advanced nations can control the *source* of these images, as companies selling them must abide by the laws of their host state. Just like the First Amendment insulates US online content even when it might violate other nations' free speech norms (Vick 2001), US laws prohibit sensitive images from being posted online and hence regulate content at its source before it is posted. For instance, one such law proscribes that "images of Israel shot by American-licensed commercial satellites be made available only at a relatively low resolution. Also, the companies' operating licenses allow the United States government to put any area off limits in the interests of national security. A 24-hour delay is mandated for images of especially high resolution" (Hafner and Rai 2005). Given that these images are already regulated at the source even before they go online, the relative imbalance in the power of the nation-states to regulate them is apparent. This difference in power is not new or surprising (Vick, 2001; Morris and Waisbord 2001) but is accentuated within a digital ecosystem wherein, as Boyd-Barrett (2006) has shown, power continues to be determined by and accrues to nations from their power in the off-line world.

Legal Jurisdiction

In addition to conflicts over security, the emerging contestations over legal jurisdiction on the internet currently playing out in countries around the world form a second key domain of tussle between nation-states and the networked digital media and represent a fundamental quandary opened up by the growth of a borderless medium in a world fragmented into nation-states. National laws become the final frontier of resistance that seeks to rein in the internet's impulse to expand and seep into national domains, and this duel has played out as much in the technological domain as in the political, cultural, and economic ones. The predicament about whose laws should prevail on a medium that presents itself as placeless and borderless is a profoundly intriguing one that has been repeatedly deliberated within parliaments, courthouses, and academic conferences and in the public domain of civil societies and popular media. However, despite innumerable technological innovations, laws passed by parliaments, and judgments pronounced by courts, disputes about legal jurisdiction that were initiated at the birth of the internet have continued unabated, throwing up new challenges in their wake. More importantly, even when laws have been made and legal orders issued, their implementation on the ground has been met with difficulties that are of a different nature than the typical challenges of implementing laws in the off-line world (Svantesson 2017; Fazlioglu 2013; Kohl and Rowland 2017). Intractable as they are, these conflicts over jurisdiction must nevertheless caution us from presuming that this is a battle between the lawless internet and the law-abiding nation-states. Instead they show us that the internet very much has laws of its own embedded within its conventions, protocols, and algorithmic regulation and that those are far more likely to be rooted in and aligned with the social, cultural, and political moorings of its sites of origin than with those of other locations and milieus. Moreover, in moments when the ethos of the web diverges from those of particular nation states, some countries have far more leverage than others in shaping the web to their own liking.

Laws in areas as distinct as those governing speech and media, criminal activities, intellectual property, and business and financial transactions have routinely run into walls of opacity, technical impenetrability, and slipperiness of the web that have led to frustration but also a desperate pushback that has taken diverse forms. A stark instance of this technological barrier was experienced in Malaysia in June 2016, when a social activist exposed the proliferation of child pornography sharing groups on the social messaging service Telegram. On investigating, local news outlets soon discovered several such groups and channels on the app that shared videos of sexual assault and abuse of young children. As the issue was picked up by the national media, police started investigating but soon hit a roadblock of encryption. In summarizing the Malaysian government's response to the difficulty, an online news site summed up the (*Today Online* 2016) position of deputy home minister of Malaysia Nur Jazlan Mohamed as saying, "It will be difficult for the police to identify the perpetrators or victims as they may not be able to trace a particular Telegram account and the forwarding of contentious materials means the source is unknown." The minister further said, "You cannot block porn on social media like Telegram unless you block total access to the country. The only way is if the service provider like Telegram blocks it themselves, but freedom of speech is an issue." He went on to add, "The government can make a request through the Communications Ministry, but up to Telegram to take action." This admission by a senior government minister as well as his echoing of the implications of the all-or-nothing option was echoed by other technology experts (Su-Lyn 2016) and was soon corroborated by unfolding events as the investigation seemed to reach a dead end in the absence of cooperation from Telegram. The Malaysian government soon set up a Special Committee on Eradicating Social Media Abuse specifically to investigate claims about pedophiles on Telegram (Malaymail 2016).

This incident of a technological barrier to legal jurisdiction is hardly an isolated one and in fact is part of a global pattern wherein the traditional means of law enforcement invariably hit a wall of encryption, thus limiting their punitive power. When law enforcement authorities were informed about a similar child pornography ring on the messaging app Telegram in the southern Indian state of Kerala in November 2017, the police were quick to arrest the administrator but soon conceded that the group had over five thousand members at large who not only actively shared sordid images of abuse of little children and toddlers (Varrier 2017) but also discussed ways of making videos and images around their locations so they could be shared. Despite this knowledge of a wider active ring of criminality and abuse, however, the police investigation stalled after the administrator's arrest as the identifiable details of other group members were hidden and hence beyond the reach of the authorities.

Arguably, the fact that the same chatting app that helped protestors organize for liberty in Iran was complicit in enabling abuse in countries such as Malaysia and India could be presented as the platform's neutrality, but the more notable point from the perspective of this chapter is that both cases reveal the limits of the classical sovereign state's ability to enforce its writ within its own borders. While Telegram has gained notoriety for its use in criminal activities and violent conflicts (also infamously making news because of its use by fighters and recruiters of ISIS) to the extent of being publicly reprimanded by world leaders (Cook 2018), it is by no means the only platform to present this kind of challenge to states' legal jurisdiction. In fact, the past two decades have presented a veritable running list of such tugs-of-war between law enforcement authorities and digital platforms and websites on the web. While some instances such as Turkey's conflict with Wikipedia and Pakistan's decision to ban YouTube are discussed in the Culture and Informational Domain section below, others, such as the use of social media to spread rumors of violence leading to an unprecedented mass exodus of people belonging to the northeastern region of India from the city of Bangalore (Srivatsa and Kurup 2012), the conflict between Google and China (Jin 2015), the conflict between Russia and Instagram (BBC 2019), and the conflict between Russia and Google as well as the European Union's ongoing conflicts with various platforms, all represent a similar broad pattern of an insurmountable technological challenge to the traditional mechanisms of law enforcement. In each such instance a nation-state's ability to avoid the binary of an "all or nothing" (Svantesson 2017) response depends on its leverage (technological, political, social, cultural, economic) to weigh in on the particular digital entity.

Perhaps the most organized and legalistic resistance to the global sway of the web and one that avoids the all-or-nothing response comes from the regional block of the European Union. Its long-running legal conflicts with platforms such as Google (Daly 2017; Bottando 2012) as well as its legislations targeting particular aspects of the web in order to align it to their preferable cultural and societal values (most recently in the case of the GDPR) present fruitful moments of conflict with rich lessons for scholars and analysts. The European Union's Right to Be Forgotten law clearly emerges from a culturally rooted difference that takes an "objectivist" approach to freedom of speech as opposed to the "skeptical" one taken in the United States (Oster 2017), and yet it has repeatedly met with technological challenges in its implementation. The law (and subsequent judgments about it) places the obligation of implementing user requests for deletion of personal information on "data controllers" who are broadly defined as "persons or entities which collect and process personal data" (Fazlioglu 2013, 151), thus making a host of intermediaries such as search engines and social media platforms enforcers of the law.

While the law's conflicts with norms of freedom of speech are well documented, critics have also pointed to its problematic attempts to introduce a logic meant for the off-line world to the internet, its delegation of matters of public importance (e.g., the balance between privacy and freedom of speech) to private entities, and its attempts to project a territorially contingent law onto the global web. What is notable from our perspective, however, are the ways in which the presumptions on which the law is based are "completely undone" (Kohl and Rowland, 2017, 101) by the internet's architecture, leading to significant and intractable challenges in its implementation. This is because the online world brings attempts at data protection far more directly into conflict with freedom of speech than was the case in the pre-internet era. Moreover, the porous boundaries between the EU and non-EU web means that the only way to ensure implementation of laws such as the Right to Be Forgotten is for it to become the global standard governing individual data protection and freedom of speech (Kohl and Rowland 2017) online.

These enduring conflicts between nation-states and the internet situate the legal domain centrally (Daly 2016) within ongoing conflicts between state sovereignty and the web. By attending to differential responses of nations in their attempts to enforce their laws, we get a far more accurate picture of the resilience of the nation-state in the digital era. Global inequities in the ability of nation-states to engage with the web help complicate notions of sovereignty and move away from imagining it as a constant and stable category that can be equally applied across the board. In this vein, it would be fitting to explore the ability of United States in responding to similar contingencies and challenges. While the United States benefits from the physical location of prominent globally dominant digital platforms within its territory, as evidenced by the ongoing political and legal deliberations to prevent a repeat of episodes like the Russian meddling in the 2016 elections, its significant leverage also accrues from its economic, political, technological, and geographical power.

The use of those powers to aid the United States in enforcing its laws outside its physical boundaries is clear in areas such as copyright enforcement (Tusikov 2017) and online gambling laws (Hurt 2017), with the latter also pointing to dual standards in global online governance. Even as many forms of gambling are allowed in the United States (e.g., lotteries, casinos, horse racing, and online gambling by companies located in certain states), the country has gone to unprecedented lengths to prevent access to online gambling sites located outside the United States. These steps, emerging from the Unlawful Internet Gambling Enforcement Act (UIGEA) of 2006, include preventing any US banks from facilitating payments to offshore gambling sites, repeatedly arresting individuals involved with those offshore sites when they are traveling inside the United States, freezing and seizing assets held in US bank accounts, and punishing any other intermediaries that help offshore gambling that, it must be mentioned, is a perfectly legal activity in their countries of location.

By excluding US-based online gambling from the UIGEA as well as allowing other forms of gambling to flourish in its territory, the US government undermines its claims about the restrictions on offshore gambling sites based in moral and ethical disapproval and instead reveals the real motive: the desire to protect the US-based gambling industry (Hurt 2017). The multipronged and aggressive efforts to limit access to offshore gambling sites in the United States, when juxtaposed with repeated calls to other countries to accept the US version of online laws in other domains (e.g., in the case of freedom of speech), reveals the world of online governance as an area where, akin to global geopolitics, power and self-interest trump notions of values, ideals, and principles. The point of this analysis, however, is to show how the latter is always a ruse to conceal the former.

Cultural and Informational Domain

The broad domain of culture and information is a third area of contestation between states and the digital domain, and while interrelated to the prior two areas of conflict, its centrality to the cultural, symbolic, and affective ideas of the nation and national imaginary have made these conflicts salient and controversial enough for them to deserve separate mention. Conflicts in this domain reveal the cultural and political orientations of the seemingly universal and acultural web that has repeatedly faced resistance from the social and cultural milieus at odds with both its content and the web's ability to disseminate that content with relative ease. Many of these conflicts veer around diverging notions of freedom of speech, which, despite being a concept enshrined in most constitutions, has varying legal and cultural definitions that are rooted in the unique historical trajectories of each culture (Oster 2017; Vick 2001). These different conceptions of free speech, however, could find expression in the online world only if it were balkanized and fragmented into multiple internets with hard boundaries separating them—an impossible proposition.

The Chinese firewall has clearly been most successful in regulating and controlling its internet's relationship with the rest (and, as explained earlier, with significant limitations), but for the rest of the world, implementing radically different norms of freedom of speech on the web has met with little success. This scenario has led to repeated episodes of conflict where the seemingly dominant notion of free speech has invariably been the Western one and, more specifically, the US First Amendment. Since the United States remains one of the largest producers of online content, both because of the location of major platforms here and because of its dominant preexisting culture industries, each time the American government or legal institutions pronounce a verdict or form a policy about freedom of speech on the web, it has reverberating consequences on the rest of the global digital sphere. And since international covenants and treaties lie below the US Constitution in the hierarchy of American law, any globally agreed-upon norm of free speech will need to meet the contours of the First Amendment, the American free speech law, for it to be accepted by the United States (Vick 2001). This not only means that US legal and policy pronouncements on free speech shape the global web but more specifically that the First Amendment emerges as the default free speech law for large parts of the global web.

Repeated instances have borne out the pitfalls of the globalization of a culturally and historically contingent idea of free speech by presenting it as the universal one. Such moves shift the culturally determined divide between the public and private, thus invariably emerging as a contentious issue. This has been most starkly illustrated in the conflicts around religious iconography and aniconism between the Islamic and Western worlds. From the Muhammad cartoons controversy (which started in the off-line world but moved online) to the various "Draw Mohammed" events (organized on Facebook and beyond) as well as the *Innocence of Muslims* film uploaded on YouTube, each of these controversies has brought two radically opposing ideologies of freedom of speech face to face that in the pre-internet era could both have coexisted in their separate spheres. These face-offs about the location of the public/private divide, the role of the sacred within that divide, and the sovereignty of cultures to determine their unique boundaries of free speech each starkly revealed the predicament of determining standards, conventions, and norms on a global and universally accessible medium and the often violent consequences of that irresolvable quandary. The conflict between the two ideologies eventually played out in the technological domain as countries sought to curtail the unregulatable architecture of the web in attempts to prevent their citizens from having access to controversial and offensive texts. Exemplifying the all-or-nothing approach resorted to in other instances, Pakistan banned an entire range of digital platforms such as Facebook, Wikipedia, YouTube, and BlackBerry services (Ahmed 2010; Yusuf 2013) to prevent images created and uploaded as a part of Everybody Draw Mohammed Day from circulating within its borders. These recurring controversies have revealed that akin to the domain of security and law, there exist wide disparities among countries' abilities and leverage to project their norms and values onto the web.

Conflicts between cultural and national values have not been restricted to the religious domain alone, as visual, textual, and cartographic portrayals of nations have also led to diverging positions and revealed the limitations of nations to control their depictions on digital platforms in ways they could in the pre-digital era. In a world where international boundaries between nations are frequently changing (e.g., those of Ukraine, Crimea, and Russia in 2014) and are often sore points of contention and differing perceptions, their depiction on digital platforms simultaneously accessible from multiple locations has led to invariable run-ins between the digital entities and countries (Glasze 2017; Kumar 2010). These conflicts have been particularly pronounced in regions that face ongoing conflicts and unsolved boundary issues such as the Israel-Palestine imbroglio (McNamara 2008), the post-Soviet bloc (BBC News 2019), and the Pakistan-India-China triangle of conflict in the state of Kashmir (Hafner and Rai 2005).

The drawing of maps has historically been a politically laden act since maps are selective representations and make real a received cultural fact through symbolically representing "the accumulated thought and labor of the past" (Wood 1992, 1). The affective investments in these symbolic representations of territoriality came to the fore as the Israeli town of Kiryat Yam decided to sue Google when its mapping platform, Google Earth, showed a description claiming that the town had been built on the ruins of an Arab village (McNamara 2008). Similarly, Pakistan, India, and China, all locked in a triangular territorial dispute, claim more territory on their maps than they have actual military control over. Maps printed and circulated within these countries therefore depict their territorial boundaries as they would want them to be rather than as they are, thus making them into political statements rather than accurate representations of the reality on the ground. More recently, Apple's acquiescence to Russia (BBC News 2019) by depicting Crimea as part of Russia on Apple Maps (instead of acknowledging Ukraine's sovereignty over it) has led to understandable backlash, especially since the changes were announced by the Russian parliament.

Google, having learned from its experience with clashes over boundary depictions on Google Earth around the world, took a more nuanced approach, showing Crimea as part of Russia when seen from within Russia, but when viewed from Ukraine it showed "no clear border between Crimea and Ukraine but also no border between Crimea and Russia" (BBC News 2019). Given this imbroglio arising from conflicting versions of reality, a universally accessible mapping platform such as Google Maps must make choices about which version of reality it will go with.

While these standoffs have been resolved in different ways, including the use of multicolored lines to show competing claims and allowing different versions to be accessed from different locations, the issue continues to present challenges that highlight how a globally accessible digital network changes the very nature of cartographic representation. In the case of the Indian state, it helps call out the state's misinformation (that most Indian citizens know to be such) about territorial boundaries, thus explaining the vehement and aggressive competition to impose their version of territorial maps in the digital sphere. One such effort is the Geospatial Information Regulation Bill, 2016 of India, deliberated but shelved for now, which would impose a prison term of seven years and a fine of up to $14 million (approximately) for wrongful depiction of India's boundaries (Bearak 2016; Srivas 2017). The bill was widely criticized for its overreach and unreal expectations, and attempts such as this symbolize the asymmetries within global power in the face of the technological novelty of the web. These conflicts over a country's representation have extended beyond the cartographic to the informational domain, as in the case of Turkey's tug-of-war with Wikipedia after the latter refused to remove an entry that classified the country as a state sponsor of terrorism (Phippen 2017). Even as all language versions of Wikipedia were blocked within the country, new mirror sites that uploaded the entire Wikipedia and used evasive technologies were soon offering the Wikipedia to Turkish citizens (Dale 2017). One such website claims to use a protocol called the InterPlanetary File System (IPFS), which, by placing Wikipedia's content on a distributed network of servers, would ensure that citizens inside Turkey could access it "even if access to the specific https://en.wikipedia.org servers is censored" (IPFS 2017). As this conflict has played out, the distributed digital network has once again revealed the insurmountable and, more importantly, differential nature of its challenge to the nation-state. This differential challenge arises, in part, from a closer alignment of the web's prevailing laws, standards, and protocols with the cultural, political, and ideological values of certain nation-states as opposed to others.

Differential Sovereignty and the Postcolonial Nation-State

The applied, on-the-ground iteration of the concept of sovereignty has rarely been true to its ideal notion and almost never a homogeneously applied and universally visible political fact. Variations from the norm across geography and across historical periods have been routine, and yet the conflicts above show the distinctness of the challenge of new and digital media technologies to the historical authority of the nation-state. In its subversive potential, the digital domain thus joins a retinue of prior challenges, marking both a continuation of and a rupture in the nature of confrontation to undermine the authority of the state, a process that has made Westphalian sovereignty an "organized hypocrisy" (Krasner 1999). Claims about the resilience of the nation-state in the face of this challenge have no doubt focused on the ways in which the same digital technologies that subvert it can be appropriated by sovereign states to police, discipline, and control their populations, allowing for their "reassertion and repositioning" (Kohl and Fox 2017, 1). But to go further and claim that "the nation state is propelling towards its heyday—a period of its greatest grip on the popular imagination" (1) is to gloss over stark disparities in nations' abilities to respond to challenges to their sovereignty, as this chapter's analysis of numerous conflicts has shown. As these case studies show, it seems a more accurate proposition to argue that in the case of a significant number of countries, the power of the nation-state has seen strident advancements in certain areas while significantly diminishing in others. The strengthening of the state in areas such as surveillance, monitoring, and propaganda can indeed occur alongside its weakening in areas such as regulating the flow of information and communication and enforcing key aspects of their legal writ within their territory. This dialectical position, which acknowledges these simultaneous yet seemingly opposing effects of the digital domain on national sovereignty, provides us with a more accurate representation of the unfolding events.

That position gains deeper historical context when we concede that the differences in states' resilience and aggressiveness of response in the face of this challenge can be understood through paying attention to the unique contingencies that bring nation-states and nationalisms into being.

The seemingly paranoid reaction of some states to the threat of subversion from digital media technologies reveals deep-seated insecurities that emerge from a particular notion of nationalism rooted within historically determined ideas of culture, territorial boundaries, and external and internal threats to sovereignty. Undeniably, nationalism has been the cause of innumerable destructive wars and continues to manifest itself in unimaginably oppressive and violent regimes today. The unifying and homogenizing tendencies of nationalisms are invariably premised on creating imagined or real Others (Robins 1996; Anderson 1983) that are, in most cases, religious, ethnic, racial, or linguistic minorities as well as dissenting voices within nation-states. This aspect is clearer today than ever before as a resurgent wave of populist nationalism has swept across the world.

However, when we juxtapose these violent manifestations of nationalism with the fact that in large parts of the world, "the national question" is "historically fused with the colonial question" (Chatterjee 1993, 18), we get a far more complex picture of the tussle. Non-Western, postcolonial nationalism, as seen in large parts of the world today, is the continuation of anti-colonial struggles that originated along with the imposition of colonialism and the modern nation-state that subverted existing community affiliations. This imposition produced an irreconcilable struggle between community and capital (Chatterjee 1993), and the emerging nation-states have often positioned themselves as barriers against continuing headwinds of cultural imperialism, capitalist exploitation, and political and economic subjugation (Kennedy 2001). To acknowledge that in many cases nationalisms have been a vantage point of colonial resistance cautions us from painting all forms of national attempts to moderate external influence (including those mediated through digital networks) with the same broad stroke. The weakening of the nation-state that can justifiably be held up as the advancement of liberty and an empowered citizenry can also open up the floodgates for the unchecked sway of neoliberal capitalism, multinational corporations, media and cultural empires, and the domination of powerful nation-states over the weaker ones.

This historical contingency locates the discomfort over unimpeded flow of digital networks within a history of skepticism toward claims of free speech that surreptitiously presented the global order as an equal playing field, thus eliding over issues of historical inequities and power. In unmasking the seductive trope of free speech to show how it advanced particular geopolitical interests, movements such as NWICO and NAM began a quest for equity and parity that fora such as the WSIS conventions have continued in the digital sphere (Bhuiyan 2008). Repeated events in the political, cultural, and economic domains lend credence to the fact that postcolonial nation-states have been particularly vulnerable to the destabilizing effects of economic dependence as well as the political and military strengths of the dominant global powers (Premnath 2003; Braziel 2006). To imagine, therefore, that the global web would remain immune to those relations of power would present the online domain as some otherworldly entity disconnected from the off-line real world where the utopian visions of equality can play out impervious from the realpolitik of dominance, power play, and expansionism that marks global geopolitics.

While the early imaginaries about the web certainly articulated those visions of distinctness, its continuing growth and expansion have situated it quite centrally within global power play and made it a site of international politics and strategic maneuverings to assert and project national power (Powers and Jablonski 2015). Given such intermeshing of the digital with the geopolitical, all the elements of global power play, including the hierarchical structure within the order of nation-states, are not just reproduced but amplified within the online domain. A cursory survey of the list of sixty-five countries (in November 2019) where Facebook offers its free and limited version of the internet, for instance, reveals a disproportionate presence of countries in the developing postcolonial world (internet.org, n.d.) that, as the chapter "Frontier" shows, highlights how the lack of connectivity in large parts of the world is being manipulated by Facebook to expand its digital empire. While the actors are no doubt private entities and platforms, the relations of power in this case are similar to the north/south divide in the off-line world but only far more disproportionate. This is so because about half of the world's population is without connectivity and has yet to have a voice on the global web.

This is visible in the disproportionate ability of major off-line powers such as the United States to shape the internet in areas ranging from free speech, 5G connectivity, and copyright to gambling laws, thus underscoring the amplified imbalance. After all, US attempts to restrain offshore gambling sites from being accessible in the country included aggressive and unapologetic use of real-world assets such as its airports, its global banking institutions, financial infrastructures, and its extensive physical and technological law-enforcement apparatus. Hurt (2017) tries to make sense of this ability to assert power through an ironic inversion: "Perhaps this is consistency: U.S. laws whether they relate to free speech or online gambling, should be respected everywhere" (83). Power in the digital domain, therefore, becomes an extension of power in the non-online real world. The thesis of resilient nation-states in the face of the onslaught of digital media entities seems inadequately representative of this complexity within the ongoing global tussles between the nation-state and the internet. A call to acknowledge differential sovereign power on the web, therefore, is also an attempt to bring theories about the relationship between the web and sovereign states far closer to the ongoing tussle between the sovereign and the digital.

Conclusions

The expansion of a borderless medium in a world carved up into delimited sovereign territories defined along cultural, linguistic, and ethnic solidarities is bound to create conflict between two competing impulses. The goal of this chapter has not been to provide a solution to that impasse but to lay out how differential power plays out in such conflicts. While the invention of media technologies has historically been accompanied by paranoid reactions emerging from drastic prognostications about their social and cultural effects, the disruptive effect of the digital revolution is perhaps second only to the invention of the printing press in human history (Eisenstein 1980). By documenting the nature of the challenge posed by this technology against a historically entrenched mode of power and the global variations in how those conflicts play out, we gain a far truer picture of the nature of sovereignty in an age of networked digital media technologies. The historical accounting of the evolution of sovereignty shows us that this is far from the first time that such a challenge has been posed, and yet its technological nature makes this challenge different and far more persistent.

Precisely because of the challenge's technological nature, the abilities of nation-states to respond to it is determined by their technological expertise, which often has to be sourced from the very technological hubs that were formative to the birth and growth of the internet. Acknowledging this disparity presents a far more nuanced and differentiated picture of the global conflict between the web and nation-states that allows us to eschew the either/or position of the declining nation-state versus a strengthening one. As the prior accounts have shown, depending on the country in question and the specific moment of conflict, we see sufficient evidence for both (weakening and strengthening sovereignty) scenarios unfolding simultaneously. While this chapter has focused primarily on the challenge the digital domain poses to nation-states, ongoing scholarship about state surveillance, cyberattacks, and cyber espionage as well as computational propaganda on the web provide sufficient evidence of how the web allows the strengthening of state power in key areas.

The only way each nation could have its off-line laws reflected on the internet is to have a balkanized web, which then defeats the very purpose of having a universal network. Such a scenario would only replicate the structure of the pre–digital media era, wherein distinct national spheres determined the nature, shape, and content of media technologies. Undeniably, the benefits of a medium that can, theoretically at least, connect the entire world simultaneously are there for all to see and cannot be emphasized enough. We see emerging before us clear signs of intense global conversations, a thriving global creator culture (Craig and Cunningham 2019), and enabling global solidarities in all aspects of social, cultural, and political life that were unimaginable in a pre-internet era. And yet, just as categories and concepts that claim a universal appeal and resonance have been historically shown to conceal and mask their parochial, cultural, and historical origins, most effectively by scholars located in the realm of postcolonial studies, so must a universally accessible technological medium be interrogated about its own cultural and political affiliations. Even as we call out untenable claims about the acultural and apolitical nature of digital infrastructures, going beyond that move to show the political and cultural valences of their standards and conventions allows us to underscore how the globalization of the web privileges particular codes, norms, and values while suppressing others. This dilemma is perhaps irresolvable, but paying attention to the contestations and sites of conflict, as this book has done, allows us to point to the traces of the irreducible Other that lurk behind the seemingly universal ethos pervading global digital cultures.

Note

1. These prohibitions are listed in Article 57 of the revised Regulation on Telecommunications of the People's Republic of China (IPKey, n.d.).

CONCLUSION

A S WE ARRIVE AT THE END OF THIS interrogation of the nature of cultural and political power on the global web, it would be remiss to ignore the consequences of an emerging scenario witnessing the rise of two distinct platform ecosystems. The Silicon Valley–led Western system finds itself increasingly at odds with the Chinese one, revealing their distinct "ideological-political" orientations (van Dijck, Poell, and De Waal 2018, 163). The commonsensical assumption that the latter privileges state interests and institutional priorities over individual liberty (no doubt true with qualifications) can often create a polarity that allows the former to evade geopolitical critiques of the global dimensions of power it represents. Since the US-led platform ecosystem is today the version of the internet that large parts of the world increasingly adopt, such a critique becomes imperative.

Analyses of the global and geopolitical dimensions of the internet (DeNardis 2014; Jin 2015; Powers and Jablonski 2015) have sought to pursue this question. The most trenchant of those critiques have emerged from the vantage point of the supranational block of the European Union (van Dijck, Poell, and De Waal 2018) that, despite not being home to any globally dominant platform, has sought to assert its cultural, political, and ideological sovereignty on the web. Laws such as the Right to be Forgotten and the GDPR have underscored the different approaches toward regulating the digital ecosystem in the interests of "public values and the common good" (165). Given the combined bargaining power that a large block of nations (such as the European Union) can exercise, these laws are already beginning to have a reverberating effect globally both in changed behavior and policies due to the deterrent effect of punitive action (e.g., fines) and in the form of similar laws being passed by other nations.

In acknowledging the leading role the European Union plays in making the dominant platforms on the internet more responsive to user concerns, this project extends and adds to those critiques from the vantage point of the postcolonial and Global South. Taking that positionality is important because such a perspective is yet to fully assert itself within the conversation about the representativeness of the global web. In tracing its lineage to the contentious debates around the NWICO, this project has sought to assert that the historical, political, and cultural vantage point of the postcolonial Global South is distinct and must remain a prominent voice in the debates about the future of the global platform ecosystem. Since their historical experiences of colonialism and appropriation combined with their contemporary lack of technological infrastructure, paucity of resources, and economic and political vulnerability diminishes their bargaining power compared to the European Union, asserting their vantage point becomes an urgent necessity.

In advancing that perspective, this book is inspired by the imagination of a truly representative global web and has sought to understand the nature of global power that citizens and states around the world experience. Its claim navigates the dialectical positions that on the one hand envision the internet as a site for creativity, emancipation, global communication, and solidarities and on the other locate it as an unprecedented form of surveillance, monitoring, and control without historical parallels. Situated in opposition to each other and yet simultaneously true, both these positions allow us to forge an interactive middle path that unravels a form of power whose deceptive and disarming modality makes it a challenge to locate its sites of operation and hence difficult to closely interrogate. Embedded within the networks and sinews making up the material and cultural architectures of the global web, this power advances through an enabling ruse of participation, interaction, and collaboration that simultaneously shapes, modulates, and nudges particular ways of knowing, being, and belonging. The transactional relationship wherein the rewards of connection, creation, and validation can be achieved only by navigating through the conventions, designs, protocols, and ideologies instantiates a covenant between users and the digital infrastructure that is a different modality of power than the disciplinary forms of surveillance and monitoring.

A New Form of Global Cultural Power

The first site where this arrangement can be seen to operate is in the material and physical realm of access, which reveals the ways in which the web's expansion through aggressive private capital investments (by four of the Big Five companies) encapsulates a logic of appropriation, usurpation, and control similar to a prior logic of colonialism. In using the metaphor of the frontier, the dividing line that demarcated the "civilized" from the "uncivilized," the conquered from the yet to be conquered, this analysis has sought to show the fecundity of the concept in historicizing the current private-led scramble to connect the world. By portraying private-led connectivity efforts as altruistic, collaborative, and beneficial, media coverage of these campaigns frames their efforts in ways that obviate any critical interrogation of the terms and conditions of access. Private control over the expanding material infrastructures of connectivity creates the grounds on which the usurpation of interactive data and the operation of cultural power can operate for perpetuity.

An instance of that operation is in the domain of knowledge wherein the book evaluates the web's promise of realizing democratized and participatory knowledge creation by closely analyzing that process on Wikipedia, the world's preeminent peer-to-peer collaborative online encyclopedia. Acknowledging its laudatory goal of creating the "sum of all human knowledge" (Slashdot 2004), the analysis also reveals insurmountable impediments to that goal given the cultural and ideological valences of its "infrastructural configuration" (Bowker 2018, 210) and the geographical and demographic distribution of its editors. Decisions such as what counts as proof and verifiable evidence, the version of English that should hold primacy over others, and which proper nouns and names supersede others reveal how the encyclopedia's rules, policies, and conventions privilege particular truths and ways of knowing while stifling others. An openness to plurality does not necessarily mean an anarchic, anything-goes system that compromises the rigor and evaluative processes necessary for separating knowledge from opinion, untruths and propaganda. Instead, such an openness calls for a self-interrogating awareness of the limits of epistemic cultures and their ways of knowing (Bowker 2018). It requires acknowledging global differences in access that affect the numbers of editors and contributors and an awareness of how disparities in media and publishing industries can make published records of knowledge, events, and histories far more abundant and readily available in some parts of the world than others.

In addition to knowledge, the domains of selfhood and sovereignty similarly reveal global dimensions of the power of the web's cultural and political architecture. The causal relationship between the global rise of social media platforms and the globalization of new aspirational norms are evident in key dimensions of digital cultures such as the selfie, lifestreaming, and influencer phenomena. The spread of these cultural practices through an incentive structure of digital rewards and rebukes, sanctions and seductions, has much in common both in its process and its end goals on the social web with a prior system of cultivating desirable norms and subjectivities (Rose 1999; Elias 2000). Just as in the past, the contours of that emerging subjectivity reveal a radical individualism created through limitless self-revelation and a carefully managed entrepreneurial digital self that takes charge of and constructs a public image designed for social validation.

Lastly, the domain of sovereignty is analyzed as the final site of conflict wherein the cultural, political, and ideological orientations of the digital network clash with the prior repository of sovereign power: the nation-state. As the centralizing, hierarchical, and centripetal tendencies of the nation-state come in conflict with the decentralized and centrifugal tendencies of the web, the power of nation-states to reassert themselves and align the web to their own interests and values is proportionate to their power in the off-line world. In posing correctives to claims that either present the picture of a resilient nation-state in the face of challenges from digital media or portray a homogenous and common challenge faced by all nation-states globally, this chapter advances the notion of differential power. The chapter underscores the weak sovereignty of postcolonial nation-states whose unique contingencies of birth and postcolonial challenges have infused a dialectical dimension to their nationalisms.

The web's emergence as a site of global contestations shows the infrastructural power accruing to the digital oligopolies from their emergence as gateways of connectivity as well as their role as the dominant platforms that become global hubs of conventions, protocols, designs, and standards regulating sociality and shaping global culture. That its hard and soft infrastructures betray affiliations to particular cultural ethos, ideologies, and world views is hardly a surprise, as any technology is first and foremost social, arising out of particular needs, expectations, and ambitions that are contingent and contextual. Prior scholars' work in pointing to the cultural values that shaped the early web, such as the "California Ideology" (Hillis, Petit, and Jarrett 2013) or the "American counterculture" (Turner 2010), already lay the groundwork for this book's argument.

Two Equally True Stories

The past two decades have witnessed a media revolution whose consequences in all dimensions of human life are there for all to see. The centrifugal ethos of the web is subversive by design, and its threats to established structures of power resonate within the news and public sphere of global geopolitics everyday. The age of information abundance, expression, and creation (Craig and Cunningham 2019) that it has heralded had long been imagined as the ideal media ecosystem by critical scholars interested in inequity, operations of power, and human emancipation. The ways in which its liberating modes of sociality can also shape, constrain, and impose is not to negate the other, equally valid narrative about the enabling side of the web. It is in fact to acknowledge that both these dialectical aspects of digital culture exist simultaneously and are inseparable aspects of the same process. It heralds a form of liberating control that is distinct from prior forms of power but arguably far more effective, precisely due to its promise of validation and reward.

Future attempts in this vein need only remind us that adoptions of all media technologies have involved similar bargains wherein their empowering dimensions have simultaneously involved destabilizing change and often a loss. As the web expands and globalizes particular ways of knowing, being, and belonging, it must do so by nudging aside preexisting culturally determined modes of life. For large parts of the world, getting on board the digital bandwagon means doing so under predetermined terms and conditions enfolded within the affordances, conventions, and protocols that mask their own parochial and contextual nature under the guise of universalism and the common global good. In unraveling the ways in which those claims of universalism conceal particular, private, and culturally rooted interests, this book's goal has been to embrace the dialectical nature of the medium rather than be deterred by its seeming contradictory effects.

Is a Balkanized Internet the Answer?

The book's argument is equally animated by the enduring quandary of a common universal network connecting a teeming number of irreducible pluralities. The advantages of a first truly global media technology that can transgress cultural, national, and linguistic boundaries while bringing untold benefits is also premised on making particular choices. As the historical conflicts over standards and conventions (Galison 2004) have shown, the very process of globalization involves questions such as "Whose conventions?," "Whose standards?," and "Whose rules?" As the conflict between the French and the British over determining global standards of time and distance showed, the choice of conventions has material, political, and cultural consequences. This is not to claim that we must forgo a universal network in favor of a fragmented or balkanized one (Mueller 2017). Instead, as this book's chapters have sought to gesture both in their distinct case studies and in the central argument running across them, the way forward is to more fully embrace the global plurality rather than erase it through making participation mandatory on conditions that are cultural, social, and political. This looks different in each case study analyzed in the book and must find expression both in how we reimagine the web and in the scholarship about it.

If universalism is almost always a guise for particularisms, scholarship about the global dimensions of the web must not be distracted by its decentralized networked ethos to entirely eschew how it also instantiates a form of global cultural power. Doing so will only signal the effectiveness of the immersed and immanent form of control that its expanding, global digital infrastructures heralds. To claim that the web has no inherent trajectory of its own and that its course is determined only by the global zeitgeist is to ignore powerful reminders from the philosophical interrogations of technology (Heidegger 1977; Ellul 2014; Ihde 1979; Winner 1980) that have repeatedly established their cultural and ideological values to show the autonomous nature of technological artifacts. No doubt global netizens remake and appropriate networked digital technologies to fit within their own lives and social milieus, but they must do so within the constraints and restrictions that are already predetermined—more often than not by corporate and geopolitical interests.

In providing concrete instantiations of the operations of global cultural power, this book's analysis should embolden visions of a plural, more globally representative web. As the next half of the world gets online, they should be empowered to do so under just as enabling conditions as did the first half living primarily within the technologically advanced regions and metropolitan centers of the world. In calling for the preservation of differences rather than their erasure, this book's argument sees differences as opportunities for global learning and growth rather than a threat. More diverse ways of knowing, being, and belonging enrich the global conversation rather than diminishing it.

BIBLIOGRAPHY

Abidin, Crystal, and Mart Ots. 2016. "Influencers Tell All? Unravelling Authenticity and Credibility in a Brand Scandal." In *Blurring the Lines: Market-Driven and Democracy-Driven Freedom of Expression*, edited by Maria Edström, Andrew T. Kenyon, and Eva-Maria Svensson, 153–61. Sweden: Nordicom.

Adas, Michael. 2009. *Dominance by Design: Technological Imperatives and America's Civilizing Mission*. Cambridge, MA: Harvard University Press.

Adorno, Theodore. 2007. *Dialectic of Enlightenment*. Stanford, CA: Stanford University Press.

Agence France Presse. 2006. "India Takes Evasive Action against Google Earth." April 5, 2006. https://www.defencetalk.com/india-takes-evasive-action-against-google-earth-5363/.

———. 2007. "Google Earth to Blur Key India Sites." February 4, 2007. https://www .spacedaily.com/2006/070204083216.t882ynto.html.

———. 2015. "Q&A: How Internet.Org Aims to Connect the World's Poor." Relaxnews, January 15, 2015. https://finance.yahoo.com/news/q-internet-org-aims-connect-worlds -poor-102202616.html

Agence France-Presse in Moscow. 2015. "'A Selfie with a Weapon Kills': Russia Launches Campaign Urging Photo Safety." *Guardian*, July 7, 2015. http://www.theguardian.com /world/2015/jul/07/a-selfie-with-a-weapon-kills-russia-launches-safe-selfie-campaign.

Aggarwal, Varun. 2018. "We're Committed to Making White-Fi Happen: Microsoft." *Hindu BusinessLine*, March 12, 2018. https://www.thehindubusinessline.com/info-tech/were -committed-to-making-white-fi-happen-microsoft/article21495498.ece.

Ahmed, Issam. 2010. "Pakistan Bans Facebook, YouTube over 'Draw Mohammad Day.'" *Christian Science Monitor*, May 20, 2010. https://www.csmonitor.com/World/Asia -South-Central/2010/0520/Pakistan-bans-Facebook-Youtube-over-Draw-Mohammad -Day.

Alexa. n.d. "The Top 500 Sites on the Web." Accessed December 15, 2017. http://www.alexa .com/topsites.org.

———. n.d. "Wikipedia.org Competitive Analysis, Marketing Mix and Traffic." Accessed July 15, 2015. https://www.alexa.com/siteinfo/wikipedia.org.

Alexander, Harriet. 2015. "France to Include 'Selfie' in New Dictionary." World, *Telegraph*, May 18, 2015. https://www.telegraph.co.uk/news/worldnews/europe/france/11614060 /France-to-include-selfie-in-new-dictionary.html.

Allen, Douglas B., ed. 2018. *Culture and Self: Philosophical and Religious Perspectives, East And West*. London: Routledge.

Amazon Jobs. n.d. "Project Kuiper." Accessed October 19, 2020. https://www.amazon.jobs /en/teams/projectkuiper.

Amazon Web Services. 2019. "Announcing General Availability of AWS Ground Station." May 23, 2019. https://aws.amazon.com/about-aws/whats-new/2019/05/announcing -general-availability-of-aws-ground-station-/.

Anderson, Benedict. 1983. *Imagined Communities*. London: Verso.

Andrejevic, Mark. 2009. "The Work of Being Watched: Interactive Media and the Exploitation of Self Disclosure." In *The Advertising and Consumer Culture Reader*, edited by Joseph Turow and Matthew P. McAllister, 385–401. New York: Routledge.

———. 2011. "Social Network Exploitation." In *A Networked Self: Identity, Community and Culture on Social Network Sites*, edited by Zizi Papacharissi, 82–102. London: Routledge.

Andrejevic, Mark, and Mark Burdon. 2015. "Defining the Sensor Society." *Television and New Media* 16 (1): 19–36. https://doi.org/10.1177/1527476414541552.

Aouragh, Miriyam, and Paula Chakravartty. 2016. "Infrastructures of Empire: Towards a Critical Geopolitics of Media and Information Studies." *Media, Culture and Society* 38 (4): 559–75. https://doi.org/10.1177/0163443716643007.

Appadurai, Arjun. 1990. "Disjuncture and Difference in the Global Cultural Economy." *Theory, Culture and Society* 7:295–310.

———. 1996. *Modernity at Large*. Minneapolis: University of Minnesota Press.

Appel, Hannah, Nikhil Anand, and Akhil Gupta. 2018. "Introduction: Temporality, Politics, and the Promise of Infrastructure." In *The Promise of Infrastructure*, edited by Hannah Appel, Nikhil Anand, and Akhil Gupta, 1–38. Durham, NC: Duke University Press.

Appiah, Anthony. 2006. *Cosmopolitanism: Ethics in a World of Strangers*. New York: W. W. Norton and Co.

Arendt, Hannah. 2013. *The Human Condition: Second Edition*. Chicago: University of Chicago Press.

Arora, Payal. 2019. *The Next Billion Users: Digital Life Beyond the West*. Cambridge, MA: Harvard University Press.

Arnold, Matthew. 1993. *Arnold: "Culture and Anarchy" and Other Writings*. Cambridge, UK: Cambridge University Press.

Ashraf, Gibran. 2015. "Why This Man Put Up a Billboard in Karachi to Thank Mark Zuckerberg for Internet.Org." *Express Tribune*, June 17, 2015. https://tribune.com.pk /story/905416/why-this-man-put-up-a-billboard-in-karachi-to-thank-mark -zuckerberg-for-internet-org/.

Assisi, C. 2005. "Google Software Exposes IAF Bases." *Times of India*, September 27, 2005. https://timesofindia.indiatimes.com/india/Google-software-exposes-IAF-bases /articleshow/1243460.cms.

Associated Press. 2005. "S Korea Discusses Security Concerns with US over Google Satellite Photo Service." TMCnet, August 30, 2005. https://www.tmcnet.com/usubmit/2005 /aug/1177560.htm.

Auletta, Ken. 2009. *Googled: The End of the World as We Know It*. London: Penguin.

Baishya, Amit Rahul. 2012. "'Counter Me, Rape Us': Bare Life and the Mimicry of the Sovereign." In *Subaltern Vision: A Study in Postcolonial Indian English Text*, edited by Aparajita De, Amrita Ghosh, and Ujjwal Jana 134–81. Newcastle upon Tyne, UK: Cambridge Scholars Publishing.

Balakrishnan, Janarthanan, and Mark D. Griffiths. 2018. "An Exploratory Study of 'Selfitis' and the Development of the Selfitis Behavior Scale." *International Journal of Mental Health and Addiction* 16 (3): 1–15. https://doi.org/10.1007/s11469-017-9844-x.

Balleste, Roy. 2015. *Internet Governance: Origins, Current Issues, and Future Possibilities*. Lanham, MD: Rowman and Littlefield.

Balwin, Richard. 2016. *The Great Convergence: Information Technology and the New Globalization*. Cambridge, MA: Harvard University Press. https://b-ok.cc/book /2874846/5122e1.

Bamman, David, Brendan O'Connor, and Noah Smith. 2012. "Censorship and Deletion Practices in Chinese Social Media." *First Monday* 17 (3). https://journals.uic.edu/ojs /index.php/fm/article/view/3943.

Banerjee, Somnath, Krishnan Ramanathan, and Ajay Gupta. 2007. "Clustering Short Texts Using Wikipedia." *Proceedings of the 30th Annual International ACM SIGIR Conference on Research and Development in Information Retrieval*, edited by Charles L. A. Clarke, Norbert Fuhr, Noriko Kando, Wessel Kraaij, and Arjen. P. de Vries, 787–88. https://doi.org/10.1145/1277741.1277909.

Bangkok Post. 2013. "Facebook Chief in Bid to Widen Global Internet Access." August 22, 2013.

Banks, Michael. 2008. *On the Way to the Web: The Secret History of the Internet and Its Founders*. Berlin: Springer.

Baraniuk, Chris. 2016. "Facebook Tests Wi-Fi Service in India." BBC News, August 8, 2016. http://www.bbc.com/news/technology-37011806.

Barbara, Juliet. 2014. "Top 10 Most Edited Pages on Wikipedia in 2014." *Diff* (Wikimedia Blog), December 30, 2014. http://blog.wikimedia.org/2014/12/30/top-10-most-edited -pages-in-2014/.

Barlow, John Perry. 1996. "A Declaration of the Independence of Cyberspace." Electronic Frontier Foundation, February 8, 1996. https://www.eff.org/cyberspace -independence.

Barlow, Karen. 2005. "Google Earth Prompts Security Fears." ABC News Online, August 8, 2005. http://web.archive.org/web/20070124105253/http://www.abc.net.au/news /indepth/featureitems/s1432602.htm.

Barwise, Patrick, and Leo Watkins. 2018. "The Evolution of Digital Dominance: How and Why We Got to GAFA." In *Digital Dominance: The Power of Google, Amazon, Facebook, and Apple*, edited by Martin Moore and Damian Tambini, 21–49. Oxford, UK: Oxford University Press.

Basu, I. 2006. "India Says No to Google Earth's Peering." United Press International, March 10, 2006. https://phys.org/news/2006-03-india-google-earth-peering.html.

Bateson, Gregory. 2006. "A Theory of Play and Fantasy." In *The Game Design Reader: A Rules of Play Anthology*, edited by Katie Salen and Eric Zimmerman, 314–28. Cambridge, MA: MIT Press.

Bayer, Tilman. 2015. "How Many Women Edit Wikipedia?" Wikimedia Blog, April 30, 2015. http://blog.wikimedia.org/2015/04/30/how-many-women-edit-wikipedia/.

BBC News. 2019. "Ukrainians Condemn Apple's Crimea Map Change." November 28, 2019. https://www.bbc.com/news/technology-50585898.

Bearak, Max. 2016. "Cartographers Beware: India Warns of $15 Million Fine for Maps It Doesn't Like." *Washington Post*, May 6, 2016. https://www.washingtonpost.com/news /worldviews/wp/2016/05/06/cartographers-beware-india-warns-of-15-million-fine-for -maps-it-doesnt-like/.

Bedi, Rahul. 2008. "Mumbai Attacks: Indian Suit against Google Earth over Image Use by Terrorists." *Telegraph*, December 8, 2008. http://www.telegraph.co.uk/news /worldnews/asia/india/3691723/Mumbai-attacks-Indian-suit-against-Google-Earth -over-image-use-by-terrorists.html.

Beer, David. 2017. "The Social Power of Algorithms." *Information, Communication and Society* 20 (1): 1–13. https://doi.org/10.1080/1369118X.2016.1216147.

Bell-Jordan, Katrina E. 2008. "*Black.White.* and a *Survivor* of *The Real World*: Constructions of Race on Reality TV." *Critical Studies in Media Communication* 25 (4): 353–72.

Benkler, Yochai. 2007. *The Wealth of Networks: How Social Production Transforms Markets and Freedom.* New Haven, CT: Yale University Press.

———. 2011. "Network Theory | Networks of Power, Degrees of Freedom." *International Journal of Communication* 5 (0): 39.

Bensmaïa, Réda. 2017. *Gilles Deleuze, Postcolonial Theory, and the Philosophy of Limit.* London: Bloomsbury.

Berg, Lawrence, and Robin Kearns. 2009. "Naming as Norming: 'Race', Gender and the Identity Politics of Naming Places in Aotearoa/New Zealand." In *Critical Toponymies*, edited by Lawrence Berg and Jani Vuolteenaho, 19–52. Farnham, UK: Ashgate.

Berg, Lawrence, and Jani Vuolteenaho, eds. 2009a. *Critical Toponymies.* Farnham, UK: Ashgate.

———. 2009b. "Toward Critical Toponymies: The Contested Politics of Place Naming." In *Critical Toponymies*, edited by Lawrence Berg and Jani Vuolteenaho, 1–18. Farnham, UK: Ashgate.

Bhabha, Homi. 1984. "Of Mimicry and Man: The Ambivalence of Colonial Discourse." *October* 28 (Spring, 1984): 125–33. https://doi.org/10.2307/778467.

———. 1997. *Location of Cultures.* UK: Routledge.

Bhuiyan, A. J. M. Shafiul Alam. 2008. "Peripheral View: Conceptualizing the Information Society as a Postcolonial Subject." *International Communication Gazette* 70 (2): 99–116.

Biel, Joan-Isaac, and Daniel Gatica-Perez. 2010. "Vlogcast Yourself: Nonverbal Behavior and Attention in Social Media." *ICMI-MLMI '10: International Conference on Multimodal Interfaces and the Workshop on Machine Learning for Multimodal Interaction* (November 2010): 1–4. https://doi.org/10.1145/1891903.1891964.

Bignall, Simone, and Paul Patton, eds. 2010. *Deleuze and the Postcolonial.* Edinburgh: Edinburgh University Press.

Bishop, Sophie. 2018. "Anxiety, Panic and Self-Optimization: Inequalities and the YouTube Algorithm." *Convergence* 24 (1): 69–84. https://doi.org/10.1177/1354856517736978.

Black, Jan Knippers. 2009. *The Politics of Human Rights Protection: Moving Intervention Upstream with Impact Assessment.* Lanham, MD: Rowman and Littlefield.

Blackton, Charles S. 1990. *Partha Chatterjee. Nationalist Thought and the Colonial World: A Derivative Discourse?* Oxford, UK: Oxford University Press.

Bolton, Herbert E. 1917. "The Mission as a Frontier Institution in the Spanish-American Colonies." *The American Historical Review* 23 (1): 42–61. https://doi.org/10.2307/1837685.

Bosker, Bianca. 2016. "The Binge Breaker." *Atlantic*, November 2016. https://www.theatlantic.com/magazine/archive/2016/11/the-binge-breaker/501122/.

Bottando, Evelyn. 2012. "Hedging the Commons: Google Books, Libraries, and Open Access to Knowledge." PhD diss., University of Iowa.

Boult, Adam. 2016. "People Who Take Selfies Regularly 'Overestimate How Attractive They Are'—Study." *Telegraph*, May 20, 2016. https://www.telegraph.co.uk/science/2016/05/20/people-who-take-selfies-regularly-overestimate-how-attractive-th/.

Bowker, Geoffrey C. 2018. "Sustainable Knowledge Infrastructures." In *The Promise of Infrastructure*, edited by Hannah Appel, Nikhil Anand, and Akhil Gupta, 203–22. Durham, NC: Duke University Press.

Boyd, Danah. 2014. *It's Complicated: The Social Lives of Networked Teens*. New Haven, CT: Yale University Press.

Boyd-Barrett, Oliver. 2006. "Cyberspace, Globalization and Empire." *Global Media and Communication* 2 (1): 21–41.

Boyle, Alan. 2019. "Jeff Bezos Explains Amazon's Bet on Project Kuiper Satellites—And Copes with an Onstage Protest." GeekWire, June 6, 2019. https://www.geekwire .com/2019/jeff-bezos-explains-amazons-bet-project-kuiper-satellites-copes-onstage -protest/.

Braman, Sandra. 2016. "Instability and Internet Design." *Internet Policy Review* 5 (3). https:// policyreview.info/articles/analysis/instability-and-internet-design.

Brantlinger, Patrick. 1985. "Victorians and Africans: The Genealogy of the Myth of the Dark Continent." *Critical Inquiry* 12 (1): 166–203. https://doi.org/10.1086 /448326.

Braziel, Jana Evans. 2006. "Haiti, Guantánamo, and the One Indispensable Nation: US Imperialism, Apparent States, and Postcolonial Problematics of Sovereignty." *Cultural Critique* 64:127–60.

Bucher, Taina. 2012. "Want to Be on the Top? Algorithmic Power and the Threat of Invisibility on Facebook." *New Media and Society* 14 (7): 1164–80. https://doi.org /10.1177/1461444812440159.

———. 2018. *If . . . Then: Algorithmic Power and Politics*. Oxford, UK: Oxford University Press.

Bucher, Taina, and Anne Helmond. 2017. "The Affordances of Social Media Platforms." In *SAGE Handbook of Social Media*. Edited by Jean Burgess, Alice Marwick, and Thomas Poell, 233–53. London: Sage.

Burgess, Jean, and Ariadna Matamoros-Fernández. 2016. "Mapping Sociocultural Controversies across Digital Media Platforms: One Week of #gamergate on Twitter, YouTube, and Tumblr." *Communication Research and Practice* 2 (1): 79–96. https://doi .org/10.1080/22041451.2016.1155338.

Burgess, Matt. 2017. "Google Quietly Shut Its Internet Drone Project Last Year." *Wired* (UK), January 12, 2017. http://www.wired.co.uk/article/google-project-titan-web-drones.

Busch, Lawrence. 2011. *Standards: Recipes for Reality*. Infrastructure Series. MIT Press.

Business Insider. 2019. "The Influencer Marketing Report." Accessed October 18, 2020. https://www.businessinsider.com/influencer-marketing-report.

———. n.d. "The Influencer Marketing Report." Business Insider Intelligence Research Store. Accessed October 27, 2019. https://store.businessinsider.com/products/the-influencer -marketing-report.

Business Today. 2018. "Railways Targets 100% Wi-Fi Enabled Stations across India by 2019 at Cost of Rs 700 Crore." January 8, 2018. https://www.businesstoday.in/current /economy-politics/railways-targets-100-percent-wifi-enabled-stations-india-2019 -cost-rs-700-crore/story/267546.html.

Callahan, Ewa. 2014. "Crosslinguistic Neutrality." In *Global Wikipedia: International and Cross-Cultural Issues in Online Collaboration*. Edited by Pnina Fichman and Noriko Hara, 69–84. New York: Rowman and Littlefield.

Canclini, Nestor Garcia. 2006. "Hybrid Cultures, Oblique Powers." In *Media and Culture Studies: Keyworks*, edited by Meenakshi Gigi Durham and Douglas Kellner, 422–44. Malden, MA: Blackwell.

Canoy, Vida, and Mark Ferdinand Lacano. 2015. "Get Information at Your Fingertips Anytime, Anywhere Even without WiFi." *Philippine Daily Inquirer*, April 10, 2015. https://technology.inquirer.net/41651/get-information-at-your-fingertips-anytime -anywhere-even-without-wifi.

Carey, J. 1992. *Communication as Culture*. New York: Routledge.

Carr, Nicholas. 2006. "The Death of Wikipedia." *ROUGH TYPE* (blog), May 24, 2006. http:// www.roughtype.com/?p=394.

———. 2011. *The Shallows: What the Internet Is Doing to Our Brains*. New York: W. W. Norton and Company.

Castells, Manuel. 2000. *The Rise of the Network Society*. 2nd edition. Oxford, UK: Wiley-Blackwell.

———. 2010. *The Information Age: Economy, Society and Culture*. Oxford, UK: Wiley-Blackwell.

———. 2013. *Communication Power*. Oxford, UK: Oxford University Press.

Chakrabarty, Dipesh. 2007. *Provincializing Europe: Postcolonial Thought and Historical Difference*. Princeton, NJ: Princeton University Press.

Chang, Emily, and Sarah Frier. 2015. "Mark Zuckerberg Q&A: The Full Interview on Connecting the World - Bloomberg." Bloomberg, February 19, 2015. https://www .bloomberg.com/news/articles/2015-02-19/mark-zuckerberg-q-a-the-full-interview -on-connecting-the-world.

Chatterjee, Partha. 1993. *Nationalist Thought and the Colonial World: A Derivative Discourse*. London: Zed Books.

Cheney-Lippold, John. 2018. *We Are Data: Algorithms and the Making of Our Digital Selves*. New York: NYU Press.

Chong, Dennis, and James N. Druckman. 2007. "Framing Public Opinion in Competitive Democracies." *American Political Science Review* 101 (4): 637–55. https://doi.org/10.1017 /S0003055407070554.

Chowdhary, Sunita Y. 2016. "Selfie Raja: Marred by Shoddy Execution." *Hindu*, July 15, 2016. http://www.thehindu.com/features/cinema/Selfie-Raja-Marred-by-shoddy-execution /article14490910.ece.

CIOL News. 2005. "Google Images Upset Thai Military." September 7, 2005. https://www.ciol .com/google-images-upset-thai-military/.

Cirucci, Angela M. 2015. "Facebook's Affordances, Visible Culture, and Anti-Anonymity." *SMSociety '15: Proceedings of the 2015 International Conference on Social Media and Society* (July 2015): 1–5. https://doi.org/10.1145/2789187.2789202.

Clement, J. 2017. "Most Famous Social Network Sites Worldwide as of September 2017, Ranked by Number of Active Users (In Millions)." Statista. Accessed December 16, 2017. https://www.statista.com/statistics/272014/global-social-networks-ranked-by -number-of-users/. Original page no longer available.

———. 2019a. "Countries with the Most Instagram Users 2019." Statista, August 29, 2019. https://www.statista.com/statistics/578364/countries-with-most-instagram-users/.

———. 2019b. "Global Social Networks Ranked by Number of Users 2019." Statista, April 24, 2020. https://www.statista.com/statistics/272014/global-social-networks-ranked-by -number-of-users/.

———. 2019c. "Number of Monthly Active Instagram Users 2013–2018." Statista, December 3, 2019. https://www.statista.com/statistics/253577/number-of-monthly-active-instagram -users/.

———. 2020. "Countries with the Most Twitter Users 2020." Statista, April 24, 2020. https:// www.statista.com/statistics/242606/number-of-active-twitter-users-in-selected -countries/.

Clinton, Hillary Rodham. 2010. "Remarks on Internet Freedom." US Department of State, January 21, 2010. https://2009-2017.state.gov/secretary/20092013clinton/rm /2010/01/135519.htm.

Coffey, Helen. 2017. "India Has the Highest Number of Selfie Deaths in the World." *Independent*, July 6, 2017. https://www.independent.co.uk/travel/news-and-advice /india-selfie-deaths-highest-number-priti-pise-marine-drive-instagram-a7827486 .html.

Cohen, Noam. 2011. "Define Gender Gap? Look Up Wikipedia's Contributor List." *New York Times*, January 30, 2011. https://www.nytimes.com/2011/01/31/business/media/31link .html.

Cole, Steve. 2014. "NASA Releases Earth Day 'Global Selfie' Mosaic of Our Home Planet." NASA, August 7, 2017. https://www.nasa.gov/press/2014/may/nasa-releases-earth-day -global-selfie-mosaic-of-our-home-planet.

Collier, Benjamin, and Julia Bear. 2012. "Conflict, Criticism, or Confidence: An Empirical Examination of the Gender Gap in Wikipedia Contributions." In *CSCW '12: Proceedings of the ACM 2012 Conference on Computer Supported Cooperative Work* (February 2012): 383–92. https://doi.org/10.1145/2145204.2145265.

Collins, Larry, and Dominique Lapiere. 1997. *Freedom at Midnight*. New York: HarperCollins.

Condliffe, Jamie. 2016. "Facebook and Google Are Racing to Supply India with Internet Access." MIT Technology Review, August 9, 2016. https://www.technologyreview .com/s/602132/facebook-and-google-are-racing-to-supply-india-with-internet-access/.

Congress.gov. 2017. "S.1989—Honest Ads Act. 115th Congress (2017–2018)." October 19, 2017. https://www.congress.gov/bill/115th-congress/senate-bill/1989/text.

Connell, Raewyn W. 2007. *Southern Theory: Social Science and the Global Dynamics Of Knowledge*. Cambridge, UK: Polity.

———. 2014. "Using Southern Theory: Decolonizing Social Thought in Theory, Research and Application." *Planning Theory* 13 (2): 210–23.

Cook, James. 2018. "Theresa May Will Single out Messaging App Telegram and Call It a 'Home to Criminals and Terrorists.'" Business Insider, January 24, 2018. http://www .businessinsider.com/theresa-may-telegram-home-to-criminals-and-terrorists -2018-1.

Cort, John, trans. 2007. *The Saving Waves of Milk White Ganga*. Calcutta: Writers Workshop.

Cotter, Kelley. 2019. "Playing the Visibility Game: How Digital Influencers and Algorithms Negotiate Influence on Instagram." *New Media and Society* 21 (4): 895–913. https://doi .org/10.1177/1461444818815684.

Couldry, Nick, and Ulises A. Mejias. 2018. "Data Colonialism: Rethinking Big Data's Relation to the Contemporary Subject." *Television and New Media* 20 (4): 336–49. https://doi .org/10.1177/1527476418796632.

———. 2019. *The Costs of Connection: How Data Is Colonizing Human Life and Appropriating It for Capitalism*. Stanford, CA: Stanford University Press.

Couture, Stephane, and Sophie Toupin. 2019. "What Does the Notion of 'Sovereignty' Mean When Referring to the Digital?" *New Media and Society* 21 (10): 2305–22. https://doi .org/10.1177/1461444819865984.

Cox, Andrew. 2016. "Flying Aquila: Early Lessons from the First Full-Scale Test Flight and the Path Ahead." Facebook Engineering, July 21, 2016. https://code.facebook.com /posts/268598690180189.

Coyle, Diane. 2018. "Platform Dominance: The Shortcomings of Antitrust Policy." In *Digital Dominance: The Power of Google, Amazon, Facebook, and Apple*, edited by Martin Moore and Damian Tambini, 50–70. Oxford, UK: Oxford University Press.

Croxton, Derek. 1999. "The Peace of Westphalia of 1648 and the Origins of Sovereignty." *The International History Review* 21 (3): 569–91.

Cunliffe, Daniel. 2007. "Minority Languages and the Internet: New Threats, New Opportunities." In *Minority Language Media: Concepts, Critiques and Case Studies*, edited by Michael J. Cormack and Niamh Hourigan, 133–50. Bristol: Multilingual Matters.

Cunningham, Stuart, and David Craig. 2019. *Social Media Entertainment: The New Intersection of Hollywood and Silicon Valley*. New York: NYU Press.

———, eds. 2021. *Creator Culture: Studying the Social Media Entertainment Industry*. New York: NYU Press.

Curtin, Michael. 2004. "Media Capitals: Cultural Geographies of Global TV." In *Television after TV: Essays on a Medium in Transition*, edited by Lynn Spiegel and Jan Olsson, 270–302. Durham, NC: Duke University Press.

Daily Independent (Nigeria). 2015. "Airtel, Facebook Launch Free Basic Services in Nigeria, Other African Countries." December 24, 2015. https://www.latestnigeriannews.com /news/2239423/airtel-facebook-launch-free-basic-services-in-nigeria-other-african -countries.html.

Daily Nation (Kenya). 2015. "Facebook Ready to Beam Free Internet in Kenya." October 5, 2015.

Daily News (Sri Lanka). 2015a. "Google to Cover Lanka with 3G Floating Balloons." July 29, 2015.

———. 2015b. "A Great Partnership." August 1, 2015.

———. 2016a. "Google's Project Loon to Begin in March." February 2, 2016.

———. 2016b. "SL to Increase Internet Penetration Upto 50%." April 11, 2016.

Daily Pakistan Today. 2015. "Karachi Billboard Put Up by Man to Thank Mark Zuckerberg for Internet.Org!" June 18, 2015. https://www.pakistantoday.com.pk/2015/06/18/karachi -billboard-put-up-by-man-to-thank-mark-zuckerberg-for-internet-org/.

Daily Record (Glasgow). 2005. "Security Fears Over Map Site." December 21, 2005.

Dalby, Andrew. 2009. *The World and Wikipedia: How We Are Editing Reality*. Somerset: Siduri Books.

Dale, Brady. 2017. "Turkey Can't Block This Copy of Wikipedia." *Observer*, May 10, 2017. http://observer.com/2017/05/turkey-wikipedia-ipfs/.

Daly, Angela. 2016. *Private Power, Online Information Flows and EU Law: Mind the Gap*. New York: Bloomsbury.

———. 2017. "Symposium on Google Search (Shopping) Decision—Beyond 'Hipster Antitrust.'" *European Competition and Regulatory Law Review* 1 (3): 188–92. https:// doi.org/10.21552/core/2017/3/4.

Dasti, Matthew, and Edwin Bryant, eds. 2014. *Free Will, Agency, and Selfhood in Indian Philosophy.* Oxford, UK: Oxford University Press.

Davies, Harry. 2015. "Ted Cruz Using Firm That Harvested Data on Millions of Unwitting Facebook Users." *Guardian*, December 11, 2015. http://www.theguardian.com/us-news/2015/dec/11/senator-ted-cruz-president-campaign-facebook-user-data.

Deibert, R. 2002. "Dark Guests and Great Firewall: The Internet and Chinese Security Policy." *Journal of Social Issues* 58 (1): 143–59.

Deibert, Ronald, John Palfrey, Rafal Rohozinski, and Jonathan Zittrain, eds. 2008. *Access Denied: The Practice and Policy of Global Internet Filtering.* Cambridge, MA: MIT Press.

———, eds. 2011. *Access Contested: Security, Identity, and Resistance in Asian Cyberspace.* Cambridge, MA: MIT Press.

Deleuze, Gilles. 1992. "Postscript on the Societies of Control." *October* 59:3–7.

———. 1995. "Control and Becoming." In *Negotiations: 1972–1990*, 169–76. Translated by Martin Joughin. New York: Columbia University Press.

———. 1998. "Having an Idea in Cinema." In *Deleuze and Guattari: New Mappings in Politics, Philosophy, and Culture*, edited by Eleanor Kaufman and Kevin Jon Heller, 14–19. Minneapolis: University of Minnesota Press.

DeNardis, Laura. 2009. *Protocol Politics: The Globalization of Internet Governance.* Cambridge, MA: MIT Press

———., ed. 2011. *Opening Standards: The Global Politics of Interoperability.* Cambridge, MA: MIT Press.

———. 2014. *The Global War for Internet Governance.* New Haven, CT: Yale University Press.

De Senarclens, Pierre. 2003. "The Politics of Human Rights." In *The Globalization of Human Rights*, edited by Jean-Marc Coicaud, Michael W. Doyle, and Anne-Marie Gardner, 137–59. Tokyo: United Nations University Press.

Deutsche Presse-Agentur. 2005. "Google Heeds Indian President's Concerns over Satellite Imagery." October 20, 2005.

Dijck, José van. 2013. *The Culture of Connectivity: A Critical History of Social Media.* Oxford, UK: Oxford University Press.

Dijck, José van, Thomas Poell, and Martijn de Waal. 2018. *The Platform Society: Public Values in a Connective World.* New York: Oxford University Press.

Dorfman, Ariel, and Armand Mattelart. 1975. *How to Read Donald Duck: Imperialist Ideology in the Disney Comic.* Amsterdam: International General.

Doshi, Vidhi. 2016. "Google, Facebook and Microsoft Race to Get 1 Billion Indians Online." *Guardian.* November 4, 2016. http://www.theguardian.com/sustainable-business/2016/nov/04/google-facebook-and-microsoft-1-billion-india-online-internet.

Duckett, Chris. 2020. "Washington Aims Clean Network Program Directly at Stopping China and Huawei." Zdnet, August 6, 2020. https://www.zdnet.com/article/washington-aims-clean-network-program-directly-at-stopping-china-and-huawei/.

Duhigg, Charles. 2012. "How Companies Learn Your Secrets." Magazine, *New York Times*, February 16, 2012. https://www.nytimes.com/2012/02/19/magazine/shopping-habits.html.

Dusek, Val. 2006. *Philosophy of Technology: An Introduction.* Vol. 90. Hoboken, NJ: Blackwell.

Ebo, Bosah Louis, ed. 2001. *Cyberimperialism? Global Relations in the New Electronic Frontier.* Westport, CT: Praeger.

Eckert, Stine, and Linda Steiner. 2013. "(Re) Triggering Backlash: Responses to News About Wikipedia's Gender Gap." *Journal of Communication Inquiry* 37 (4): 284–303.

Economic Times. 2014. "Goa DGP Assures Fair Probe in Anti-Modi Facebook Post Case." May 26, 2014. http://economictimes.indiatimes.com//articleshow/35618419.cms.

———. 2016. "Facebook Tests 'Express Wifi' in India." November 27, 2016. https:// economictimes.indiatimes.com/tech/internet/facebook-tests-express-wifi-in-india /articleshow/55649460.cms.

———. 2019. "RailTel Turns 1600 Railway Stations into RailWire Wi-Fi Zone." April 10, 2019. https://economictimes.indiatimes.com/industry/transportation/railways /railtel-turns-1600-railway-stations-into-railwire-wi-fi-zone/articleshow/68810682 .cms?from=mdr.

Economist. 2009. "It's a Man's World." May 21, 2009. http://www.economist.com/node /13717514?story_id=13717514.

Edelman, Benjamin. 2014. "Leveraging Market Power Through Tying: Does Google Behave Anti-Competitively?" *Journal of Competition Law and Economics* 11 (2): 365–400. https://doi.org/10.1093/joclec/nhv016.

Edwards, Paul N., Geoffrey C. Bowker, Steven J. Jackson, and Robin Williams. 2009. "Introduction: An Agenda for Infrastructure Studies." *Journal of the Association for Information Systems* 10 (5): 6.

Eisenstein, Elizabeth L. 1980. *The Printing Press as an Agent of Change*. Vol. 1. Cambridge, UK: Cambridge University Press.

Elias, Norbert. 2000. *The Civilizing Process: Sociogenetic and Psychogenetic Investigations*. Hoboken, NJ: Wiley.

Ellul, Jacques. 2014. "The 'Autonomy' of the Technological Phenomenon." In *Philosophy of Technology: The Technological Condition*, edited by Robert C Scharff and Val Dusek, 430–41.

Entman, Robert M. 1993. "Framing: Toward Clarification of a Fractured Paradigm." *Journal of Communication* 43 (4): 51–58. https://doi.org/10.1111/j.1460-2466.1993.tb01304.x.

———. 2010. "Media Framing Biases and Political Power: Explaining Slant in News of Campaign 2008." *Journalism* 11 (4): 389–408. https://doi.org/10.1177/1464884910367587.

Etehad, Melissa. 2017. "Telegram Was the App Where Iranians Talked Politics. Then the Government Caught On." *Los Angeles Times*, March 13, 2017. http://www.latimes.com /business/la-fi-telegram-iran-20170313-story.html.

Eubanks, Virginia. 2018. *Automating Inequality: How High-Tech Tools Profile, Police, and Punish the Poor*. New York: St. Martin's Press.

Evans, Tony. 2005. *The Politics of Human Rights: A Global Perspective*. Pluto Press.

Ewen, Stuart. 1996. *PR!: A Social History of Spin*. New York: Basic Books.

Express Wi-Fi by Facebook. n.d. "Fast, Affordable, and Reliable Wi-Fi Connection." Accessed October 21, 2020. https://expresswifi.fb.com/.

Eyal, Nir. 2014. *Hooked: How to Build Habit-Forming Products*. Scotts Valley, CA: CreateSpace.

Ezekiel, Nissim. 2006. *Collected Poems*. 2nd ed. New Delhi: Oxford University Press.

Facebook for Developers. n.d. "Free Basics Platform." Accessed October 21, 2020. https:// developers.facebook.com/docs/internet-org.

Facebook Help Center. n.d. "What Is Our Action Plan against Foreign Interference?" Accessed February 25, 2018. https://www.facebook.com/help/1991443604424859. Page no longer available.

Facebook Investor Relations. 2019. "Facebook Reports Fourth Quarter and Full Year 2018 Results." January 30, 2019. https://investor.fb.com/investor-news/press-release-details /2019/Facebook-Reports-Fourth-Quarter-and-Full-Year-2018-Results/default.aspx.

Facebook Newsroom. 2015. "Announcing the Internet.org Platform." May 12, 2015. https:// about.fb.com/news/2015/05/announcing-the-internet-org-platform/.

Fanon, Frantz. 2008. *Black Skin, White Masks*. Translated by Richard Philcox. New York; Berkeley, CA: Grove Press.

Farooq, O. 2005. "Google Satellite Photo Service Can Be Misused: Kalam." *Hindustan Times*, October 16, 2005.

Fazlioglu, Muge. 2013. "Forget Me Not: The Clash of the Right to Be Forgotten and Freedom of Expression on the Internet." *International Data Privacy Law* 3 (3): 149–57.

Federal Communications Commission. n.d. "White Space Database Administrators Guide." Accessed October 21, 2020. https://www.fcc.gov/general/white-space-database -administrators-guide.

Feenberg, Andrew. 1991. *Critical Theory of Technology*. Oxford, UK: Oxford University Press.

Fichman, Pnina, and Noriko Hara. 2014. *Global Wikipedia: International and Cross-Cultural Issues in Online Collaboration*. Lanham, MD: Rowman and Littlefield.

Financial Express. 2015. "Bangladesh Launches 'Free' Mobile Internet." May 10, 2015.

Fink, Bruce. 1997. *The Lacanian Subject: Between Language and Jouissance*. Princeton, NJ: Princeton University Press.

Fiske, John. 2010. *The John Fiske Collection: Reading the Popular*. London; New York: Routledge.

Flammia, Madelyn, and Carol Saunders. 2007. "Language as Power on the Internet." *Journal of the American Society for Information Science and Technology* 58 (12): 1899–1903. https://doi.org/10.1002/asi.20659.

Flew, Terry. 2019. "The Platformized Internet: Issues for Internet Law and Policy." *Journal of Internet Law* 22 (May): 3–16.

Foer, Franklin. 2017. "Facebook's War on Free Will." Technology, *Guardian*, September 19, 2017. http://www.theguardian.com/technology/2017/sep/19/facebooks-war-on-free-will.

Fonternel, Ernst. 2015. "Facebook's Internet.org Has More Pros Than Cons." *Cape Times*, July 13, 2015. https://www.iol.co.za/capetimes/opinion/facebooks-internetorg-has-more -pros-than-cons-1884198.

Forbes. n.d. "Forbes Lists." Accessed October 18, 2020. https://www.forbes.com/lists /#67098d26370e.

——— n.d. "Top Influencers." Accessed October 18, 2020. https://www.forbes.com/top -influencers/#67cc5ddd72dd.

Forte, Andrea, Judd Antin, Shaowen Bardzell, Leigh Honeywell, John Riedl, and Sarah Stierch. 2012. "Some of All Human Knowledge: Gender and Participation in Peer Production." *CSCW '12: Proceedings of the ACM 2012 Conference on Computer Supported Cooperative Work Companion* (February 2012): 33–36. http://dl.acm.org /citation.cfm?id=2141530.

Foucault, Michel. 1970. *The Order of Things: An Archaeology of the Human Sciences*. New York: Vintage Books.

———. 1972. *Archaeology of Knowledge*. New York: Pantheon Books.

———. 1980. *Power/Knowledge: Selected Interviews and Other Writings, 1972–1977*. New York: Pantheon Books.

———. 1995. *Discipline and Punish*. 2nd Edition. New York: Vintage Books.

Foucault, Michel, and Robert Hurley. 1990. *The History of Sexuality: An Introduction*. New York: Vintage Books.

Fraser, Nancy. 1990. "Rethinking the Public Sphere: A Contribution to the Critique of Actually Existing Democracy." *Social Text* 25–26: 56–80.

Frenke, Sheera. 2018. "Iranian Authorities Block Access to Social Media Tools." *New York Times*, January 2, 2018. https://www.nytimes.com/2018/01/02/technology/iran-protests -social-media.html.

Freud, Sigmund. 2004. *Civilization and Its Discontents*. London: Penguin UK.

Friederici, Nicolas, Sanna Ojanperä, and Mark Graham. 2017. "The Impact of Connectivity in Africa: Grand Visions and the Mirage of Inclusive Digital Development." *The Electronic Journal of Information Systems in Developing Countries* 79 (1): 1–20. https:// doi.org/10.1002/j.1681-4835.2017.tb00578.x.

Frosh, Paul. 2015. "Selfies The Gestural Image: The Selfie, Photography Theory, and Kinesthetic Sociability." *International Journal of Communication* 9 (22): 1607–28.

Fuchs, Christian. 2010. "New Imperialism: Information and Media Imperialism?" *Global Media and Communication* 6 (1): 33–60. https://doi.org/10.1177/1742766510362018.

Fuchs, Christian, and Vincent Mosco, eds. 2017. *Marx in the Age of Digital Capitalism*. Chicago: Haymarket Books.

Gadamer, Hans. 2004. *Truth and Method*. London; New York: Bloomsbury Academic.

Gadgets Now. 2020. "These Are the Top Smartphone Brands in India." October 28, 2020. https://www.gadgetsnow.com/slideshows/these-are-the-top-smartphone-brands-in -india/photolist/78920261.cms.

Gajjala, Radhika. 2013. *Cyberculture and the Subaltern: Weavings of the Virtual and Real*. Lanham, MD: Rowman and Littlefield.

Galison, Peter. 2004. *Einstein's Clocks and Poincare's Maps: Empires of Time*. New York: W. W. Norton and Company.

Galloway, Alexander. 2006. *Protocol: How Control Exists After Decentralization*. Cambridge, MA: MIT Press.

Galloway, Alexander R., and Eugene Thacker. 2007. *The Exploit: A Theory of Networks*. Vol. 21. Minneapolis: University of Minnesota Press.

Gandhi, Leela. 1998. *Postcolonial Theory*. New York: Columbia University Press.

Gardner, Sue. 2011. "Nine Reasons Women Don't Edit Wikipedia (in Their Own Words)." *Sue Gardner's Blog*, February 19, 2011. http://suegardner.org/2011/02/19/nine-reasons-why -women-dont-edit-wikipedia-in-their-own-words/.

Garside, Juliette. 2014. "Facebook Buys UK Maker of Solar-Powered Drones to Expand Internet." Tech, *Guardian*, February 28, 2014. https://www.theguardian.com /technology/2014/mar/28/facebook-buys-uk-maker-solar-powered-drones-internet.

Gerrand, Peter. 2006. "A Short History of the Catalan Campaign to Win the .Cat Internet Domain, with Implications for Other Minority Languages." *Digithum* 8. https://www .raco.cat/index.php/Digithum/article/view/39462.

———. 2007. "Estimating Linguistic Diversity on the Internet: A Taxonomy to Avoid Pitfalls and Paradoxes." *Journal of Computer-Mediated Communication* 12 (4): 1298–1321.

Gibson, Margaret. 2016. "YouTube and Bereavement Vlogging: Emotional Exchange between Strangers." *Journal of Sociology* 52 (4): 631–45. https://doi.org/10.1177/1440783315573613.

Gillespie, Tarleton. 2017. "Algorithmically Recognizable: Santorum's Google Problem, and Google's Santorum Problem." *Information, Communication and Society* 20 (1): 63–80. https://doi.org/10.1080/1369118X.2016.1199721.

GitHub. n.d. "Geo-search-tool." Accessed December 27, 2017. https://github.com/youtube/geo
-search-tool.

Gittinger, Juli L. 2014. "Is There Such a Thing as 'Cyberimperialism'?" *Continuum* 28 (4):
509–19. https://doi.org/10.1080/10304312.2014.907873.

Glaser, April. 2016. "Here's Why Facebook's Massive Drone Crashed in the Arizona Desert."
Recode, December 18, 2016. https://www.recode.net/2016/12/18/13998900/facebooks
-drone-crash-aquila-arizona-structural-failure.

———. 2017. "You Can Now Check if You Interacted with Russian Agents on Facebook."
Slate, December 22, 2017. https://slate.com/technology/2017/12/you-can-now-check-if
-you-interacted-with-russian-agents-on-facebook.html.

Glasze, Georg. 2017. "Geoinformation, Cartographic (Re)Presentation and the Nation State:
A Co-Constitutive Relation and Its Transformation in the Digital Age." In *The Net and
the Nation State: Multidisciplinary Perspectives on Internet Governance*, edited by Uta
Kohl, 218–40. Cambridge, UK: Cambridge University Press.

Goggin, Gerard, and Mark McLelland. 2009. "The Internationalization of the Internet and Its
Implications for Media Studies." In *Internationalizing Media Studies*, edited by Daya
Kishan Thussu, 277–93. London: Routledge.

———. 2017. *The Routledge Companion to Global Internet Histories.* New York: Taylor and Francis.

Goldsmith, Jack L. 1997. "The Internet and the Abiding Significance of Territorial
Sovereignty." *Indiana Journal of Global Legal Studies.* 5:475–91.

Goldsmith, Jack, and Tim Wu. 2006. *Who Controls the Internet? Illusions of a Borderless
World.* Oxford, UK: Oxford University Press.

Google AdSense. n.d. "How AdSense Works." Accessed October 22, 2020. https://support
.google.com/adsense/answer/6242051?hl=en.

Google Station. n.d. "Connect to So Much More." Accessed October 22, 2020. https://station
.google.com/.

Google Transparency Report. n.d. "Global Requests for User Information." Accessed October
22, 2020. https://transparencyreport.google.com/user-data/overview?user_requests
_report_period=series:requests,accounts;authority:US&lu=user_requests_report_period.

Grasswick, Heidi E. 2011. "Introduction: Feminist Epistemology and Philosophy of Science
in Twenty First Century." In *Feminist Epistemology and Philosophy of Science: Power
in Knowledge*, edited by Heidi E. Grasswick, xiii–xxx. Berlin: Springer Science and
Business Media.

Gray, Richard. 2016. "What a Vain Bunch We Really Are! 24 Billion Selfies Were Uploaded to
Google Last Year." *Daily Mail*, June 1, 2016. http://www.dailymail.co.uk/sciencetech
/article-3619679/What-vain-bunch-really-24-billion-selfies-uploaded-Google-year
.html.

Grewal, David Singh. 2008. *Network Power: The Social Dynamics of Globalization.* New
Haven, CT: Yale University Press.

Griffin, Andrew. 2015. "Wikipedia's Most Edited Articles: WWE and George W Bush Take
Spot as Encyclopedia's Most Controversial Topics." *Independent*, June 25, 2015. http://
www.independent.co.uk/life-style/gadgets-and-tech/news/wikipedias-most-edited
-articles-wwe-and-george-w-bush-take-spot-as-encyclopedias-most-controversial
-topics-10343162.html.

Guardian. 2017. "Turkey Blocks Wikipedia under Law Designed to Protect National
Security." April 29, 2017. https://www.theguardian.com/world/2017/apr/29/turkey
-blocks-wikipedia-under-law-designed-to-protect-national-security.

Guha, Ramachandra. 2002. *History at the Limit of World-History*. New York: Columbia University Press.

Guins, Raiford. 2009. *Edited Clean Version: Technology and the Culture of Control*. Minneapolis: University of Minnesota Press.

Guldbrandsson, Lennart. 2013. "Swedish Wikipedia Surpasses 1 Million Articles with Aid of Article Creation Bot." June 17, 2013. http://blog.wikimedia.org/2013/06/17/swedish -wikipedia-1-million-articles/.

Hafner, K., and Saritha Rai. 2005. "Google Offers a Bird's-Eye View, and Some Governments Tremble." *New York Times*, December 20, 2005, A1.

Halfaker, Aaron, R. Stuart Geiger, Jonathan T. Morgan, and John Riedl. 2013. "The Rise and Decline of an Open Collaboration System How Wikipedia's Reaction to Popularity Is Causing Its Decline." *American Behavioral Scientist* 57 (5): 664–88. https://doi.org /10.1177/0002764212469365.

Hall, Stuart. 1997. "The Local and the Global: Globalization and Ethnicity." *Cultural Politics* 11:173–87.

Harcourt, Alison, and Robert G. Picard. 2009. "Policy, Economic, and Business Challenges of Media Ownership Regulation." *Journal of Media Business Studies* 6 (3): 1–17.

Harding, Thomas. 2007a. "Google Blots Out Iraq Bases on Internet." *Telegraph*, January 20, 2007. https://www.telegraph.co.uk/news/worldnews/1540039/Google-blots-out-Iraq- bases-on-internet.html.

———. 2007b. "Terrorists 'Use Google Maps to Hit UK Troops.'" *Telegraph*, January 13, 2007. http://www.telegraph.co.uk/news/worldnews/1539401/Terrorists-use-Google-maps-to- hit-UK-troops.html.

Hardt, Michael, and Antonio Negri. 2000. *Empire*. Cambridge, MA: Harvard University Press.

Harindranath, Ramaswami. 2003. "Reviving 'Cultural Imperialism': International Audiences, Global Capitalism, and the Transnational Elite." *Planet TV: A Global Television Reader*, edited by Lisa Parks and Shanti Kumar, 155–68. New York: NYU Press.

Harris, Tristan. 2016. "How Technology Is Hijacking Your Mind—From a Magician and Google Design Ethicist." Thrive Global, May 19, 2016. https://medium.com/thrive -global/how-technology-hijacks-peoples-minds-from-a-magician-and-google-s -design-ethicist-56d62ef5edf3.

Hasan, Heather. 2011. *Wikipedia, 3.5 Million Articles and Counting: Using and Assessing the People's Encyclopedia*. New York: Rosen.

Havenstein, Heather. 2007. "Wikipedia Founder Rejects His 'Ignore All Rules' Mantra in New Online Project." Computerworld. April 2, 2007. http://www.computerworld.com /article/2553395/networking/wikipedia-founder-rejects-his--ignore-all-rules--mantra -in-new-online-project.html.

Heidegger, Martin. 1977. *The Question Concerning Technology, and Other Essays*. New York: Harper and Row.

Held, D. 2004. *Global Covenant: The Social Democratic Alternative to the Washington Consensus*. Cambridge, MA: Cambridge Press.

Herman, Lawrence. 2009. "The Aloha State: Place Names and the Anti-conquest of Hawai'i." In *Critical Toponymies*, edited by Lawrence D. Berg and Jani Vuolteenaho. 101–36. Farnham, UK: Ashgate.

Hernandez, Javier C. 2010. "Google Calls for Action on Web Limits." *New York Times*, March 24, 2010. https://www.nytimes.com/2010/03/25/technology/25google.html.

Herring, Susan. 2011. "Communication Styles Make a Difference." *New York Times*, February 4, 2011. http://www.nytimes.com/roomfordebate/2011/02/02/where-are-the-women-in -wikipedia/communication-styles-make-a-difference.

Hill, Benjamin Mako, and Aaron Shaw. 2013. "The Wikipedia Gender Gap Revisited: Characterizing Survey Response Bias with Propensity Score Estimation." *PLoS ONE* 8 (6): e65782. https://doi.org/10.1371/journal.pone.0065782.

Hillis, Ken, Michael Petit, and Kylie Jarrett. 2013. *Google and the Culture of Search*. Abingdon: Routledge.

Hindu. 2014. "India Has Slowest Internet Penetration Growth in APAC." June 5, 2014. http://www.thehindu.com/sci-tech/technology/internet/india-has-slowest-internet -penetration-growth-in-apac/article6085420.ece.

———. 2016. "After Rumours, Northeast People Flee Bangalore." July 1, 2016. http://www .thehindu.com/news/national/karnataka/after-rumours-northeast-people-flee -bangalore/article3776549.ece.

Hinsley, Francis Harry. 1986. *Sovereignty*. Cambridge, UK: Cambridge University Press.

Hobart Mercury. 2005. "Google Faces Terror Claim." October 17, 2005.

Hume, David. 1965. *Of the Standard of Taste and Other Essays*. Indianapolis: Bobbs-Merrill.

Hund, Emily. 2017. "Measured Beauty: Exploring the Aesthetics of Instagram's Fashion Influencers." *#SMSociety17: Proceedings of the 8th International Conference on Social Media and Society* 44 (July 2017): 1–5. https://doi.org/10.1145/ 3097286.3097330.

Hurt, Christine. 2017. "Protecting Gamblers or Protecting Gambling? The Economic Dimension of Borderless Online 'Speech.'" In *The Net and the Nation State: Multidisciplinary Perspectives on Internet Governance*, edited by Uta Kohl, 81–92. Cambridge, UK: Cambridge University Press.

Hutchby, Ian. 2001. *Conversation and Technology: From the Telephone to the Internet*. Cambridge, UK; Malden, MA: Polity.

Ihde D. 1979. "Heidegger's Philosophy of Technology." In *Technics and Praxis*, 103–29. Boston Studies in the Philosophy of Science, vol. 24. Dordrecht: Springer. https://doi .org/10.1007/978-94-009-9900-8_9.

Indo-Asian News Service. 2005. "Google Takes India's Concerns over Satellite Imaging 'Very Seriously.'" October 18, 2005. https://www.dnaindia.com/world/report-google-takes -india-s-concerns-seriously-agrees-to-dialogue-6248.

Ingenta. 2014. "IPA Report Says Global Publishing Productivity Is Up, but Growth Is Down." October 31, 2014. https://www.ingenta.com/blog-article/ipa-report-says-global -publishing-productivity-is-up-but-growth-is-down-2/.

Innis, Harold A. 2008. *The Bias of Communication*. Toronto: University of Toronto Press.

International Telecommunication Union. 2019. *Measuring Digital Development: Facts and Figures 2019*. Geneva, Switzerland: ITU Publications. https://www.itu.int/en/ITU-D /Statistics/Documents/facts/FactsFigures2019.pdf.

———. n.d. "Country Classifications." Accessed October 21, 2020. https://www.itu.int/en /ITU-D/Statistics/Pages/definitions/regions.aspx.

Internet Live Stats. n.d. "Internet Users." Accessed October 21, 2020. http://www.internetlivestats .com/internet-users/.

Internet.org. n.d. "Where We've Launched." Accessed October 22, 2020. https://info.internet
.org/en/story/where-weve-launched/.

Internet World Stats. n.d. "Internet Users Distribution in the World—2020 Q1." Accessed
April 15, 2020. http://www.internetworldstats.com/stats.htm.

IPFS. 2017. "Uncensorable Wikipedia on IPFS." May 4, 2017. https://ipfs.io/blog
/24-uncensorable-wikipedia/.

———. n.d. "IPFS Powers the Distributed Web." Accessed October 15, 2020. https://ipfs.io/.

IPKey. n.d. "IP Resources." Accessed October 22, 2020. http://www.ipkey.org/en/ip-law
-document/download/2324/3148/23.

Ippolita. 2013. *The Dark Side of Google*. Amsterdam: Institute of Network Cultures.

Irish Independent. 2005. "The Spy in the Sky with a Sinister Twist." November 23, 2005.
https://www.pressreader.com/ireland/irish-independent/20051123/282282430702132.

Jacobs, Jane. 2003. "Earth Honoring: Western Desires and Indigenous Knowledges." In
Feminist Postcolonial Theory: A Reader, edited by Reina Lewis and Sara Mills, 667–91.
New York: Routledge.

Jaggar, Alison M. 1989. "Love and Knowledge: Emotion in Feminist Epistemology." *Inquiry*
32 (2): 151–76. https://doi.org/10.1080/00201748908602185.

Jameson, Frederic. 1998. "Notes on Globalization as Philosophical Issue." In *The Cultures
of Globalization: Post-Contemporary Interventions*, edited by Frederic Jameson and
Masao Miyoshi, 54–80. Durham, NC: Duke University Press.

Jamie. 2019. "65+ Social Networking Sites You Need to Know About." Make a Website Hub,
June 5, 2019. https://makeawebsitehub.com/social-media-sites/.

Jemielniak, Dariusz. 2014. *Common Knowledge? An Ethnography of Wikipedia*. Stanford, CA:
Stanford University Press.

Jenkins, Henry. 2008. *Convergence Culture: Where Old and New Media Collide*. New York:
NYU.

Jenner, Mareike. 2018. *Netflix and the Re-Invention of Television*. London: Palgrave
Macmillan.

Jin, Dal Yong. 2015. *Digital Platforms, Imperialism and Political Culture*. New York:
Routledge.

Joseph, Manu. 2015. "Vyapam Corruption Case Mystifies India." *New York Times*, July 8, 2015.
http://www.nytimes.com/2015/07/09/world/asia/vyapam-corruption-case-mystifies
-india.html.

Kang, Cecilia. 2016. "Court Backs Rules Treating Internet as Utility, Not Luxury."
Technology, *New York Times*, June 14, 2016. https://www.nytimes.com/2016/06/15
/technology/net-neutrality-fcc-appeals-court-ruling.html.

———. 2017. "F.C.C. Repeals Net Neutrality Rules." Technology, *New York Times*, December 14,
2017. https://www.nytimes.com/2017/12/14/technology/net-neutrality-repeal-vote.html.

Kennedy, Paul. 2001. "Introduction: Globalization and the Crisis of Identities?" In
Globalization and National Identities, edited by Paul Kennedy and Catherine Danks,
1–28. New York: Palgrave Macmillan.

Kildall, Scott, and Nathaniel Stern. 2011. "Wikipedia Art: Citation as Performative Act." In
Critical Point of View: A Wikipedia Reader, edited by Geert Lovink and Nathaniel
Tkacz, 165–90. Amsterdam: Institute of Network Cultures.

Kitchin, Rob, and Martin Dodge. 2011. *Code/Space: Software and Everyday Life*. Cambridge,
MA: MIT Press.

Kittler, Friedrich A. 1999. *Gramophone, Film, Typewriter*. Stanford, CA: Stanford University Press.

Kittur, Aniket, Ed Chi, Bryan A. Pendleton, Bongwon Suh, and Todd Mytkowicz. 2007. "Power of the Few vs. Wisdom of the Crowd: Wikipedia and the Rise of the Bourgeoisie." *World Wide Web* 1 (2): 19.

Kittur, Aniket, and Robert E. Kraut. 2008. "Harnessing the Wisdom of Crowds in Wikipedia: Quality through Coordination." *CSCW '08: Proceedings of the 2008 ACM Conference on Computer Supported Cooperative Work* (November 2008): 37–46. https://doi .org/10.1145/1460563.1460572.

Kittur, Aniket, Bongwon Suh, Bryan A. Pendleton, and Ed H. Chi. 2007. "He Says, She Says: Conflict and Coordination in Wikipedia." *CHI '07: Proceedings of the SIGCHI Conference on Human Factors in Computing Systems* (April 2007): 453–62. https://doi .org/10.1145/1240624.1240698.

Kleinwachter, Wolfgang. 1989. "Three Waves of the Debate." In *The Global Media Debate: Its Rise, Fall and Renewal*, edited by G. Gerbner, H. Mowlana, and K. Nordenstreng, 13–20. Norwood, NJ: Ablex.

Knapton, Sarah. 2017. "'Selfitis'—the Obsessive Need to Post Selfies—Is a Genuine Mental Disorder, Say Psychologists." *Telegraph*, December 15, 2017. https://www.telegraph.co .uk/science/2017/12/15/selfitis-obsessive-need-post-selfies-genuine-mental-disorder/.

Koh, Adeline, and Roopika Risam. n.d. *Postcolonial Digital Humanities* (blog). Accessed January 8, 2014. http://dhpoco.org/blog/.

Kohl, Uta. 2017. *The Net and the Nation State: Multidisciplinary Perspectives on Internet Governance*. Cambridge, UK: Cambridge University Press.

Kohl, Uta, and Carrie Fox. 2017. "Introduction: Internet Governance and the Resilience of the Nation State." In *The Net and the Nation State: Multidisciplinary Perspectives on Internet Governance*, edited by Uta Kohl, 1–24. Cambridge, UK: Cambridge University Press.

Kohl, Uta, and Diane Rowland. 2017. "Censorship and Cyberborders through EU Data Protection Law." In *The Net and the Nation State: Multidisciplinary Perspectives on Internet Governance*, edited by Uta Kohl, 93–119. Cambridge, UK: Cambridge University Press.

Kohs, Gregory. 2011. "Wikipedia Biographies Favor Men." *Examiner*, January 12, 2011. http://www.examiner.com/article/wikipedia-biographies-favor-men. Page no longer available.

Kraidy, Marwan. 2001. "From Imperialism to Glocalization: A Theoretical Framework for the Information Age." In *Cyberimperialism? Global Relations in the New Electronic Frontier*, edited by Bosah Louis Ebo, 27–42. Westport, CT: Praeger.

———. 2007. *Hybridity, or the Cultural Logic of Globalization*. Delhi: Pearson Education India.

Kramer, Adam D. I., Jamie E. Guillory, and Jeffrey T. Hancock. 2014. "Experimental Evidence of Massive-Scale Emotional Contagion through Social Networks." *Proceedings of the National Academy of Sciences* 111 (24): 8788–90. https://doi.org/10.1073/pnas.1320040111.

Krasner, Stephen D. 1995. "Compromising Westphalia." *International Security* 20 (3): 115–51.

———. 1999. *Sovereignty: Organized Hypocrisy*. Princeton, NJ: Princeton University Press.

Kreijen, Gerard. 2004. *State Failure, Sovereignty and Effectiveness: Legal Lessons from the Decolonization of Sub-Saharan Africa*. Vol. 50. Leiden: Martinus Nijhoff.

Kuchler, Hannah. 2016. "Facebook, Google and the Race to Sign up India." *Financial Times*, March 18, 2016. https://www.ft.com/content/91539fc4-ebc5-11e5-888e-2eadd5fbc4a4.

Kuhn, Thomas. 1970. *The Structure of Scientific Revolutions*. Chicago: University of Chicago Press.

Kumar, Sangeet. 2010. "Google Earth and the Nation State: Sovereignty in the Age of New Media." *Global Media and Communication* 6 (2): 154–76.

———. 2014. "Articulation as a Site of Discursive Struggle: Globalization and Nationalism in an Indian Media Debate." *Journal of Communication Inquiry* 38 (2): 113–30.

———. 2016. "The Global as the Postcolonial: Desire, Identity, and Liminality in Indian Rock." *International Journal of Communication* 10:3106–23.

———. 2017. "A River by Any Other Name: Ganga/Ganges and the Postcolonial Politics of Knowledge on Wikipedia." *Information, Communication and Society* 20 (6): 809–24. https://doi.org/10.1080/1369118X.2017.1293709.

———. 2019. "The Algorithmic Dance: YouTube's Adpocalypse and the Gatekeeping of Cultural Content on Digital Platforms." *Internet Policy Review* 8 (2). https://policyreview.info/articles/analysis/algorithmic-dance-youtubes-adpocalypse-and-gatekeeping-cultural-content-digital.

Kumar, Sangeet, and Radhika Parameswaran. 2018. "Charting an Itinerary for Postcolonial Communication and Media Studies." *Journal of Communication* 68 (2): 347–58. https://doi.org/10.1093/joc/jqx025.

Lacan, Jacques, Héloïse Fink, and Bruce Fink. 2006. *Ecrits: The First Complete Edition in English*. New York: W. W. Norton and Company.

Lam, Shyong (Tony) K., Anuradha Uduwage, Zhenhua Dong, Shilad Sen, David R. Musicant, Loren Terveen, and John Riedl. 2011. "WP:Clubhouse? An Exploration of Wikipedia's Gender Imbalance." *WikiSym '11: Proceedings of the 7th International Symposium on Wikis and Open Collaboration* (October 2011): 1–10. https://doi.org/10.1145/2038558.2038560.

Lamba, Hemank, Varun Bharadhwaj, Mayank Vachher, Divyansh Agarwal, Megha Arora, and Ponnurangam Kumaraguru. 2016. "Me, Myself and My Killfie: Characterizing and Preventing Selfie Deaths." *ArXiv:1611.01911 [Cs]* (November 7, 2016). http://arxiv.org/abs/1611.01911.

Landes, Joan B. 1988. *Women and the Public Sphere in the Age of the French Revolution*. Ithaca, NY: Cornell University Press.

Laniado, David, Andreas Kaltenbrunner, Carlos Castillo, and Mayo Fuster Morell. 2012. "Emotions and Dialogue in a Peer-Production Community: The Case of Wikipedia." *WikiSym '12: Proceedings of the Eighth Annual International Symposium on Wikis and Open Collaboration* (August 2012): 1–10. https://doi.org/10.1145/2462932.2462944.

Larkin, Brian. 2008. *Signal and Noise*. Durham, NC: Duke University Press.

Latour, Bruno. 2005. *Reassembling the Social: An Introduction to Actor-Network-Theory*. Oxford, UK: Oxford University Press.

———. 2011. "Network Theory| Networks, Societies, Spheres: Reflections of an Actor-Network Theorist." *International Journal of Communication* 5 (0): 15.

Legters, Lyman H. 1988. "The American Genocide." *Policy Studies Journal* 16 (4): 768–77.

Leitch, Thomas. 2014. *Wikipedia U: Knowledge, Authority, and Liberal Education in the Digital Age*. Baltimore: John Hopkins University Press.

Leslie, Ian. 2016. "The Scientists Who Make Apps Addictive." *1843*, October 20, 2016. https://www.1843magazine.com/features/the-scientists-who-make-apps-addictive.

Lewis, Reina, and Sara Mills. 2003. *Feminist Postcolonial Theory: A Reader.* New York: Routledge.

Liebes, Tamar, and Elihu Katz. 1994. *The Export of Meaning: Cross-Cultural Readings of Dallas.* Cambridge, UK: Polity.

Lindsay, Brendan C. 2012. *Murder State: California's Native American Genocide, 1846–1873.* Lincoln: University of Nebraska Press.

Lipman, Victor. 2013. "The World's Most Active Twitter Country? (Hint: Its Citizens Can't Use Twitter)." *Forbes*, May 1, 2013. http://www.forbes.com/sites/victorlipman /2013/05/01/the-worlds-most-active-twitter-country-hint-its-citizens-cant-use-twitter/.

Locke, John. 2003. *Two Treatises of Government and a Letter Concerning Toleration.* Edited by Ian Shapiro. New Haven, CT; London: Yale University Press.

Loon.com. n.d. "The Loon Flight System." Accessed September 14, 2020. https://loon.com /technology/flight-systems/.

Lovink, Geert. 2008. *Zero Comments: Blogging and Critical Internet Culture.* New York: Routledge.

Luers, Will. 2007. "Cinema without Show Business: A Poetics of Vlogging." *Post Identity* 5 (1). http://hdl.handle.net/2027/spo.pid9999.0005.105.

MacBride, S., and C. Roach. 1989. "The New International Information Order." In *The Global Media Debate: Its Rise, Fall and Renewal*, edited by G. Gerbner, H. Mowlana, and K. Nordenstreng, 3–11. New York: Ablex.

MacKinnon, Rebecca. 2013. *Consent of the Networked: The Worldwide Struggle for Internet Freedom.* New York: Basic Books.

Maguire, Yael. 2015. "Building Communications Networks in the Stratosphere." Facebook Engineering, July 30, 2015. https://code.facebook.com/posts/993520160679028/building -communications-networks-in-the-stratosphere/.

Mahapatra, D. 2005. "Google Earth Under Govt Scrutiny." *Times of India*, October 17, 2005. https://timesofindia.indiatimes.com/india/Google-earth-under-govt-scrutiny /articleshow/1264698.cms.

Malaymail. 2016. "MCMC: Special Committee Probing Claims of Paedophile Group on Telegram." June 3, 2016. https://www.malaymail.com/news/malaysia/2016/06/03/mcmc -special-committee-probing-claims-of-paedophile-on-telegram/1133461.

Malaysiakini. 2016. "Special Panel Probing Telegram Messaging by Local Paedophiles." June 3, 2016. https://www.malaysiakini.com/news/344001.

Manovich, Lev. 2001. *The Language of New Media.* Cambridge, MA: MIT press.

Marcuse, Herbert. 2014. "The New Forms of Control." In *Philosophy of Technology: The Technological Condition*, edited by Robert C. Scharff and Val Dusek, 449–55. Malden, MA: Blackwell.

Marwick, Alice E. 2013. *Status Update: Celebrity, Publicity, and Branding in the Social Media Age.* New Haven, CT: Yale University Press.

Mattingly, Marybeth J., and Suzanne M. Blanchi. 2003. "Gender Differences in the Quantity and Quality of Free Time: The U.S. Experience." *Social Forces* 81 (3): 999–1030. https:// doi.org/10.1353/sof.2003.0036.

McLuhan, Marshall. 2003. *Understanding Media.* Corte Madera, CA: Gingko Press.

———. 2011. *The Gutenberg Galaxy: The Making of Typographic Man.* Toronto: University of Toronto Press.

McNamara, Paul. 2008. "Israeli City Demands That Google Earth Erase Palestinian Claim— Google Says No." *Network World*, February 11, 2008. https://www.networkworld.com /article/2350780/israeli-city-demands-that-google-earth-erase-palestinian-claim---- google-says-no.html.

Metz, Cade. 2016. "Facebook's Giant Internet-Beaming Drone Finally Takes Flight." *Wired*, July 21, 2016. https://www.wired.com/2016/07/facebooks-giant-internet-beaming -drone-finally-takes-flight/.

———. 2017. "Machine Learning Invades the Real World on Internet Balloons." *Wired*, February 17, 2017. https://www.wired.com/2017/02/machine-learning-drifting-real -world-internet-balloons/.

Microsoft 4Afrika. n.d. "How 4Afrika Is Improving Quality of Life." Accessed October 22, 2020. https://www.microsoft.com/africa/4afrika/.

———. n.d. "Our Story." Accessed October 24, 2020. https://www.microsoft.com/africa /4afrika/about-us.aspx.

Microsoft White Spaces Database. n.d. "White Spaces Database." Accessed October 24, 2020. http://whitespaces.microsoftspectrum.com/.

Mignolo, Walter D. 2003. *The Darker Side of the Renaissance: Literacy, Territoriality, and Colonization.* 2nd Edition. Ann Arbor: University of Michigan Press.

———. 2011. *The Darker Side of Western Modernity: Global Futures, Decolonial Options.* Durham, NC: Duke University Press Books.

Milani, Leo. 2015. "Millions of Facebook Users Have No Idea They're Using the Internet." Quartz, February 9, 2015. https://qz.com/333313/milliions-of-facebook-users-have-no -idea-theyre-using-the-internet/.

Miller, Daniel, Elisabetta Costa, Nell Haynes, Tom McDonald, Razvan Nicolescu, Jolynna Sinanan, Juliano Spyer, Shriram Venkatraman, and Xinyuan Wang. 2016. *How the World Changed Social Media.* London: UCL Press.

Miller, Mara. 2018. "Views of Japanese Selfhood: Japanese and Western Perspectives." In *Culture and Self: Philosophical and Religious Perspectives, East and West,* edited by Douglas Alle, 145–62. New York: Routledge.

Miller, Toby. 2005. "Anti-Americanism and Popular Culture." Anti-Americanism Working Papers. Budapest: Central European University.

———. 2009. "Cybertarians of the World Unite: You Have Nothing to Lose but Your Tubes!" In *The Youtube Reader,* edited by P. Snickars and P. Vondereau, 424–40. Stockholm: National Library of Sweden. http://researchrepository.murdoch.edu.au/id/ eprint/26705/.

Miller, Toby, Nitin Govil, John McMurria, Richard Maxwell, and Ting Wang. 2004. *Global Hollywood 2.* 2nd ed. London: British Film Institute.

Milne, David, and Ian H. Witten. 2008. "Learning to Link with Wikipedia." *CIKM '08: Proceedings of the 17th ACM Conference on Information and Knowledge Management* (October 2008): 509–18. https://doi.org/10.1145/1458082.1458150.

Mims, Christopher. 2012. "Facebook's Plan to Find Its next Billion Users: Convince Them the Internet and Facebook Are the Same." Quartz, September 24, 2012. https:// qz.com/5180/facebooks-plan-to-find-its-next-billion-users-convince-them-the -internet-and-facebook-are-the-same/.

Miranda, Leticia. 2019. "These Are All the Businesses You Never Knew Were Owned by Amazon." BuzzFeed News, July 5, 2019. https://www.buzzfeednews.com/article /leticiamiranda/these-are-all-the-businesses-you-never-knew-were-owned-by.

Mirani, Leo. 2015. "Millions of Facebook Users Have No Idea They're Using the Internet." Quartz, February 9, 2015. https://qz.com/333313/milliions-of-facebook-users-have-no -idea-theyre-using-the-internet/.

Mitchell, Lincoln A. 2012. *The Color Revolutions*. Philadelphia: University of Pennsylvania Press.

Morozov, Evgeny. 2012. *The Net Delusion: The Dark Side of Internet Freedom*. New York: PublicAffairs.

———. 2014. "Facebook's Gateway Drug." Opinion, *New York Times*, August 2, 2014. https://www.nytimes.com/2014/08/03/opinion/sunday/evgeny-morozov-facebooks-gateway-drug.html.

———. 2015. "Facebook Isn't a Charity. The Poor Will Pay by Surrendering Their Data." *Guardian*, April 25, 2015. http://www.theguardian.com/commentisfree/2015/apr/26/facebook-isnt-charity-poor-pay-by-surrending-their-data.

Morris, John B., Jr. 2011. "Injecting the Public Interest into Internet Standards." In *Opening Standards: The Global Politics of Interoperability*, edited by Laura DeNardis, 3–12. Cambridge, MA: MIT Press.

Morris, Nancy, and Silvio Waisbord. 2001. "Rethinking Media Globalization and State Power." In *Media and Globalization: Why the State Matters*, edited by Nancy Morris and Silvio Waisbord. vii–xvi. Lanham, MD: Rowman and Littlefield.

Mountjoy, Shane. 2009. *Manifest Destiny: Westward Expansion*. New York: Infobase.

Mowshowitz, Abbe, and Akira Kawaguchi. 2002. "Assessing Bias in Search Engines." *Information Processing and Management* 38 (1): 141–56. https://doi.org/10.1016/S0306-4573(01)00020-6.

Mueller, Milton. 2017. *Will the Internet Fragment? Sovereignty, Globalization and Cyberspace*. Hoboken, NJ: John Wiley and Sons.

Mumford, Lewis. 1934. *Technics and Civilization*. London: Routledge and Kegan Paul.

Murgu, Andreea. 2015. "Was YouTube's Autoplay Feature a Bad Idea?" Softpedia, March 21, 2015. https://news.softpedia.com/news/Youtube-s-Autoplay-Feature-476400.shtml.

Nash, Catherine. 1993. "Remapping and Renaming: New Cartographies of Identity, Gender and Landscape in Ireland." *Feminist Review* 44 (July): 39–57. https://doi.org/10.2307/1395194.

———. 2009. "Irish Place Names: Postcolonial Locations." In *Critical Toponymies*, edited by Lawrence Berg and Jani Vuolteenaho, 137–52. Farnham, UK: Ashgate.

Nation (Thailand). 2013a. "Facebook Boss Wants to Get the World Online." August 25, 2013.

———. 2013b. "Internet Balloons to Benefit Small Firms: Google." June 20, 2013.

———. 2014. "Linking up World's Unconnected Two-Thirds." October 28, 2014.

NDTV. 2015. "Watch Full Video: Facebook's Mark Zuckerberg's townhall in Delhi." Filmed at the Indian Institute of Technology, Delhi. YouTube video, 58:12. https://www.youtube.com/watch?v=-C507xSES_g.

News Today. 2013. "Facebook's Gift to the Entire World." August 23, 2013.

New York Times. 2011. "Where Are the Women in Wikipedia?" February 2, 2011. https://www.nytimes.com/roomfordebate/2011/02/02/where-are-the-women-in-wikipedia.

———. 2015. "Dangerous Corruption in India." July 12, 2015. http://www.nytimes.com/2015/07/13/opinion/dangerous-corruption-in-india.html.

New Zealand Herald. 2013a. "Google Launches Project Loon." June 15, 2013. https://www.nzherald.co.nz/nz/google-launches-project-loon/GFHWZAK4J2KNWU6IEPVC35TBIY/.

———. 2013b. "Loon Project Brings the Web to Billions." June 16, 2013. https://www.nzherald.co.nz/technology/loon-project-brings-the-web-to-billions/BEK663C6FM6TXPGK274VMGHH5A/#.

———. 2015. "Google's Project Loon Gains Some Lift." April 22, 2015. https://www.nzherald
.co.nz/business/googles-project-loon-gains-some-lift/HOXKT2QIRYSA3D3HG
KMDGA22SA/.

Ní Aodha, Gráinne. 2017. "Wikipedia's Community Is 85% Male, and Founder Jimmy Wales
Isn't Sure How to Fix It." TheJournal.ie, October 29, 2017. https://www.thejournal.ie
/wikipedia-founder-gender-imbalance-3668767-Oct2017/.

Nieborg, David B, and Thomas Poell. 2018. "The Platformization of Cultural Production:
Theorizing the Contingent Cultural Commodity." *New Media and Society* 20 (11):
4275–92. https://doi.org/10.1177/1461444818769694.

Niederer, Sabine, and José van Dijck. 2010. "Wisdom of the Crowd or Technicity of Content?
Wikipedia as a Sociotechnical System." *New Media and Society* 12 (8): 1368–87. https://
doi.org/10.1177/1461444810365297.

Noble, David W. 1965. *Historians against History: The Frontier Thesis and the National
Covenant in American Historical Writing since 1830.* Minneapolis: University of
Minnesota Press.

Noble, Safiya. 2018. *Algorithms of Oppression: How Search Engines Reinforce Racism.* New
York: NYU Press.

Northon, Karen. 2014. "NASA Releases Earth Day 'Global Selfie' Mosaic of Our Home
Planet." NASA, May 22, 2014. http://www.nasa.gov/press/2014/may/nasa-releases
-earth-day-global-selfie-mosaic-of-our-home-planet.

Nov, Oded. 2007. "What Motivates Wikipedians?" *Communications of the ACM* 50 (11):
60–64. https://doi.org/10.1145/1297797.1297798.

Obeyesekere, Gananath. 1997. *The Apotheosis of Captain Cook: European Mythmaking in the
Pacific.* Princeton, NJ: Princeton University Press.

Ochieng, Lilian. 2015. "Coming Soon: Free Internet to Rural Areas." *Daily Nation* (Kenya),
November 16, 2015. https://www.knowledgebylanes.co.ke/%EF%BB%BFcoming-soon
-free-internet-to-rural-areas/.

O'Neil, Mathieu. 2011. "The Sociology of Critique in Wikipedia." *Journal of Peer Production,*
no. 0, 1–20. http://peerproduction.net/issues/issue-0/peer-reviewed-papers/sociology
-of-critique/.

Open Source Center. 2008. *The Google Controversy—Two Years Later.* July 30, 2008. http://
www.fas.org/irp/dni/osc/google.pdf.

Osiander, Andreas. 2001. "Sovereignty, International Relations, and the Westphalian Myth."
International Organization 55 (2): 251–87.

Oster, Jan. 2017. "Which Limits on Freedom of Expression Are Legitimate? Divergence of
Free Speech Values in Europe and the United States." In *The Net and the Nation State:
Multidisciplinary Perspectives on Internet Governance,* edited by Uta Kohl, 39–47.
Cambridge, UK: Cambridge University Press.

O'Sullivan, Dan. 2009. *Wikipedia: A New Community of Practice?* Farnham, UK:
Ashgate.

Pace, Jonathan. 2018. "The Concept of Digital Capitalism." *Communication Theory* 28 (3):
254–69. https://doi.org/10.1093/ct/qtx009.

Pak Banker. 2014. "Facebook Ready to Spend Billions to Bring Whole World Online."
September 8, 2014.

Pakistan Today. 2015. "Facebook's Zuckerberg in India to Get 'Next Billion Online.'" October
28, 2015.

Parameswaran, Radhika. 2002. "Local Culture in Global Media: Excavating Colonial and Material Discourses in National Geographic." *Communication Theory* 12 (3): 287–315. https://doi.org/10.1111/j.1468-2885.2002.tb00271.x.

———. 2008. "The Other Sides of Globalization: Communication, Culture, and Postcolonial Critique." *Communication, Culture and Critique* 1 (1): 116–25.

Parks, Lisa, and Nicole Starosielski. 2015. *Signal Traffic: Critical Studies of Media Infrastructures.* University of Illinois Press.

Pasquale, Frank. 2015. *The Black Box Society.* Cambridge, MA: Harvard University Press.

Perks, Lisa Glebatis. 2014. *Media Marathoning: Immersions in Morality.* Washington, DC: Lexington Books.

Perrin, Andrew, and Monica Anderson. 2019. "Share of US Adults Using Social Media, Including Facebook, Is Mostly Unchanged since 2018." Pew Research Center, April 10, 2019. https://www.pewresearch.org/fact-tank/2019/04/10/share-of-u-s-adults-using-social-media-including-facebook-is-mostly-unchanged-since-2018/.

Perritt, Henry H., Jr. 1998. "The Internet as a Threat to Sovereignty? Thoughts on the Internet's Role in Strengthening National and Global Governance." *Indiana Journal of Global Legal Studies* 5:423–42.

Peters, Benjamin. 2016. *How Not to Network a Nation: The Uneasy History of the Soviet Internet.* Cambridge, MA: MIT Press.

Peters, John Durham. 2015. *The Marvelous Clouds: Toward a Philosophy of Elemental Media.* Chicago: University of Chicago Press.

———. 2017. "'You Mean My Whole Fallacy Is Wrong': On Technological Determinism." *Representations* 140 (1): 10–26.

Pfeil, Ulrike, Panayiotis Zaphiris, and Chee Siang Ang. 2006. "Cultural Differences in Collaborative Authoring of Wikipedia." *Journal of Computer-Mediated Communication* 12 (1): 88–113. https://doi.org/10.1111/j.1083-6101.2006.00316.x.

Pham, Sherisse. 2020. "India Bans More Chinese Apps as Tensions Remain High." CNN, November 25, 2020. https://www.cnn.com/2020/11/25/tech/india-bans-chinese-apps-hnk-intl/index.html.

Phillipson, Robert. 1992. *Linguistic Imperialism.* Oxford, UK: Oxford University Press.

———. 2008. "The Linguistic Imperialism of Neoliberal Empire 1." *Critical Inquiry in Language Studies* 5 (1): 1–43.

———. 2009. *Linguistic Imperialism Continued.* Hyderabad, India; New York: Orient Blackswan Private Ltd.

Philippine Daily Inquirer. 2015a. "Mai-Mai's World." October 18, 2015. https://www.pressreader.com/philippines/philippine-daily-inquirer/20151018/281771333034448.

———. 2015b. "Pinoys Using Facebook's Internet.org Breach 4.5 Million Mark, Says TNT." July 8, 2015. https://technology.inquirer.net/43037/pinoys-using-facebooks-internet-org-breach-4-5m-mark-says-tnt.

Philpott, Daniel. 1995. "Sovereignty: An Introduction and Brief History." *Journal of International Affairs* 48 (2): 353–68.

Phippen, J. Weston. 2017. "Why Turkey Blocked Access to Wikipedia." *Atlantic*, April 29, 2017. https://www.theatlantic.com/news/archive/2017/04/turkey-blocks-wikipedia/524859/.

Pieterse, Jan Nederveen. 2006. "Globalization as Hybridization." In *Media and Culture Studies: Keyworks,* edited by Meenakshi Gigi Durham and Douglas Kellner, 658–80. Malden, MA: Blackwell.

Pimienta, Daniel, Daniel Prado, and Álvaro Blanco. 2009. *Twelve Years of Measuring Linguistic Diversity in the Internet: Balance and Perspectives.* Paris: UNESCO. http://www.ifap.ru/pr/2010/n100305c.pdf.

Plantin, Jean-Christophe, Carl Lagoze, Paul N. Edwards, and Christian Sandvig. 2018. "Infrastructure Studies Meet Platform Studies in the Age of Google and Facebook." *New Media and Society* 20 (1): 293–310. https://doi.org/10.1177/1461444816661553.

Plantin, Jean-Christophe, and Aswin Punathambekar. 2019. "Digital Media Infrastructures: Pipes, Platforms, and Politics." *Media, Culture and Society* 41 (2): 163–74. https://doi.org/10.1177/0163443718818376.

Poovey, Mary. 1998. *A History of the Modern Fact: Problems of Knowledge in the Sciences of Wealth and Society.* Chicago: University of Chicago Press.

Powers, Shawn M., and Michael Jablonski. 2015. *The Real Cyber War: The Political Economy of Internet Freedom.* Champaign: University of Illinois Press.

Premnath, Gautam. 2003. "The Weak Sovereignty of the Postcolonial Nation-State." In *World Bank Literature,* edited by Amitava Kumar, 253–64. Minneapolis: Minnesota University Press.

Press Trust of India. 2006. "Google Talking to Govt to Dispel Security Concerns." April 3, 2006.

———. 2007. "Home Ministry Meet Reviews Threat from Google Earth." June 6, 2007.

Price, Rob. 2017. "Billionaire Ex-Facebook President Sean Parker Unloads on Mark Zuckerberg and Admits He Helped Build a Monster." *Independent,* November 16, 2017. https://www.independent.co.uk/news/people/sean-parker-mark-zuckerberg-facebook-president-friends-reality-build-a8058751.html.

Punathambekar, Aswin, and Sriram Mohan. 2019. "Introduction: Mapping Global Digital Cultures." In *Global Digital Cultures: Perspectives from South Asia,* edited by Aswin Punathambekar and Sriram Mohan, 1–34. Ann Arbor: University of Michigan Press.

Rai, Saritha. 2016. "Google Outpaces Facebook on Getting India Connected to Internet." Bloomberg, August 4, 2016. https://www.bloomberg.com/news/articles/2016-08-05/google-outpaces-facebook-on-getting-india-connected-to-internet.

RailTel. n.d. "Full Scale Superlative RailWire Wi-Fi Experience." Accessed October 18, 2020. http://www.railtelindia.com/key-projects/station-wi-fi-project.html.

Reagle, Joseph Michael. 2010. *Good Faith Collaboration: The Culture of Wikipedia.* Cambridge, MA: MIT Press.

Rieder, Bernhard, and Guillaume Sire. 2013. "Conflicts of Interest and Incentives to Bias: A Microeconomic Critique of Google's Tangled Position on the Web." *New Media and Society* 16 (2): 195–211. https://doi.org/10.1177/1461444813481195.

Robins, Kevin. 1996. "Interrupting Identities: Turkey/Europe." In *Questions of Cultural Identity,* edited by Stuart Hall and Paul du Gay, 61–86. London: Sage Publications

Rogers, Everett M. 1983. *Diffusion of Innovations.* New York: Free Press.

Rogers, Richard. 2013. *Digital Methods.* Cambridge, MA: MIT Press.

Rose, Nikolas. 1996. *Inventing Our Selves: Psychology, Power, and Personhood.* UK: Cambridge University Press.

———. 1999. *Governing the Soul: The Shaping of the Private Self.* London: Free Association Books.

———. 2000. "Government and Control." *The British Journal of Criminology* 40 (2): 321–39. https://doi.org/10.1093/bjc/40.2.321.

Rosenau, J. 1999. *States, Sovereignty, and Diplomacy in the Information Age.* Washington, DC: United States Institute of Peace.

Rosenblat, Alex. 2018. *Uberland: How Algorithms Are Rewriting the Rules of Work.* Berkeley: University of California Press.

Rosenzweig, Roy. 2006. "Can History Be Open Source? *Wikipedia* and the Future of the Past." *The Journal of American History* 93 (1): 117–46. https://doi.org/10.2307/4486062.

Rushdie, Salman. 1981. *Midnight's Children.* London: Cape.

Ryann, Johnny. 2010. *A History of the Internet and the Digital Future.* London: Reaktion Books.

Said, Edward W. 1979. *Orientalism.* Princeton, NJ: Vintage.

———. 1994. *Culture and Imperialism.* New York: Vintage.

Sanger, Larry. 2004. "Why Wikipedia Must Jettison Its Anti-Elitism." December 31, 2004. https://larrysanger.org/2004/12/why-wikipedia-must-jettison-its-anti-elitism/.

Sassen, Saskia. 1998. "On the Internet and Sovereignty." *Indiana Journal of Global Legal Studies* 5 (2): 545–59.

———. 2007. "A Sociology of Globalization." New York: Norton and Company.

Sayer, Liana C. 2005. "Gender, Time and Inequality: Trends in Women's and Men's Paid Work, Unpaid Work and Free Time." *Social Forces* 84 (1): 285–303. https://doi.org/10.1353/sof.2005.0126.

Schiller, Herbert 1985. "Electronic Information Flows: New Basis for Global Domination?" *Television in Transition* (1985): 11–20.

———. 1992. *Mass Communication and American Empire.* Boulder, CO: Westview Press.

Schmitt, Carl. 1985. *Political Theology: Four Chapters on the Concept of Sovereignty.* Chicago: University of Chicago Press.

———. 2003. *The Nomos of the Earth in the International Law of the Jus Publicum Europaeum.* Translated by G. L Ulmen. New York: Telos Press.

Schonfeld, Erick. 2010. "Zuckerberg: 'We Are Building a Web Where the Default Is Social.'" TechCrunch, April 21, 2010. https://techcrunch.com/2010/04/21/zuckerbergs-buildin-web-default-social/.

Schroeder, Ralph. 2016. "The Globalization of On-Screen Sociability: Social Media and Tethered Togetherness." *International Journal of Communication* 10: 5626–5643.

———. 2018. *Social Theory after the Internet: Media, Technology, and Globalization.* London: University College London Press.

Schüll, Natasha Dow. 2012. *Addiction by Design: Machine Gambling in Las Vegas.* Princeton, NJ: Princeton University Press.

Seaver, Nick. 2019. "Captivating Algorithms: Recommender Systems as Traps." *Journal of Material Culture* 24 (4): 421–36. https://doi.org/10.1177/1359183518820366.

Sen, Sunny. 2016. "How Google Changed Itself for India in a 'Mission to Connect the World.'" *Hindustan Times,* November 14, 2016. https://www.hindustantimes.com/business-news/how-google-changed-itself-for-india-in-a-mission-to-connect-the-world/story-jMDLkztPtW9OUoWR4Zs9SJ.html.

Senarclens, Pierre de. 2003. "The Politics of Human Rights." In *The Globalization of Human Rights,* edited by Jean-Marc Coicaud, Michael W. Doyle, and Anne-Marie Gardner, 137–59. Tokyo: United Nations University Press.

Senft, Theresa M. 2008. *Camgirls: Celebrity and Community in the Age of Social Networks.* Bern: Peter Lang.

Senft, Theresa M., and Nancy K. Baym. 2015. "What Does the Selfie Say? Investigating a Global Phenomenon." *International Journal of Communication* 9 (19): 1588–606.

Servon, Lisa J. 2008. *Bridging the Digital Divide: Technology, Community and Public Policy.* Hoboken, NJ: John Wiley and Sons.

Shaban, Hamza, Craig Timberg, and Elizabeth Dwoskin. 2017. "Facebook, Google and Twitter Testified on Capitol Hill. Here's What They Said." *Washington Post*, October 31, 2017. https://www.washingtonpost.com/news/the-switch/wp/2017/10/31/facebook-google-and-twitter-are-set-to-testify-on-capitol-hill-heres-what-to-expect/.

Shahmah, D. 2007. "Security and Other Secrets at Google Earth." *Jerusalem Post*, October 9, 2007. https://www.jpost.com/business/business-features/digital-world-security-and-secrets-at-google.

Sheetz, Michael. 2019. "Amazon Wants to Launch Thousands of Satellites so It Can Offer Broadband Internet from Space." CNBC, April 4, 2019. https://www.cnbc.com/2019/04/04/amazon-project-kuiper-broadband-internet-small-satellite-network.html.

Shome, Raka. 2019. "When Postcolonial Studies Interrupts Media Studies." *Communication, Culture and Critique* 12 (3): 305–22. https://doi.org/10.1093/ccc/tcz020.

Shome, Raka, and Radha S. Hegde. 2002. "Postcolonial Approaches to Communication: Charting the Terrain, Engaging the Intersections." *Communication Theory* 12 (3): 249–70. https://doi.org/10.1111/j.1468-2885.2002.tb00269.x.

Shreeve, J. L. 2005. "I Spy with My Little Laptop; It's Supposed to Be a Tool for Fun and Research, but Now Governments Fear It May Be Helping Terrorists." *Independent*, December 21, 2005. https://www.independent.co.uk/news/science/i-spy-with-my-little-laptop-520316.html.

Siliconindia. 2005. "India Protests Google Kashmir Map." December 1, 2005. http://www.siliconindia.com/shownews/India-protests-Google-Kashmir-map-nid-30097-cid-Top.html.

Silver, Laura, and Aaron Smith. 2019. "In Some Countries, Many Use the Internet without Realizing It." Pew Research Center, May 2, 2019. https://www.pewresearch.org/fact-tank/2019/05/02/in-some-countries-many-use-the-internet-without-realizing-it/.

Silverman, Ellie. 2017. "Facebook's First President, on Facebook: 'God Only Knows What It's Doing to Our Children's Brains.'" The Switch, *Washington Post*, November 9, 2017. https://www.washingtonpost.com/news/the-switch/wp/2017/11/09/facebooks-first-president-on-facebook-god-only-knows-what-its-doing-to-our-childrens-brains/.

Simonite, Tom. 2013. "The Decline of Wikipedia: Even as More People Than Ever Rely on It, Fewer People Create It." MIT Technology Review, October 22, 2013. https://www.technologyreview.com/2013/10/22/175674/the-decline-of-wikipedia/.

Simonton, Stell. 2018. "Where Are the Women of Wikipedia?" HowStuffWorks, August 2, 2018. https://computer.howstuffworks.com/internet/basics/where-are-women-of-wikipedia.htm.

Singh, Harmeet Shah, and Jethro Mullen. 2015. "Alarm in India over Dozens of Deaths of People Linked to Vyapam Scandal." CNN, July 7, 2015. http://www.cnn.com/2015/07/07/asia/india-vyapam-scandal-deaths/index.html.

Slashdot. 2004. "Wikipedia Founder Jimmy Wales Responds." July 28, 2004. http://slashdot.org/story/04/07/28/1351230/wikipedia-founder-jimmy-wales-responds.

Smyrnaios, Nikos. 2018. *Internet Oligopoly: The Corporate Takeover of Our Digital World.* Bingley, UK: Emerald.

Smyser, A. A. 1991. "Questions Remain on Hawaiian Immersion." *Honolulu Star-Bulletin*, March 19, 1991.

Solomon, Brian. 2014. "Facebook Follows Amazon, Google into Drones with $60 Million Purchase." *Forbes*, March 4, 2014. https://www.forbes.com/sites/briansolomon /2014/03/04/facebook-follows-amazon-google-into-drones-with-60-million -purchase/#65806cfe60b8.

Sowetan. 2013. "Facebook Aims to Get World Online." August 23, 2013. https://www .pressreader.com/south-africa/sowetan/20130823/281900180863637.

Spivak, Gayatri Chakravorty. 1999. *A Critique of Postcolonial Reason: Toward a History of the Vanishing Present*. Cambridge, MA: Harvard University Press.

———. 2013. *An Aesthetic Education in the Era of Globalization*. Cambridge, MA: Harvard University Press.

Srinivasan, Ramesh. 2013. "Re-Thinking the Cultural Codes of New Media: The Question Concerning Ontology." *New Media and Society* 15 (2): 203–23. https://doi.org/10.1177 /1461444812450686.

Srivas, Anuj. 2017. "How the Controversial Geospatial Bill Snowballed—and Was Then Shoved into Cold Storage." The Wire, March 7, 2017. https://thewire.in/114584 /controversial-geospatial-bill-snowballed-shoved-cold-storage/.

Srivatsa, Sharath S., and Deepa Kurup. 2012. "After Rumours, Northeast People Flee Bangalore." *Hindu*, August 16, 2012. http://www.thehindu.com/news/national/karnataka/after-rumours -northeast-people-flee-bangalore/article3776549.ece.

Stannard, David E. 1992. *American Holocaust: The Conquest of the New World*. Oxford, UK: Oxford University Press.

Starkey, Armstrong. 2002. *European and Native American Warfare 1675–1815*. London: Routledge.

Statesman. 2005. "Kalam's Google Alert Wakes Up Security Agencies." October 19, 2005.

Stein, Janice Gross, Robert Faris, Nart Villeneuve, Ross Anderson, Steven Murdoch, Mary Rundle, and Malcolm Birdling. 2008. *Access Denied: The Practice and Policy of Global Internet Filtering*. Edited by Ronald Deibert, John Palfrey, Rafal Rohozinski, and Jonathan Zittrain. Cambridge, MA: MIT Press.

Sterling, T. 2005. "Dutch Lawmakers Question Whether Terrorists Could Use Google Earth Soft-Ware." Associated Press Worldstream, August 17, 2005.

Straumann, Ralph K., and Mark Graham. 2016. "Who Isn't Online? Mapping the 'Archipelago of Disconnection.'" *Regional Studies, Regional Science* 3 (1): 96–98. https:// doi.org/10.1080/21681376.2015.1116960.

Suciu, Peter. 2016. "Google's Loons to Glide Over India." *E-Commerce Times*, March 8, 2016. https://www.ecommercetimes.com/story/83202.html.

Su-Lyn, Boo. 2016. "Cops' Hands Tied over Telegram Child Porn, Rape Videos, Tech Experts Say." *Malay Mail Online*, June 17, 2016. http://www.themalaymailonline. com/malaysia/article/cops-hands-tied-over-telegram-child-porn-rape-videos-tech -experts-say.

Svantesson, Dan Jerker B. 2017. "Cyberborders through 'Code': An All-or-Nothing Affair?" In *The Net and the Nation State: Multidisciplinary Perspectives on Internet Governance*, edited by Uta Kohl, 110–24. Cambridge, UK: Cambridge University Press.

Svoboda, E. 2005. "Google's Open Skies Raise Cries." *Christian Science Monitor*, December 1, 2005. https://www.csmonitor.com/2005/1201/p13s01-stct.html.

Taneja, Harsh, and Angela Xiao Wu. 2014. "Does the Great Firewall Really Isolate the Chinese? Integrating Access Blockage with Cultural Factors to Explain Web User Behavior." *The Information Society* 30 (5): 297–309.

Taylor, Charles. 1989. *Sources of the Self: The Making of the Modern Identity.* Cambridge, MA: Harvard University Press.

Thaler, Richard H., and Cass R. Sunstein. 2008. *Nudge: Improving Decisions about Health, Wealth, and Happiness.* New Haven, CT: Yale University Press.

Thiagarajan, Kamala. 2017. "India Declares War on Unsafe Selfies." NPR, November 14, 2017. https://www.npr.org/sections/goatsandsoda/2017/11/14/563255936/india-declares-war-on-unsafe-selfies.

Thien, Vee Vian, Heike Jensen, Jac sm Kee, Gayathri Venkiteswaran, Sonia Randhawa, Pirongrong Ramasoota, Erwin A. Alampay, et al. 2011. *Access Contested: Security, Identity, and Resistance in Asian Cyberspace.* Edited by Ronald Deibert, John Palfrey, Rafal Rohozinski, and Jonathan Zittrain. Cambridge, MA: MIT Press.

This Day. 2014. "Facebook to Be Free on All Mobile Networks in East Africa." April 27, 2014.

Thussu, Daya Kishan. 2005. "From Macbride to Murdoch: The Marketisation of Global Communication." *Javnost—The Public* 12 (3): 47–60. https://doi.org/10.1080/13183222.2005.11008894.

———. 2015. "Digital BRICS: Building a NWICO 2.0?" In *Mapping BRICS Media*, edited by K. Nordenstreng and Daya Kishan Thussu, 242–63. London: Routledge. https://doi.org/10.4324/9781315726212-16.

———. 2018. *International Communication: Continuity and Change.* New York: Bloomsbury.

Tifentale, Alise. 2014. "The Selfie: Making Sense of the 'Masturbation of Self-Image' and the 'Virtual Mini-Me.'" Selfiecity.net, February 2014. http://d25rsf93iwlmgu.cloudfront.net/downloads/Tifentale_Alise_Selfiecity.pdf.

Times of India. 2005. "Google's Soul-Searching on Kalam Worries." October 19, 2005. https://timesofindia.indiatimes.com/india/Googles-soul-searching-on-Kalams-worries/articleshow/1268405.cms.

———. 2006. "Google Earth Images to Be Masked." March 10, 2006. https://timesofindia.indiatimes.com/city/delhi/Google-Earth-images-to-be-masked/articleshow/1444939.cms.

Tkacz, Nathaniel. 2015. *Wikipedia and the Politics of Openness.* Chicago: University of Chicago Press.

Tkacz, Nathaniel, and Geert Lovink, eds. 2011. *Critical Point of View a Wikipedia Reader.* Amsterdam: Institute of Network Cultures.

Today Online. 2016. "Monsters among Us: Malaysians Are Sharing Child Porn, Rape Videos on Telegram." June 16, 2016. http://www.todayonline.com/world/asia/monsters-among-us-malaysians-are-sharing-child-porn-rape-videos-telegram.

Tomlinson, John. 1995. *Cultural Imperialism a Critical Introduction.* Baltimore: Johns Hopkins University Press.

Tomlinson, Simon. 2014. "Is This the World's Most Prolific Writer? Meet the Swedish Physicist Who Has Written 8.5% of Everything on Wikipedia." *Mail Online*, July 15, 2014. http://www.dailymail.co.uk/news/article-2693129/Is-worlds-prolific-writer-Meet-Swedish-physicist-written-8-5-Wikipedia.html.

Trachtman, Joel P. 1998. "Cyberspace, Sovereignty, Jurisdiction, and Modernism." *Indiana Journal of Global Legal Studies* 5 (2): 561–81.

Tufekci, Zeynep. 2017. *Twitter and Tear Gas: The Power and Fragility of Networked Protest.* New Haven, CT: Yale University Press.

Turkle, Sherry. 2017. *Alone Together: Why We Expect More from Technology and Less from Each Other.* London: Hachette UK.

Turner, Fred. 2010. *From Counterculture to Cyberculture: Stewart Brand, the Whole Earth Network, and the Rise of Digital Utopianism.* Chicago: University of Chicago Press.

Turner, Frederick Jackson. 1920. *The Frontier in American History.* New York: Holt, Rinehart and Winston.

Turow, Joseph. 2011. *The Daily You: How the New Advertising Industry Is Defining Your Identity and Your Worth.* New Haven, CT: Yale University Press.

Tusikov, Natasha. 2017. *Chokepoints: Global Private Regulation on the Internet.* Berkeley, CA: University of California Press.

Udupa, Sahana. 2016. "Archiving as History-Making: Religious Politics of Social Media in India." *Communication, Culture and Critique* 9 (2): 212–30. https://doi.org/10.1111/cccr.12114.

United Nations News. 2015. "Mark Zuckerberg Addresses the UN Sustainable Development Summit." September 26, 2015. Facebook video, 03:55. https://www.facebook.com/UN.News.Centre/videos/mark-zuckerberg-addresses-the-un-sustainable-development-summit/10153252006166872.

Uttam, Payal. 2015. "Death by Selfie? Russian Police Release Safety Brochure." CNN, July 8, 2015. https://edition.cnn.com/2015/07/08/asia/russia-selfie-death-brochure/index.html.

Vaidhyanathan, Siva. 2012. *The Googlization of Everything:(and Why We Should Worry).* Berkeley: University of California Press.

——. 2018. *Antisocial Media: How Facebook Disconnects Us and Undermines Democracy.* New York: Oxford University Press.

Valby, Karen. 2011. "Wikipedia's Librarian to the World." *Fast Company*, April 4, 2011. http://www.fastcompany.com/1739776/wikipedias-librarian-world.

Valcke, Peggy. 2009. "From Ownership Regulations to Legal Indicators of Media Pluralism: Background, Typologies and Methods." *Journal of Media Business Studies* 6 (3): 19–42.

Varrier, Megha. 2017. "How a Secret Telegram Group of Child Sexual Predators Was Busted: A TNM Exclusive." *The News Minute*, December 22, 2017. https://www.thenewsminute.com/article/how-secret-telegram-group-child-sexual-predators-was-busted-tnm-exclusive-73603.

Vergano, Dan. 2013. "Study: Wikipedia Is Driving Away Newcomers." *USA Today*, January 3, 2013. http://www.usatoday.com/story/tech/2013/01/03/wikipedia-rules-new-editors/1801229/.

Vick, Douglas. 2001. "Exporting the First Amendment to Cyberspace: The Internet and State Sovereignty." In *Media and Globalization: Why the State Matters*, edited by N. Morris and S. Waisbord, 3–21. New York: Rowman and Littlefield.

Viegas, F. B., M. Wattenberg, J. Kriss, and F. van Ham. 2007. "Talk before You Type: Coordination in Wikipedia." *40th Annual Hawaii International Conference on System Sciences*, edited by Ralph H. Sprague Jr., 78. https://doi.org/10.1109/HICSS.2007.511.

Vincent, James. 2013. "Facebook: Mark Zuckerberg's Hunt for 5 Billion New Friends." *Independent on Saturday*, August 22, 2013. https://www.independent.co.uk/life-style/gadgets-and-tech/news/facebook-mark-zuckerberg-s-hunt-for-five-billion-new-friends-8778024.html.

Viswanathan, Gauri. 1997. "Currying Favor: The Politics of British Educational and Cultural Policy in India, 1813–54." In *Dangerous Liaisons: Gender, Nation, and Postcolonial Perspectives*, edited by Anne McClintock, Aamir Mufti, and Ella Shohat, 113–30. Minneapolis: University of Minnesota Press.

Walden, Celia. 2016. "We Take 1 Million Selfies Every Day—but What Are They Doing to Our Brains?" *Telegraph*, May 24, 2016. https://www.telegraph.co.uk/women/life/we-take-1-million-selfies-every-day---but-what-are-they-doing-to/.

Wallerstein, Immanuel Maurice. 2004. *World-Systems Analysis: An Introduction*. Durham, NC: Duke University Press.

Warschauer, Mark. 2004. *Technology and Social Inclusion: Rethinking the Digital Divide*. Cambridge, MA: MIT Press.

Waterloo Region Record. 2015. "Google to Deliver Internet Service to Indonesia via Balloons." October 29, 2015. https://www.therecord.com/business/2015/10/29/google-to-deliver-internet-service-to-indonesia-via-balloons.html.

Wei, Lulu. 2017. "Gatekeeping Practices in the Chinese Social Media and the Legitimacy Challenge." In *The Net and the Nation State: Multidisciplinary Perspectives on Internet Governance*, edited by Uta Kohl, 69–80. Cambridge, UK: Cambridge University Press.

West, Darrell M. 2015. "Digital Divide: Improving Internet Access in the Developing World through Affordable Services and Diverse Content." Washington, DC: Brookings Institution.

Wickman, Forrest. 2014. "What Was 'Poking'?" *Slate*, February 4, 2014. http://www.slate.com/articles/technology/technology/2014/02/facebook_s_poke_function_still_a_mystery_on_the_social_network_s_10th_anniversary.html.

Wikimania. 2013. "Submissions/WMF's New Global South Strategy." Accessed April 15, 2020. https://wikimania2013.wikimedia.org/wiki/Submissions/WMF%27s_New_Global_South_Strategy.

Wikimedia. 2011. *Editor Survey Report*. Wikimedia.org, April 2011. https://upload.wikimedia.org/wikipedia/commons/7/76/Editor_Survey_Report_-_April_2011.pdf

———. 2018a. "Wikipedia Statistics." December 31, 2018. https://stats.wikimedia.org/EN/Sitemap.htm.

———. 2018b. "Wikimedia Traffic Analysis Report—Wikipedia Page Views per Country—Breakdown." October 25, 2018. https://stats.wikimedia.org/wikimedia/squids/SquidReportPageViewsPerCountryBreakdown.htm.

———. 2019. "Wikipedia Statistics All Languages." January 31, 2019. https://stats.wikimedia.org/EN/TablesWikipediaZZ.htm.

———. n.d. "List of Wikipedias." Accessed October 20, 2020. https://meta.wikimedia.org/wiki/List_of_Wikipedias.

———. n.d. "Polls Are Evil." Accessed November 25, 2020. https://meta.wikimedia.org/wiki/Polls_are_evil.

———. n.d. "Wikimedia Statistics." Accessed October 20, 2020. https://stats.wikimedia.org/v2/#/all-projects/reading/pageviews-by-country.

———. n.d. "Wikimedia Statistics: Active Editors." Accessed November 25, 2020. https://stats.wikimedia.org/#/en.wikipedia.org/contributing/active-editors/normal|line|2-year|~total|monthly.

———. n.d. "Wikimedia Statistics: Monthly Overview." Accessed October 20, 2020. https://stats.wikimedia.org/v2/#/all-projects.

Wikipedia. n.d. "Deletionism and Inclusionism in Wikipedia." Accessed November 17, 2020. https://en.wikipedia.org/wiki/Deletionism_and_inclusionism_in_Wikipedia.

———. n.d. "Ignore All Rules." Accessed October 20, 2020. https://en.Wikipedia.org/wiki/Ignore_all_rules.

———. n.d. "List of Countries by English-Speaking Population." Accessed October 20, 2020. https://en.Wikipedia.org/wiki/List_of_countries_by_English-speaking_population.

———. n.d. "List of Wikipedias." Accessed November 25, 2020. https://en.wikipedia.org/wiki/List_of_Wikipedias.

———. n.d. "Wikipedia: Article Titles." Accessed June 30, 2015. https://en.Wikipedia.org/wiki/Wikipedia:Article_titles.

——— n.d. "Wikipedia: Pages with the Most Revisions" Accessed November 25, 2020. https://en.wikipedia.org/wiki/Special:MostRevisions.

———.n.d. "Wikipedia: Please Do Not Bite the Newcomers" Accessed November 25, 2020. https://en.wikipedia.org/wiki/Wikipedia:Please_do_not_bite_the_newcomers.

———n.d. "Wikipedia: Reliable Sources" Accessed July 30, 2015. https://en.wikipedia.org/wiki/Wikipedia:Reliable_sources.

———. n.d. "Wikipedia: Independent Sources." Accessed October 20, 2020. https://en.Wikipedia.org/wiki/Wikipedia:Third-party_sources.

———. n.d. "Wikipedia: No Original Research." Accessed November 17, 2020. https://en.wikipedia.org/wiki/Wikipedia:No_original_research.

———. n.d. "Wikipedia: Notability." Accessed November 17, 2020. https://en.wikipedia.org/wiki/Wikipedia:Notability.

———. n.d. "Wikipedia: Polling Is Not a Substitute for Discussion." Accessed October 20, 2020. https://en.wikipedia.org/wiki/Wikipedia:Polling_is_not_a_substitute_for_discussion.

———. n.d. "Wikipedia: Search Engine Test." Accessed October 20, 2020. https://en.Wikipedia.org/wiki/Wikipedia:Search_engine_test.

———. n.d. "Wikipedia: There Is a Deadline." Accessed October 20, 2020. https://en.Wikipedia.org/wiki/Wikipedia:There_is_a_deadline.

———. n.d. "Wikipedia: Top 25 Report." Accessed October 20, 2020. https://en.wikipedia.org/wiki/Wikipedia:Top_25_Report.

———. n.d. "Wikipedia: Verifiability." Accessed October 20, 2020. https://en.Wikipedia.org/wiki/Wikipedia:Verifiability#What_counts_as_a_reliable_source.

Wilkinson, Dennis M., and Bernardo A. Huberman. 2007. "Cooperation and Quality in Wikipedia." *WikiSym '07: Proceedings of the 2007 International Symposium on Wikis* (October 2007): 157–64. https://doi.org/10.1145/1296951.1296968.

Willett, Megan. 2015. "Poking Someone on Facebook Is No Longer a Creepy or Lazy Way to Flirt with Someone." Business Insider, August 3, 2015. https://www.businessinsider.com.au/wheres-the-facebook-poke-now-2015-7.

Willson, Michele. 2017. "Algorithms (and the) Everyday." *Information, Communication and Society* 20 (1): 137–50.

Winner, Langdon. 1980. "Do Artifacts Have Politics?" *Daedalus* 109 (1): 121–36.

Wood, Alex J, Mark Graham, Vili Lehdonvirta, and Isis Hjorth. 2019. "Good Gig, Bad Gig: Autonomy and Algorithmic Control in the Global Gig Economy." *Work, Employment and Society* 33 (1): 56–75. https://doi.org/10.1177/0950017018785616.

Wood, W. 1992. *The Power of Maps*. New York: Guilford Press.

Woollaston, Victoria. 2015. "Do YOU Think 'Facebook Is the Internet'? Two Thirds of Users Do—And Millions Don't Know They're on the Web When They Log In." *Mail Online*, February 11, 2015. https://www.dailymail.co.uk/sciencetech/article-2948923/Do-think-Facebook-internet-Two-thirds-users-millions-don-t-know-web-log-accounts.html.

Wriston, Walter B. 1997. "Bits, Bytes, and Diplomacy." *Foreign Affairs*, September 1, 1997. https://www.foreignaffairs.com/articles/1997-09-01/bits-bytes-and-diplomacy.

X—The Moonshot Factory. n.d. "X—The Moonshot Factory." Accessed September 6, 2020. https://x.company.

Yahoo Finance. 2015. "Q&A: How Internet.Org Aims to Connect the World's Poor." January 15, 2015. https://finance.yahoo.com/news/q-internet-org-aims-connect-worlds-poor -102202616.html.

Yang, Qinghua, and Yu Liu. 2014. "What's on the Other Side of the Great Firewall? Chinese Web Users' Motivations for Bypassing the Internet Censorship." *Computers in Human Behavior* 37:249–57.

Yeung, Karen. 2017. "'Hypernudge': Big Data as a Mode of Regulation by Design." *Information, Communication and Society* 20 (1): 118–36. https://doi.org/10.1080/136911 8X.2016.1186713.

Young, Robert J. C. 1995. *Colonial Desire: Hybridity in Theory, Culture and Race*. London: Routledge.

YouTube-GitHub. n.d. "About the Geo Search Tool." Accessed Dec 27, 2017. http://youtube .github.io/geo-search-tool/about.html.

Yusuf, Huma. 2013. *Mapping Digital Media: Pakistan*. NYC: Open Society Foundations. https://www.opensocietyfoundations.org/publications/mapping-digital-media -pakistan#publications_download.

Zuckerberg, Mark. 2017. "I just went live a minute ago. Here's what I said." Facebook, September 21, 2017. https://www.facebook.com/zuck/posts/10104052907253171.

———. n.d. "Is Connectivity a Human Right?" Facebook. Accessed November 22, 2020. https://www.facebook.com/isconnectivityahumanright.

INDEX

Project Kuiper, 47, 50, 56
Project Loon, 42, 44, 59–60, 63, 65–66
protest movement, 185, 189–90
protocols: of algorithmic systems, 40–41; of digital networks, 16–17; globalization of, 24; TCP/IP, 178
psychographic profiles, 71–72
public opinion, 47–48, 164–67
public/private divide, 198
public utility, 55
published sources, 92, 96
Putin, Vladimir, 90

quality control, of Wikipedia, 83–84
Quartz study, 69

Ramamurthy, V. S., 190
ranking guidelines, 70
rationality, 79
regulatory bodies, 46
regulatory mechanisms, 182–83
Right to be Forgotten, 181, 195–96
Rogers, Richard, 94–95
Rose, Nicholas, 124, 136–37, 141, 154, 158
rules for control, 15–16
Rushdie, Salman, 103, 120n5

sanctions, in digital infrastructures, 123, 149
Sanger, Larry, 82
Saruhashi, Katsuko, 90
Satanic Verses, The (Rushdie), 120n5
Sazhin, Leonid, 188
Schmitt, Carl, 14, 174
Schmitt, Eric, 51
Schmitt, Karl, 19–21, 174
Schroeder, Ralph, 130, 142
Schüll, Natasha Dow, 140
search engine optimization (SEO), 70
search engines, 31, 97–98, 127
security risks, 192
seductions, in digital infrastructures, 123
self-disclosure, 151
self-entrepreneurism, 124, 165
self-expression, 158
self-favoring bias, 156
selfhood/subjectivity, 31; affordances and algorithms in, 167; default

settings in, 167; in digital culture, 126–27; on digital domains, 132–34; on digital infrastructures, 150; on digital platforms, 148–49; foundational characteristics of, 134–37; global digital self, 150–67; globalizing aspirational, 131–37; ideal subject emerging in, 134–37; on internet, 124; normative subjects in, 132–34; prize and penalty from, 123–24; on social media, 121, 130–31; technology of, 136
Selfie Raja (film), 155
selfies, 154–57, 163–64
self-interrogating awareness, 208
selfitis, 156
self-regulation, 182
self-reliance, 137
self-revelation, 32
semiotic acts, 143–44
semipermeable membrane, 182
sensitive sites, 189
SEO. *See* search engine optimization
shared-revenue model, 43
small and medium enterprises (SMEs), 46
Snapchat, 121, 142, 157, 161
social behaviors, 14–15
social life, 9–10
social media: affordances of, 141–44; aspirational norms of, 208–9; buttons on, 143–44; countries usage of, 151–52; customers needs on, 69–70; in digital cultures, 158; economic values of, 147–48; Euro-American origins of, 4; global role of, 121–22, 130–31; insurrections within, 184; lifestreaming and selfies on, 163–64; nudge on globalizing, 142; as public utility, 55; rewards and incentives of, 140–41, 149–50; selfhood on, 121, 130–31; selfies on, 154; semiotic acts on, 143–44; sign out steps on, 147; US dominance of, 130; user behaviors on, 127–28; website popularity on, 129
Social Network, The (film), 61
social networking, 157
social problems, 40, 48–49
sociocultural layers, 158
soft counterparts, 22–23

SANGEET KUMAR is Associate Professor of Media Studies in the Department of Communication at Denison University. He also serves as Director of the International Studies program at Denison. Prior to his academic career, he worked as a journalist with a daily in New Delhi, India.